STUDY GUIDE

to accompany

MACROECONOMICS
ELEVENTH EDITION

Robert J. Gordon

Mihajlo Balic
Palm Beach Community College

Andrew Foshee
McNeese State University

PEARSON

Addison
Wesley

Boston San Francisco New York
London Toronto Sydney Tokyo Singapore Madrid
Mexico City Munich Paris Cape Town Hong Kong Montreal

Reproduced by Pearson Addison Wesley from electronic files supplied by author.

Copyright © 2009 Pearson Education, Inc.
Publishing as Pearson Addison Wesley, 75 Arlington Street, Boston, MA 02116

ISBN-13   978-0-321-60957-1
ISBN-10   0-321-60957-3

1 2 3 4 5 6 OPM 11 10 09 08

Contents

Answers to Study Guide Questions

Preface

■ To The Student

Why A Study Guide?

The purpose of this study guide is to help you learn macroeconomic theory by working your way through problems and questions that parallel the presentation in the text. Most study guides for economics texts separate questions within a chapter by type of question, e.g., true-false, multiple-choice, short-answer, and so on. In this study guide, however, the chapter is segmented according to content. A typical chapter is divided into six or seven questions, with each question covering a specified topic. The question might present a further exposition of a theoretical model introduced in the text. Alternatively, it might require the development of an algebraic approach to complement the graphical approach used in the text. In some cases, it might ask you to examine current data sources to examine relationships studied in the text. Using this study guide to complement Gordon's text will help you learn macroeconomic theory.

How To Use The Study Guide

The structure of the chapters in the study guide closely parallels the structure of the chapters in the textbook. The two books can and should be used together. Within each question, there are a variety of formats used. If a question is followed by one or more blank lines, your answer may range from one word or numerical value to a short essay. Sometimes you need only circle the correct answer. The study guide also contains questions that require you to draw graphs. Too often, students will look at a graph in a text and be convinced that they understand it. It is only later that they discover (usually on an exam) that they in fact did not understand the graph. The graphical questions give you the opportunity to put together your own diagrams; after doing so, you will definitely understand the diagram.

Throughout the study guide, there are questions (or parts of questions) that have an asterisk (*) after the question number or the question part that requires data. To answer these questions, you must use current data. These questions are included because you should learn the magnitude of macroeconomic variables, relationships among them, and their data sources. The following table lists the location of the asterisked questions and the data source that can be used to answer each question.

Chapter	Question	Data Source	Comment
1	2a	SCB	—
1	2b	SCB	—
2	6a	SCB	—
6	2d	WSJ	Be sure to use the amount of foreign currency per dollar.
13	4h	SCB and FRB	For the discount rate, use the rate at the Federal Reserve Bank of New York.
14	3a	SCB	—
15	5e	SCB	—
16	1a	SCB	Use quarterly data in 2000 dollars. To find real 2000 consumer durable expenditures, divide the current dollar amount by the implicit price deflator for consumer durables for that quarter.
16	1b	SCB	—

Key: SCB, *Survey of Current Business*, U.S. Department of Commerce; FRB, *Federal Reserve Bulletin*, Board of Governors, Federal Reserve System; WSJ, *Wall Street Journal*, Dow Jones and Company.

To The Instructor

Good luck with your use of the study guide. Addison Wesley would appreciate hearing from you regarding errors, omissions, suggested questions, and innovative uses of the study guide. Address your correspondence to Alison Eusden, Supplements Coordinator, Economics, Addison Wesley, 75 Arlington Street, Suite 300, Boston, Massachusetts 02116.

Chapter 1
What Is Macroeconomics?

Macroeconomics deals with some of the most important and most discussed issues of our times. In macroeconomics, we learn about inflation and unemployment, and about how the standard of living in a country can grow. We learn about these key issues by developing theories that can help us understand how the macroeconomy works. But first, we must understand the basic terms we will be using and get a feel for the size of the economic magnitudes with which we are concerned. An introduction to the basic concepts and concerns of macroeconomics is the subject of this first chapter.

Question 1

Answer the questions on basic macroeconomic principles or complete the statements by filling in the blanks with the correct word or words.

a. *Macro* comes from a Greek word meaning _____

Define *macroeconomics*. _____

_____

_____

Micro comes from a Greek word meaning _____

Define *microeconomics*. _____

_____

_____

b. Indicate whether each of the following is a macroeconomic or microeconomic question.

_____ What is the level of real output that will not make the rate of inflation change?

_____ Why do surgeons have higher incomes than janitors?

_____ What is the effect of a sales tax on the price and output of beer?

_____ Would a steady rate of growth in the money supply have a stabilizing effect on the economy?

_____ Are price controls effective in stopping an increase in inflation?

c. One of the most used and most important terms in macroeconomics is GDP, which stands for _____

_____

Define GDP. _____

_____

_____

Question 2*

Use recent economic data to answer the following questions on real and nominal GDP, the rate of inflation, and the unemployment rate. In Chapter 2, you will learn about the relationship between real and nominal magnitudes. For this question, simply find and record the appropriate data.

a. In the following table, list the values in the four most recent quarters for which data are available for the economic variables shown. (*Note*: The inflation rate is the change, at an annual rate, in the implicit GDP deflator.)

Period (Year: Quarter)	Nominal GDP ($Billions)	Real GDP (in 2000 dollars)	GDP Deflator (2000 = 1.00)	Rate of Inflation (%)
20:Q				
20:Q				
20:Q				
20:Q				

b. List the unemployment rate for the most recent six months for which data are available.

Period (Month, Year)	Unemployment Rate (%)	Period (Month, Year)	Unemployment Rate (%)
, 20		, 20	
, 20		, 20	
, 20		, 20	

Question 3

Answer the following questions on basic concepts in macroeconomics, or complete the statements by filling in the correct word or words.

a. The historical record of natural and actual real GDP (see Gordon, Figure 1-6) shows a long-run upward trend. Nevertheless, there have been many short-run fluctuations in the levels of both natural and actual real GDP. A main objective of government policy is to stabilize real GDP so that it reaches natural real GDP.

What is actual real GDP? _____

_____

Why is it undesirable for real GDP to be too high? _____

_____

_____

Why is undesirable for real GDP to be too low? _____

_____

_____

b. What is the natural level of real GDP? _____

_____

_____

What is the natural rate of unemployment? _____

_____

_____

c. Describe the relationship between the actual rate of unemployment and the natural rates of unemployment from 1960 to 2007 (use the annual data in the text's Appendix A, Table A-1).

_____

_____

_____

d. We call the aggregates that society cares most about (such as inflation, unemployment, and long-term growth) _____variables.

When the actual value for these goals deviates from the desired values, what can be used in an attempt to achieve the needed changes?

Policy instruments fall into three broad categories:

1. _____

2. _____

3. _____

e. Economic theory is used for both positive economics and normative economics. Briefly explain how theory can be used for each type of economics.

1. Positive economics: _____

_____

_____

2. Normative economics: _____

_____

_____

Most disagreements among economists are on *positive/normative* issues.

Question 4

Distinguish between short-run and long-run macroeconomics. _____

_____

_____

_____

Question 5

Gordon discusses specific examples of depression, hyperinflation, and economic growth as cases of macroeconomics at the extremes. Why does he consider economic growth to be the most significant case for the long run? Explain. _____

_____

Question 6

Not too many years ago, textbooks in macroeconomics treated the national economy as a closed economy, whereas today most textbooks devote much more space to open-economy macroeconomics.

a. What does the term *closed economy* mean? _____

_____

_____

b. What does the term *open economy* mean? _____

_____

_____

c. Why have macroeconomics textbooks oriented to a United States audience become more concerned with describing an open economy?

_____

_____

_____

_____

Chapter 2
The Measurement of Income, Prices, and Unemployment

In this chapter we examine the definition and measurement of gross domestic product (GDP) and its associated output and income measures. We show how the National Income and Product Accounts (NIPA) are constructed, with an emphasis on what is included in the NIPA and what is not. We also deal with the conversion of nominal measures of output and income to real measures, and with how unemployment is defined and measured.

Question 1

Answer the following questions on the development of national income concepts, or complete the statements by filling in the blanks with the correct word or words.

a. In a simple economy consisting only of households and business firms and in which households spend their entire income, consumption expenditure (C) would be *greater than/less than/equal to* income (Y), and saving (S) would be *negative/positive/zero*.

Consumer expenditure and income are flow magnitudes. Define a flow magnitude. _____

_____

_____

Define a stock magnitude. _____

_____

b. Give three examples of stock magnitudes commonly used in economics. _____

_____

Do the NIPA deal with stocks or flows? Explain. _____

_____

_____

c. There are three major requirements in the rule for including items in GDP. These requirements are:

1. _____

_____

2. _____

_____

3. _____

_____

d. Instead of excluding intermediate goods from final product totals, why can't we merely add up the total goods and services produced during a period by all the firms in the economy?

_____

_____

_____

e. Another way to compute GDP is to add up the value added at each stage of production. Define value added.

_____

_____

f. Suppose that Ned Dustman finds various interesting pieces of the environment (old beer cans, rusted-out bumpers, etc.) that he collects and sells (improving the quality of the environment at the same time) for $100 to Mr. Solomon Deli, the currently fashionable artist whose specialty is "found sculpture." Using his creative genius, the great Deli assembles these pieces into a masterpiece, "Vision 2008," which he sells to his art-dealer friend, Mr. Leo Jelli, for $1,500. Mr. Jelli, in turn, retails Vision 2008 to the well-known art collector, Dr. Sullivan Psnob, for the modest sum of $5,000.

What is the value of total receipts for all stages of production of Vision 2008? _____

Does this value correctly measure the contribution of Vision 2008 to GDP? _____

What is the value added to final product at each step of production of Vision 2008?

Step	Amount
Ned Dustman	
Solomon Deli	
Leo Jelli	
TOTAL	

Does this total correctly measure the contribution of Vision 2005 to GDP? _____

g. Let us return to the simple economy of Part a, consisting only of households and firms. Now, however, households do not spend all of their income. Instead, they refrain from spending 20 percent of it. The unconsumed portion of household income, called_____, is channeled through the capital market. There, it is transferred to business firms, which spend it for private capital formation, called _____.

These funds are channeled to business firms in two basic ways. List these ways:

1. _____

2. _____

If income (Y) is $200,000, fill in the blanks in the following diagram:

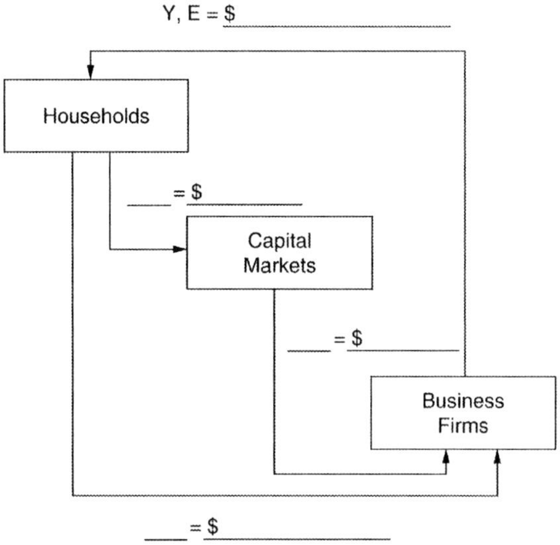

Y, E = $ _____

Figure 2A

Question 2

The GDP for an economy is the total value of production taking place in that economy during some period. One way of estimating GDP is to sum the total expenditures (sales) for final goods and services during that same period. This approach presents a problem when goods are produced but not sold during the period. In this question we show how that problem is handled in national income accounting.

a.   Assume that there are three companies in the economy: Ajax Tool Company, Beeline Honey Company, and Coastal Towel Company. Complete the following table.

Item	Ajax	Beeline	Coastal
Inventory as of 12/31/07	$400	$700	$ 300
Production during 2008	$350	$650	$1800
Sales during 2008	$300	$900	$1200
Inventory as of 12/31/08			
Change in inventory during 2008			

What is the total dollar value of goods produced during 2005 by the three companies? _____

b.   Assume that Ajax sells only to other businesses, while Beeline and Coastal sell to consumers.

Fill in the following table.

Item	Value of Actual Sales
Consumption	—
Honey	
Towels	
Investment	—
Tools	
TOTAL	

Is the sum of total consumption and investment a good measure of GDP for this economy? Why or why not? _____

_____

_____

c. Since GDP measures the value of all goods and services produced during the year, goods that are produced but not sold should be included in the GDP.

If we define *change in inventory* as a type of investment, what is the amount of inventory investment in the economy during 2008?

_____

Using our definition of investment to include both sales to other businesses and change in inventory, what is the level of investment for 2008?

_____

If we now sum the total consumption and investment during 2008, what is our total?

_____

Is this a good measure of GDP? Why or why not? _____

_____

_____

Question 3

The following table contains hypothetical amounts for items included in the National Income and Product Accounts. *Note:* Gross national product is gross domestic product plus receipts of factor income from the rest of the world minus payments of factor income to the rest of the world.

Item	Amount ($Billions)
Gross private domestic investment	243.0
Corporate profits after tax	62.7
Corporate income tax	64.3
Social Security contributions	125.1
Personal consumption expenditures	1,090.2
Capital consumption allowance	177.8
Government transfer payments and interest	209.9
Personal income tax	196.5
Government purchases of goods and services	359.5
Corporate dividends	37.9
Indirect business taxes	163.1
Net foreign investment (net exports)	7.4
Personal interest payments (personal transfers)	26.0
Receipts of factor income from the rest of the world	30.0
Payments of factor income to the rest of the world	27.0

Using the above data, complete the following table.

Item	Amount ($Billions)
Gross domestic product	
Gross national product	
Net domestic product	
Domestic income	
Undistributed corporate profits	
Personal income	
Personal disposable income	

Question 4

Give three possible implications of the government budget deficit. (*Hint*: refer to the Magic Equation.)

_____

_____

_____

Question 5

Because we often want to compare measurements of income and expenditure at different times, it is important to measure these magnitudes in *real* terms, that is, after adjustment for the effects of price changes. This question examines how nominal GDP and chain-weighted real GDP are measured.

a.   What is a nominal magnitude? _____

_____

What is a real magnitude? _____

_____

There are two possible reasons for nominal GDP to increase. What are they?

1.   _____

2.   _____

b.   Assume an economy has only three products: beer, cheese, and calculators. The table below contains relevant price and output data for 2007 and 2008.

Calculate nominal GDP for 2007. _____

Calculate nominal GDP for 2008. _____

c.   Calculate constant dollar expenditures for 2007 and 2008 at 2007 prices, and then at 2008 prices.

_____

d. What is the percentage change in nominal GDP between 2007 and 2008? _____

What is the percentage change in real GDP between 2007 and 2008 at 2007 prices, and at 2008 prices?

Explain why one percentage change is higher than the other. _____

_____

	2007		2008	
Item	**Price**	**Quantity**	**Price**	**Quantity**
Beer, six-pack	$ 1.25	4,000	$ 1.50	4,400
Cheese, pound	$ 2.00	1,000	$ 2.10	1,400
Calculators, each	$60.00	30	$65.00	50

e. Calculate the chain-weighted or geometric average increase in real GDP between 2007 and 2008.

_____

f. Calculate the chain-weighted real GDP for 2008. _____

g. If the chain-weighted percentage change in real GDP for 2006–07, 2007–08, and 2008–09 are 5 percent, 3 percent, and 6 percent, and nominal GDP for 2006 is $2500 billion, then the chain-weighted real GDP 2009 is _____.

Question 6*

a. Complete the following table for real GDP and its components for the four most recent quarters for which complete data are available.

		Amount ($Billions)			
Date	**GDP**	**Personal Consumption Expenditures**	**Gross Private Domestic Investment**	**Net Exports**	**Government Purchases of Goods and Services**
20:Q					
20:Q					
20:Q					
20:Q					

b. Briefly describe the movements of real GDP and its components during the four-quarter period.

_____

_____

_____

_____

Question 7

Data regarding the unemployment rate are readily available in newspapers, magazines, and other media. To interpret these data correctly, we must understand how the unemployment rate is measured. In this question, we examine how individuals in different situations would be classified in the employment statistics. For each description, place an "X" in the appropriate column of the following table.

Description	Employed	Unemployed	Not in Labor Force
1. Lars is currently working in a part-time job but would like to have a full-time job.			
2. Craig is currently in school but is looking for a part-time job.			
3. Kevin is a househusband and would look for a job if the economy, which is in a slump, improves.			
4. Gina has just graduated summa cum laude from college and is looking for her first job.			
5. Matthew is an honor student in college and is working through the school's internship program.			
6. Ceci, who does not want to work on a permanent basis, is currently working on a two-week assignment.			
7. Christina would like to work but is ill.			
8. Bill has been laid off and is not looking for other work.			
9. Jennifer has quit her job and is not looking for other work.			
10. Linda has just graduated from law school and is working as a lawyer.			
11. Francis would like to work but is in jail.			

Question 8

Why is it possible for the household survey to register a faster increase in employment than payroll survey? (Refer to "Conflicting Measurements; was the 2002–07 Recovery Jobless or Not?" case study.)

_____

_____

_____

Chapter 3
Spending, Income, and Interest Rates

In this chapter we develop a simple theory for the determination of the level of real GDP, often called the "simple Keynesian model." We begin by examining the nature of the multiplier process. The multiplier gives the change in equilibrium of real GDP due to a change in autonomous planned spending. Then we expand the simple two-sector model by including government expenditures, taxation, and the foreign sector.

In the development of the simple Keynesian model, we make two important assumptions. First, we rule out any effect of the interest rate on the level of spending. Second, we ignore any effects that price changes would have on the level of real income and spending. Specifically, we assume that the price level is constant.

Finally, we develop the *IS* curve. The *IS* curve depicts the relationship between equilibrium real output and the interest rate. The *IS* curve, however, is not a complete model as it does not permit the determination of the endogenous variables, r and Y. To do that requires another relationship, the *LM* curve, which will be covered in Chapter 4.

Question 1

This question examines the relationship between disposable income and consumption. Assume that $a = 200$, $c = 0.8$, and $T = 0$.

a. Write the equation of the consumption function. _____

b. Graph the consumption function in Figure 3A, and label it C.

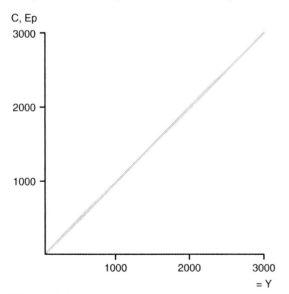

Figure 3A

c. Graph the induced saving function in Figure 3B and label it *S*.

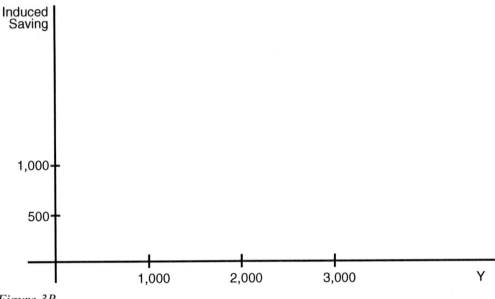

Figure 3B

Question 2

This question adds planned investment expenditure (I_p) to the consumption function of Question 1. With this two-sector model of the economy, we can find the equilibrium level of real GDP. Assume that the consumption function parameters are the same as in Question 1, that taxes are still zero, and that $I_p = 300$.

a. What is the value of planned autonomous expenditures? _____

b. What is the planned expenditure equation? The induced consumption equation? _____

c. Plot in Figure 3A the planned expenditure function derived in Part b. Label the curve E_p. Plot in Figure 3B the autonomous planned expenditure function. Label the curve A_p. In both graphs label the equilibrium level of real GDP Point *B*.

d. Give the algebraic formula for the equilibrium level of real GDP. $Y =$ _____

Solve for the equilibrium level of real GDP. $Y =$ _____

e. Complete the following table.

Real GDP Y	Total Planned Expenditure E_p	Unintended Inventory Accumulation I_u	Autonomous Planned Expenditure A_p	Induced Saving sY
1,000				
1,500				
2,000				
2,500				
3,000				

f.   If $Y = 1,500$, what effect will this have on business production decisions? _____

_____

_____

_____

g.   If $Y = 3,000$, what effect will this have on business production decisions? _____

_____

_____

_____

h.   Based on your answers to Parts e–g, the equilibrium level of real GDP is _____

Explain why this is the equilibrium level. _____

_____

_____

_____

Question 3

Now we allow the level of planned autonomous expenditure to increase from the level in the previous
question. This change in A_p will cause a change in the equilibrium level of real GDP through the
multiplier process. In the economy described in Question 2, assume that the level of planned investment
increases from 300 to 500. We label the variables referring to the original situation in Question 2 with the
subscript 0 and the new variables with the subscript 1.

a.   What is the value of A_{p_1}? _____

b.   What is the value of the multiplier? $k =$ _____

c.   Complete the following table.

Explanation	General Form	Numerical Form
New equilibrium	$Y_1 = A_{p_1}/s$	$Y_1 =$
less		
Old equilibrium (Question 2h)	$Y_0 =$	$Y_0 = 500/0.2 = 2,500$
equals		
Change in equilibrium $(\Delta Y = Y_1 - Y_0)$	$\Delta Y =$	$\Delta Y =$

Question 4

Up to this point we have ignored the role of the government in the economy. Now we include the
government sector. Continue to assume $a = 200$ and $c = 0.8$; however, assume $I_p = 400$. We label initial
values and equations with subscript 0s and subsequent values and equations with subscript 1s.

a.   We start with no government expenditure or taxes.

$A_{p_0} =$ _____

$E_{p_0} =$ _____

Graph the E_{p_0} equation in Figure 3C. Graph the A_{p_0} equation and induced saving function in Figure 3D.

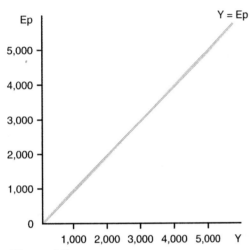

Figure 3C

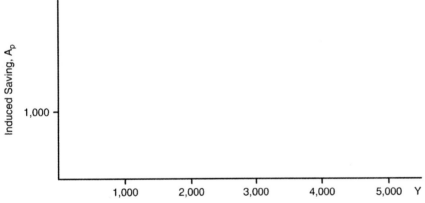

Figure 3D

What is equilibrium real GDP? _____

Label the equilibrium point as *B* in Figure 3C and Figure 3D.

b.   Now suppose there are government expenditures of 300, but everything else is the same as in Part a.

$A_{p_1} =$ _____

$E_{p_1} =$ _____

Graph the E_{p_1} equation in Figure 3C and A_{p_1} in Figure 3D.

What is the new equilibrium real GDP? _____

Label the new equilibrium point as *J* in Figure 3C and Figure 3D.

How much did *Y* change because of the change in *G*? _____

How much did *G* change? _____

What is the value of the government-expenditure multiplier? _____

c.   In Figure 3E and Figure 3F, redraw the planned spending function and the autonomous planned spending function from Part b, and again show the equilibrium position as Point *J*. Now assume that the government decides to levy autonomous taxes (T_0) of 250. We label new values and equations with subscript 2.

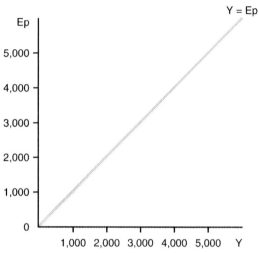

Figure 3E

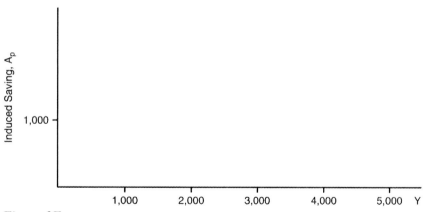

Figure 3F

$A_{p2} =$ _____

$E_{p2} =$ _____

Graph the E_{p2} equation in Figure 3E and the A_{p2} equation in Figure 3F.

What is the new equilibrium level of real GDP? _____

Label the new equilibrium point as K.

How much did Y change because of the change in T_0? _____

How much did T change? _____

What is the value of the autonomous-tax multiplier? _____

d. If the natural level of real GDP is 3,500 and the economy is at the equilibrium shown in Part a, what is the size of the GDP gap?

_____

Now suppose government increases expenditure (G) by 300 and raises autonomous taxes (T_0) by 250, so that the economy arrives at the equilibrium shown in Part c (Point K in Figure 3E).

Now what is the size of the GDP gap? _____

Why did the change in the gap occur? _____

_____

_____

Question 5

This question reviews what types of events affect autonomous spending.

a. List and briefly identify five possible causes of a change in autonomous planned spending (A_p):

1. _____

2. _____

3. _____

4. _____

5. _____

b. For each of the following events, state whether A_p rises or falls. Which of the four causes listed in Part a is responsible for the change in A_p? What was the direction of change for each "cause?" Show by writing the appropriate variable followed by a directional arrow, as illustrated for the first "cause" given below.

$A_p \uparrow I_p \uparrow$ 1. Optimistic forecasts of future demand cause business to expand spending for plant and equipment.

_____   2. Renewed trouble in the Middle East causes a 10 percent increase in defense spending (without reductions elsewhere in the federal budget).

_____   3. In an election year Congress votes to double the personal exemption in the personal income tax.

_____   4. A belief in "the classic joys of abstinence" becomes popular, and households at every income level increase their level of saving.

_____   5. The Federal Reserve makes it difficult for mortgage lenders to obtain funds and forces a sharp increase in the interest rate on new residential mortgages.

_____   6. Budget limitations force a reduction in the size of unemployment compensation payments.

_____   7. A new gas-saving engine is developed by Detroit automakers, and export sales increase dramatically.

c. Do all of the probable changes in A_p listed above produce the same multiplier? If not, which ones are different and why?

_____

_____

_____

d. Improved stability of the U.S. economy since 1985 is termed "Great Moderation." List possible causes for this improvement.

_____

_____

_____

Question 6

Previously, we have unrealistically assumed that tax revenues are set at a predetermined level. Because income, sales, property values, and other tax bases change when national income changes (as do some types of transfer payments), it is more realistic to assume that net taxes (T) are a function of real GDP. This adaptation of the model is presented in the appendix to Chapter 3.

Assume the following equations and values:

$$C = 200 + 0.8(Y - T)$$
$$I_p = 400$$
$$T = 50 + 0.1Y$$
$$G = 350.$$

a. What is the equation for disposable income? $Y - T =$ _____

b. What is the value of A_p? _____

c. Define the *marginal leakage rate (MLR)*. _____

_____

_____

d. What is the value of the MLR? _____

e. What is the equilibrium level of Y? _____

f. What is the government surplus at the equilibrium level of Y? _____

g. What is the value of the government-expenditure multiplier? _____

Why does the multiplier found in this question differ from that found in Question 3? _____

_____

Question 7

Use the same equations and values as in Question 6, but assume that the foreign sector is represented by the net export function, $NX = 65 - 0.02Y$. This adaptation of the model is presented in the appendix to Chapter 3.

a. What is the value of Ap? _____

b. What is the value of MLR? _____

c. What is equilibrium Y? _____

d. What is the value of k? _____

Explain why the value of this multiplier differs from the value found in Question 6. _____

_____

e. What is the foreign trade balance? _____

Question 8

The next three questions examine the effect of the interest rate on autonomous spending. Before we study that relationship, however, we want to learn how interest rates and bond prices are related. That is the subject of this question.

A bond is a promise to pay a fixed amount (principal) at some later date, along with interest payments at designated intervals during the period. The current value (price) of the bond is the present value of the promised future stream of payments (interest plus principal). For example, to find the price of a three-year bond, we must solve this equation:

$$\text{Present value} = [V_1/(1 + r)] + [V_2/(1 + r)^2] + [V_3/(1 + r)^3] + R/(1 + r)^3,$$

where the present value of the bond is its price in the market; V_1, V_2, and V_3 are annual interest payments; r is the prevailing interest rate; and R is the principal that is to be repaid in the third year.

a.   Assume that there is a three-year bond issued when the interest rate is 10 percent. If the issuer wishes to raise $1,000, he or she must offer a yearly payment of $100 and a promise to pay the $1,000 principal at the end of the third year. To prove this, we solve the above equation with V_1, V_2, and V_3 equal to $100, $R = \$1,000$, and $r = 10$ percent.

$$\text{Price} = \$90.91 + \$82.64 + \$75.13 + \$751.31 = \$1,000.00.$$

b.   If the interest rate falls from 10 percent to 7 percent, a *new* bond issued for $1000 would have to offer an annual payment of _____

Prove that this is the case by setting V_1, V_2, and $V_3 = \$70$, $r = 7$ percent, and $R = \$1,000$; then solve the equation. _____

c.   Assume for now that the bond in Part a still has three years to run until maturity. What would be the current price for that *existing* bond after the interest rate dropped to 7 percent?

_____

d.   When the interest rate falls, the price of existing bonds *increases/decreases*. This change in the value of the bond is due to the combined effect of a *fixed/variable* value for the yearly payment and the *fixed/variable* interest rate at which the payment is discounted.

Question 9

To find the percentage rate of return from an investment project, we compare the dollar return from that project with the cost of the project. If the project has a one-year life, the following formula is used: $r =$ (gross return—cost of project)/cost of project, where $100r$ is the percentage rate of return. We can rewrite the formula this way: gross return/cost of project $= 1 + r$, or cost of project $=$ gross return/$(1 + r)$. This last formulation will be useful when solving the problems in Parts b–d of this question.

a.   Assume that a given project costs $2,800 and that the gross return is $3,200. What is the percentage rate of return? $r =$ _____

b.   If the return on the investment does not take place all in one year, we have to modify the formula. For example, if the return in the first year (R_1) equals $1,600 and the return in the second year (R_2) equals $1,600, then the percentage rate of return is the r that solves the following equation:

$$\$2800 = [\$1600/(1 + r)] + [\$1600/(1 + r)^2].$$

The value on the right-hand side of the equation is the *discounted value of the stream of returns*. To solve this problem, find the r that makes the discounted value of the stream of returns equal $2,800. (*Hint*: This equation is not easily solved algebraically. The best approach is to choose alternative values of r, then compute the discounted value, and finally, choose the r that yields a discounted value closest to $2,800.)

Complete the following table (round off the last three columns to the nearest dollar).

r	(1 + r)	(1 + r)²	$1600/(1 + r)	$1600/(1 + r)²	Discounted Value[a]
0.07	1.07	1.1449			
0.08					
0.09					
0.10					
0.11					
0.12					

[a] Sum of columns four and five.

What is the percentage rate of return for this project? $r =$ _____

What would happen to r if the cost of the project increased to $2,890? _____

What would happen to r if the cost of the project decreased to $2,740? _____

c. Assume that we have three projects with the characteristics listed in the table below. Complete the table by calculating the rates of return for the various projects. (*Hint*: The rates of return are between 7 percent and 12 percent, so that the table you completed in Part b will be helpful. Begin by choosing a value for r and calculating the discounted value for the project. If the discounted value is greater than the cost, the value for r is too low; choose a higher r and calculate again.)

Project	Cost	Return, Year 1	Return, Year 2	Rate of Return
A	$2,000	$1,180	$1,120	
B	2,000	600	1,700	
C	3,000	1,610	1,740	

Project A and Project B both cost $2,000 and yield gross returns of $2,300, yet they have different rates of return. Why? _____

_____

_____

Which projects would be undertaken if the interest rate were 11 percent? _____

What would be the dollar value of the project chosen? _____

Which projects would be undertaken if the interest rate were 9 percent? _____

What would be the dollar value of the projects chosen? _____

Which projects would be undertaken if the interest rate were 7 percent? _____

What would be the dollar value of the projects chosen? _____

d. Assume that the Council of Economic Advisers publishes a report predicting that growth rates for the economy for the next three years will be higher than previously predicted. Because of this new information, firms revise their estimates of the expected returns from Projects A, B, and C. Calculate the rates of return for this new set of data.

Project	Cost	Return, Year 1	Return, Year 2	Rate of Return
A	$2,000	$1,200	$1,160	
B	2,000	610	1,750	
C	3,000	1,650	1,770	

e. Complete the following table.

Interest Rate (%)	Before CEA Report		After CEA Report	
	Projects Undertaken	Total Value of Investment	Projects Undertaken	Total Value of Investment
11.0				
9.0				
7.0				

Question 10

Question 10 examined the relationship between the rate of interest and the level of autonomous spending. In this question we extend the analysis to include the multiplier. The multiplier process links the rate of interest and the level of real GDP.

Both consumers and producers are affected by the interest rate when making their spending decisions. Assume that the following equations summarize their behavior:

Autonomous consumption spending: $a = 220 - 5r$
Autonomous planned investment: $I_p = 380 - 20r$.

a. Complete the following table, listing the amounts of spending that would be undertaken at different interest rates.

r (%)	I_p	a	A_p
10.0			
8.0			
6.0			
4.0			
2.0			
0.0			

b. What is the algebraic equation for A_p? $A_p = $ _____

c. Assume that the marginal propensity to consume is 0.8 and that there is no income tax and no foreign sector.

    What is the multiplier? _____

d. Using your answers from Parts a–c above, complete the following table.

r (%)	A_p	$Y = kA_p$	Induced Saving (sY)
10.0			
8.0			
6.0			
4.0			
2.0			
0.0			

e. Plot the relationship between *r* and A_p on the left-hand side of Figure 3G, and label the relationship A_p *Demand Curve.* Plot the relationship between *r* and *Y* on the right-hand side of Figure 3G, and label the curve *IS.*

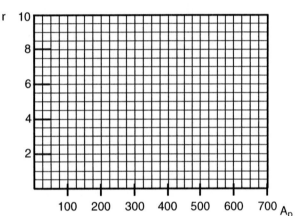 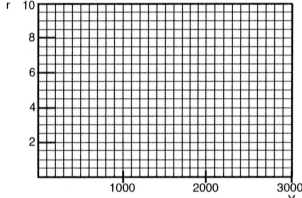

Figure 3G

f. What is the relationship between *Induced Saving* and A_p at each point along the *IS* curve? _____

g. What is the equation of the *IS* curve? _____

h. Complete the following table. Identify the four points (*A, B, C, D*) on your *IS* diagram.

Point	r	Y	sY	A_p	I_u
A	8.0	1,600			
B	8.0	2,200			
C	4.0	2,200			
D	4.0	2,800			

i. Use the information from the table in Part h to answer the following. Both Points *A* and *C* are to the *right of/left of/on* the *IS* curve. If the economy were at either *A* or *C*, autonomous planned spending would be *greater than/less than/equal to* induced saving, and there would be a(n) *unplanned decrease/unplanned increase/no change* in inventories. There would be a tendency for output to *increase/decrease/remain unchanged.*

If *r* = 8, the equilibrium level of real GDP would be _____

If *r* = 4, the equilibrium level of real GDP would be _____

Chapter 4
Monetary and Fiscal Policy in the *IS-LM* Model

In this chapter we will develop the *LM* curve. Before we can develop the *LM* curve we need to develop a model of the "money market." The interest rate is determined in the money market as a result of the interaction between the demand for money and the supply of money. In this simple model of the money market, the demand for money is inversely related to the interest rate and directly related to real GDP. The money supply is determined by the Federal Reserve and is independent of the interest rate and of real GDP. Thus, for a given level of real GDP and money supply, the interest rate is determined by the interaction of the demand and supply of money. As real GDP changes for a given money supply, the demand for money will shift, and therefore the interest rate will change. The *LM* curve represents the various combinations of the interest rate and real GDP consistent with equilibrium in the money market.

We know the interest rate affects the level of real GDP through its effect on autonomous spending. We also know real GDP affects the interest rate through the demand for money. Thus, the equilibrium levels of real GDP and the rate of interest are determined simultaneously. This is what the *IS-LM* model shows. The model allows us to study the implications of this simultaneous determination. We shall use it to study the effects of monetary and fiscal policies on real GDP and the interest rate.

Question 1

In the last chapter (Question 10) we derived the *IS* curve. In this question we examine the *IS* curve more carefully, with an emphasis on how the *IS* curve would be affected by changes in the underlying spending functions. Assume that the spending plans of the different sectors of the economy can be described by the following equations:

$$c(Y - T) = 0.75(Y - T)$$

$$Ca = 190 - 15r$$

$$I_p = 300 - 25r$$

$$G = 180$$

$$T_0 = 160.$$

a.   What is the value of the marginal propensity to consume? _____

What is the equation of A_p? A_p = _____

Define A_0. _____

What is the value of A_0 in this question? _____

What is the level of autonomous planned spending when $r = 10$? _____

When $r = 5$? _____

What is the equilibrium level of Y associated with:

$r = 10$? _____

$r = 5$? _____

$r = 0$? _____

Plot the *IS* curve in Figure 4A. Identify the curve by labeling it IS_1 and noting in brackets the values of A_0 and k.

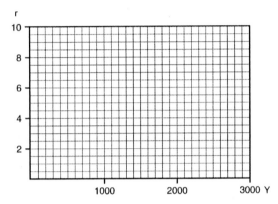

Figure 4A

By how much does the equilibrium value of Y change when r changes by one percentage point?

_____

b. Assume that government spending increases by 30 ($G = 210$) and that all other variables remain at the same levels as in Part a.

What is the new value for A_0? _____

What is the new equation for A_p? $A_p =$ _____

What is the new level of A_p when:

$r = 10$? _____

$r = 5$? _____

$r = 0$? _____

Describe what happens to the A_p curve when government spending increases by 30. _____

_____

By how much does Y change when r changes by one percentage point? _____

How would your answers to the above questions change if government spending had remained at 180 but if the new equation describing autonomous investment were $I_p = 330 - 25r$?

_____

_____

_____

By how much would autonomous tax revenues have to change to produce the same effect on Y as the change in G of 30? _____

c. Assume that the values of a, I_p, G, and T_0 are the same as in Part a. Assume that the marginal propensity to consume is now 0.8, instead of 0.75.

What is the value of the multiplier? _____

What is the value of A_p when:

$r = 10$? _____

$r = 5$? _____

$r = 0$? _____

Compare these answers to the values for A_p found in Part a. What do you conclude about the relationship of A_p to a change in the multiplier (k)?

_____

_____

What is the equilibrium Y when:

$r = 10$?_____

$r = 5$?_____

$r = 0$?_____

Plot the new *IS* curve in Figure 4A. Label it IS_2. Note in brackets the level of A_0 and k relating to this curve.

By how much does Y change when r changes by one percentage point? _____

Compare this answer to your answer in Part a. Explain any differences between the two answers.

_____

_____

_____

_____

_____

d. Assume that all variables have the same values as in Part a. Draw the A_p curve on the left-hand side of Figure 4B. Draw the *IS* curve on the right-hand side of Figure 4B. Label both curves with the subscript 1.

Now assume that there is a change in autonomous investment so that $I_p = 300 - 15r$.

What is the algebraic formula for A_p? $A_p = $ _____

What is the level of A_p when:

$r = 10$? _____

$r = 5$? _____

$r = 0$? _____

Plot the new A_p curve on the left-hand side of Figure 4B and label it A_{p3}.

The change in the A_p curve from A_{p1} to A_{p3} represents a change in A_p responsiveness. What does this mean? _____

_____

_____

Plot the *IS* curve on the right-hand side of Figure 4B and label it IS_3.

What is the change in *Y* when *r* changes by one percentage point? _____

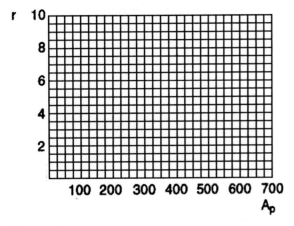 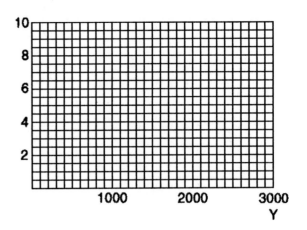

Figure 4B

Question 2

The previous question concentrated on equilibrium conditions in the "real" sector. We learned that when the interest rate changes, the level of autonomous spending changes. When autonomous spending changes, the real GDP changes. Thus, there is an equilibrium level of real GDP corresponding to each interest rate. The *IS* curve is the locus of all these pairs of interest rate and real GDP combinations. This question shifts our attention to the monetary sector. Again, we concentrate on equilibrium relationships between the interest rate and real GDP, but this time we examine the equilibrium conditions in the money market. Assume that the demand for real money balances can be written: $(M/P)^d = 0.25Y - 25r$.

a. If $Y = 2,400$, what is the demand for real balances when:

$r = 10$? _____

$r = 8$? _____

$r = 4$? _____

b. In the left-hand side of Figure 4C, plot the answers from Part a. Connect the points, and label the resulting curve L_1.

The curve L_1 is called a _____

c. Assume that the real money supply is 500. Plot the money-supply curve on the left-hand side of Figure 4C.

When $r = 6$, what is the demand for money? _____

Is there an excess demand for money or an excess supply of money when $r = 6$?

_____

By how much? _____

Explain what will take place in the money market as a result of this situation.

_____

_____

_____

What is the equilibrium rate of interest for these given conditions? _____

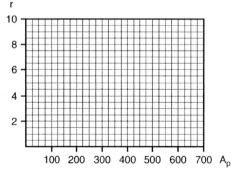
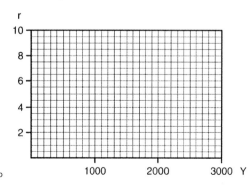

Figure 4C

d. If Y increases to 2,800, how much money will be demanded at:

$r = 8$? _____

$r = 4$? _____

Plot the new money-demand curve associated with $Y = 2,800$, and designate it L_2 in Figure 4C. Given this new level of Y, what is the relationship between money demand and money supply at the equilibrium interest rate you found in Part c?

_____

What will happen in the money market as a result of this situation? _____

_____

_____

What will be the equilibrium level of r when $Y = 2,800$? _____

e. Assume that real GDP increases again to a new level of 3,000.

What is the equation of the new money-demand curve? _____

Draw the demand-for-money curve associated with this level of real GDP, and label it L_3.

What is the new equilibrium level of r? _____

f. On the right-hand side of Figure 4C, plot the level of Y and the corresponding equilibrium level of r that you found in Parts c, d, and e. Connect these points and label the curve *LM*.

g. Each point along the *LM* curve meets the following condition: $(M/P)^d = (M^s/P)$. Using the demand-for-money function given at the beginning of this question and assuming that the real money supply is 500, calculate the numerical equation for the *LM* curve.

$Y =$ _____

Why does the *LM* curve have an upward slope? _____

_____

_____

_____

h. What is the velocity of money when:

$Y = 2,400$? _____

$Y = 2,800$? _____

$Y = 3,000$? _____

How does your answer to this question relate to your previous answer (in Part g) regarding the slope of the *LM* curve?

_____

_____

_____

i. Locate the point where $r = 7$ and $Y = 3,000$ on both parts of Figure 4C. Label that point with an *F*. Is there an excess demand or excess supply of money at this pair of r and Y?

_____

If Y remains at 3,000 (and the money supply remains unchanged), what must happen to r to bring the money market into equilibrium?

_____

Explain _____

_____

j. Locate the point where $r = 7$ and $Y = 2,200$ on both parts of Figure 4C. Label that point with a *G*. Is there an excess demand or excess supply of money at this pair of r and Y?

_____

If Y remains at 2,200 (and money supply remains unchanged), what must happen to r to bring the money market into equilibrium?

_____

Explain. _____

_____

k. In each of the following three questions, fill in the correct answer. For the first part of each question, choose among the following answers: *to the right of*; *to the left of*; *on*. For the second part of each question, choose among the following answers: *increase*; *decrease*; *remain unchanged*.

1. When the money market is in equilibrium, the existing r and Y are _____

the *LM* curve, and there is a tendency for the interest rate to _____

2. When there is an excess demand for money, the existing r and Y are _____

the *LM* curve and there is a tendency for the interest rate to _____

3. When there is an excess supply of money, the existing r and Y are _____

the *LM* curve, and there is a tendency for the interest rate to _____

Question 3

This question examines the *LM* curve more carefully. We change both the money supply and the parameters of the demand-for-money function and observe the changes that take place in the location and the shape of the *LM* curve. Assume that $(M/P)^d = 0.4Y - 20r$ and $(M^s/P) = 320$.

a. For $Y = 1,000$, the equation of money demand is: $(M/P)^d$ _____

Plot the $(M/P)^d$ curve and the (M^s/P) curve on the left-hand side of Figure 4D for the case where $Y = 1,000$. Label the demand curve L_1 and the supply curve M^s/P.

What is the equilibrium interest rate? _____

Label this point with a *G*.

b. What is the numerical equation for the *LM* curve? $Y =$ _____

Plot this *LM* curve on the right-hand side of Figure 4D, and label it LM_1. Locate the initial equilibrium point found in Part a, and label it with a *G*.

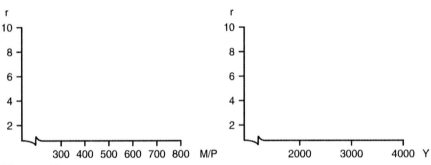

Figure 4D

c. Describe the situation in the money market if the Federal Reserve now decreases the real money supply to 280.

_____

_____

_____

Assuming that *Y* remains at 1,000, what is the new equilibrium rate of interest?

_____

Locate this point on both parts of Figure 4D and label it with an *H* in each graph. Alternatively, assume that in response to the lowered money supply, the interest rate does *not* change from the initial equilibrium level found in Part a.

What is the new level of real GDP required to bring the money market back into equilibrium?

_____

Label this point with an *I* on both parts of Figure 4D.

Neither Point H nor Point I is on the original LM curve. When the money supply changes, they both become equilibrium positions for the new money supply; therefore, they both become points on the new LM curve, LM_2.

What is the equation of LM_2? $Y =$ _____

Plot LM_2 in Figure 4D.

d. The coefficient of r in the money-demand equation indicates the responsiveness of money demand to changes in the interest rate. In Figure 4D draw the money-demand and money-supply curves associated with the following information (assume $Y = 1,000$): $(M/P)^d = 0.4Y - 40r$ and $M^s/P = 320$.

Label the demand curve L_3. How does this curve differ from L_1? _____

_____

What is the equation of the new LM curve? _____

In Figure 4D draw the LM curve associated with the money-demand and money-supply curves given above. Label this curve LM_3. How does LM_3 differ from LM_1? Explain.

_____

_____

e. The slope of the LM curve also depends on the sensitivity of money demand to real GDP. Assume that once again, the coefficient of r in the money-demand equation is 20, but now assume that the demand for money is less sensitive to changes in the level of real GDP. The money-demand equation is now $(M/P)^d = 0.25Y - 20r$, and $M^s/P = 170$.

What is the equation of the LM curve? _____

Plot the LM curve in Figure 4D, and label it LM_4.

In what ways are LM_4 to LM_1 the same, and in what ways are they different? _____

_____

_____

Question 4

The IS curve represents the Y and r combinations that are consistent with equilibrium in the commodity market. The LM curve represents the Y and r combinations that are consistent with equilibrium in the money market. For the economy to be in a "general" equilibrium, both the commodity and the money markets must be in equilibrium simultaneously. To achieve a general equilibrium, we must bring the IS and LM curves together.

a. Assume $C = 120 + 0.6Y$ and $I_p = 840 - 80r$. What is the level of A_0? _____

$A_p =$ _____

What is the multiplier? $k =$ _____

What is the equation of the IS curve? $Y =$ _____

Plot the IS curve in Figure 4E and label it IS.

b. Assume $(M^s/P)^d = 0.25Y - 25r$ and $(M^s/P) = 150$. What is the equation of the *LM* curve?

$Y =$ _____

Plot the *LM* curve in Figure 4E and label it *LM*.

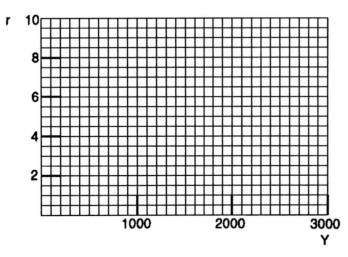

Figure 4E

c. In Figure 4E, locate the point of intersection between the *IS* and *LM* curves, and label it E_0.

At E_0, $Y =$ _____

and $r =$ _____

At E_0, what is the quantity of money demanded? _____

What is the size of the money supply? _____

How would you describe the situation in the money sector? _____

What is the level of A_p and of Induced Saving (sY)? _____

How would you describe the situation in the commodity sector? _____

d. As a way of proving that E_0 is the only general-equilibrium point, complete the following table, which compares the alternative combinations of Y and r.

Point in Fig. 4F	Y	r	M^s/P	$(M/P)^d$	Condition in Money Market	I_p	Auto C	sY	Condition in Goods Market
G	1,000	4	150						
H	1,400	8	150						
J	1,000	7	150						
K	1,400	5	150						

Use the following abbreviations: equilibrium = *EQ*, excess demand = *ED*, excess supply = *ES*, unintended inventory accumulation = $+\Delta I_u$, unintended inventory decumulation = $-\Delta I_u$.

Plot Points *G*, *H*, *J*, and *K* in Figure 4E.

e. At Point *J*, the money market *is/is not* in equilibrium. Because of this situation, there will be a tendency for the interest rate to *increase/decrease*, which will cause A_p to *increase/decrease* and *Y* to *increase/decrease*.

The new equilibrium is reached at Point _____

By how much will *r* change? _____

This change will cause the quantity demanded of money to *increase/decrease*.

By how much? _____

By how much will *Y* change? _____

This change will cause the demand for money to *increase/decrease* by _____

The total *increase/decrease* in the quantity demanded of money will be _____

The original excess *demand/supply* was equal to _____

f. At Point *G*, the commodity market *is/is not* in equilibrium. Because of this, there will be a tendency for output to *increase/decrease*.

The new equilibrium is reached at Point _____

By how much will *Y* change? _____

This change in *Y* will cause the demand for money to *increase/decrease*.

By how much? _____

To keep the money market in equilibrium, there must be an opposite impact on the demand for money. This impact will come through the interest rate's *increasing/decreasing*.

By how much? _____

This will cause the quantity demanded of money to *increase/decrease*.

By how much? _____

Question 5

Question 5 examines the case in which the demand for money is inelastic with respect to the interest rate.

a. Assume the *IS* curve is given by the equation $Y = 4,000 - 200r$, where $A_p = 800 - 40r$ and $k = 5$, and the *LM* curve is given by the equation $Y = 1,600 + 100r$, where $M^s = 400$, $P = 1$, and $(M/P)^d = 0.25\,Y - 25r$. What are the equilibrium levels of real GDP and the rate of interest?

$Y =$ _____

$r =$ _____

Plot these *IS* and *LM* curves in Figure 4F, and label them IS_1 and LM_1.

b. What is the velocity of money at the equilibrium level of real GDP? _____

c. If the real money supply increases by 150 ($M^s = 550$, $P = 1$), what is the equation for the new LM curve? _____

Plot the new LM curve in Figure 4F and label it LM_2.

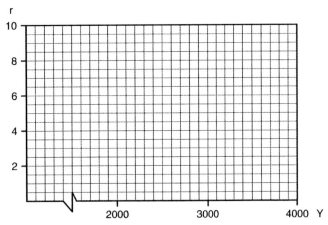

Figure 4F

What are the new equilibrium levels of real GDP and the rate of interest?

$Y =$ _____

$r =$ _____

What is the ratio of the change in real GDP to the change in the real money supply?

$\Delta Y / \Delta (M^s / P) =$ _____

d. When the real money supply equals 550, what is the velocity of money at the equilibrium level of real GDP? _____

Explain any difference between this value of velocity and that found in Part b above.

_____

e. Assume that there is a change in the demand-for-money function. The new function is $(M/P)^d = 0.25Y$. What is the effect of a change in the interest rate on the demand for money with this new demand for money function?

_____

If the real money supply equals 600, what is the equation of the LM curve? $Y =$ _____

Plot the new *LM* curve in Figure 4F, and label it LM_3. What are the equilibrium levels of real GDP and the rate of interest?

$Y =$ _____

$r =$ _____

Now what is the velocity of money at the equilibrium level of real GDP? _____

f. Suppose that the real money supply increases by 150 so that $M^s/P = 750$ while $(M/P)^d = 0.25Y$. What is the equation for the new *LM* curve?

$Y =$_____

Plot the new *LM* curve in Figure 5F and label it LM_4. What are the equilibrium levels of real GDP and the rate of interest?

$Y =$ _____

$r =$ _____

What is the velocity of money at the new equilibrium level of real GDP? _____

How does it compare with the velocity found in Part e above? _____

g. What is the ratio of change in real GDP to the change in the real money supply?

$\Delta Y/\Delta(M^s/P) =$_____

Compare the value of this ratio with the ratio you found in Part c. Explain why the ratios are different.

_____

_____

_____

Question 6

Previous question examined the case where monetary policy is extremely potent. Now we examine situations in which monetary policy is impotent and fiscal policy is very potent.

a. Assume the following: The level of induced consumption is 80 percent of disposable income, autonomous consumption is 200, planned autonomous investment is 300, government expenditure is 260, and the level of autonomous tax revenue is 200. The real money supply is 550. The equation of the demand for money is: $(M/P)^d = 0.25Y - 25r$.

What is the value of planned autonomous spending? _____

How does the level of planned autonomous spending respond to a change in the interest rate?

_____

What is the value of the multiplier? _____

What is the equation of the *IS* curve? _____

What is the equation of the *LM* curve? _____

Plot the *IS* and *LM* curves in Figures 4G. Label the *LM* curve LM_1. What are the equilibrium levels of real GDP and the rate of interest?

$Y =$ _____

$r =$ _____

b. If the real money supply increases by 150 to $M^s/P = 700$ so that the *LM* curve becomes $Y = 2,800 + 100r$, what are the equilibrium levels of real GDP and the rate of interest?

$Y =$ _____

$r =$ _____

Plot the new *LM* curve in Figure 4G. Label this curve LM_2.

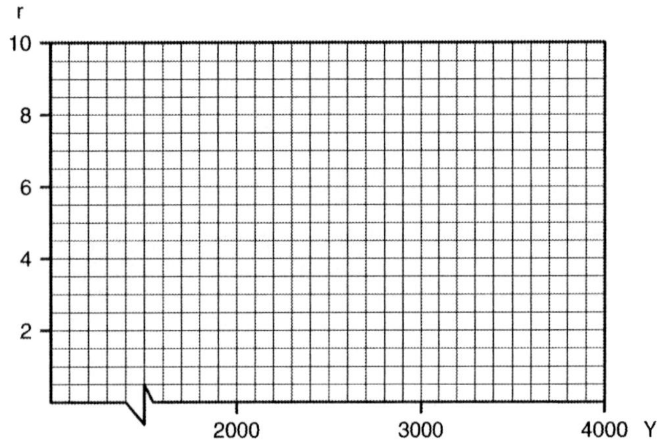

Figure 4G

c. What is the responsiveness of real GDP to the change in the real money supply?

$\Delta Y/\Delta(M^s/P) =$ _____

d. In previous question, Part g, there was also a change in money supply equal to 150. Explain why the responsiveness of real GDP to the change in money supply found there differs from the responsiveness found in Part c above.

_____

_____

_____

e. Now assume that the equation of the *IS* curve is $Y = 3{,}000 - 200r$ ($A_0 = 600$ and $k = 5$). The real money supply equals 400, and the equation of the *LM* curve is $r = 2$. What is the shape of the *LM* curve?

_____

If the *LM* curve has this shape, how do bond prices and interest rates respond to an increase in the real money supply? Explain.

_____

_____

_____

_____

f. What are the equilibrium level of real GDP and the rate of interest?

$Y = $ _____

$r = $ _____

Plot the *IS* and *LM* curves in Figure 4H. Label the *IS* curve IS_0.

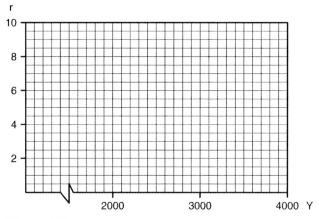

Figure 4H

If the natural level of real GDP (Y^N) is 3,200, what is the size of the gap between the equilibrium Y and Y^N?

_____

g. Explain how the Federal Reserve can change the money supply to remove the GDP gap found in Part f.

_____

_____

_____

h. If fiscal policy is used to try to remove the GDP gap, by how much should government expenditure be changed (taxes held constant)?

_____

If government expenditure were held constant, by how much should taxes be changed to remove the GDP gap?

_____

i. In this question, monetary policy was important. What must be the shapes of the *IS* or *LM* curves for this result?

_____

Do you think it is likely that the *IS* or *LM* curves would actually have such shapes? Explain.

_____

_____

_____

Question 7

This question examines the impact of discretionary fiscal policy on the economy. Expansionary fiscal policy not only affects induced spending (through its effect on income), but can also affect autonomous spending through a change in the interest rate. Use the following equations in answering this question:

$$c(Y - T) = 0.8(Y - T); a = 300 - 10r; I_p = 400 - 30r; G = 180;$$

$$T_0 = 250; (M/P)^d = 0.25Y - 25r; M^s = 550; P = 1.$$

a. What is the equation of A_p? _____

What is the equation for the *IS* curve? $Y = $ _____

What is the equation for the *LM* curve? $Y = $ _____

Plot the *IS* and *LM* curves in Figure 4I. Label the curves IS_0 and LM_0. Label the point of intersection E_0. What are the equilibrium levels of real GDP and the rate of interest?

$Y = $ _____

$r = $ _____

b. If government expenditure increases by 120 so that now $G = 300$, what is the equation for the new *IS* curve? $Y =$ _____

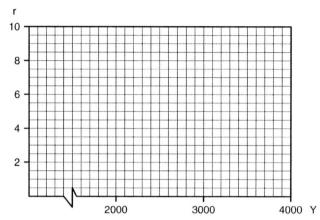

Figure 4I

Plot the new *IS* curve in Figure 4I. Label the curve IS_1. Label the point of intersection of IS_1 and LM_0 as Point E_1. What are the new equilibrium levels of real GDP and the rate of interest?

$Y =$ _____

$r =$ _____

c. If the original interest rate had not changed and the full government expenditure multiplier had taken place, what would have been the equilibrium level of real GDP?

$Y =$ _____

Label this hypothetical level of real GDP as E_2 in Figure 4I.

Explain why the economy does not move to Point E_2. _____

_____

_____

d. Complete the following table, comparing the old and new equilibrium positions.

Item	E_0	E_1
Private autonomous spending, $a + I_p$		
Government expenditure, G		
Autonomous taxes, T_0		
Total planned autonomous spending, $a - cT_0 + I_p + G$		
Real GDP, Y		

Indicate the amount of crowding out in Figure 4I. Do total private expenditures fall as a result of the increase in government expenditure? Explain.

_____

_____

_____

_____

e. Assume the same original conditions and changes concerning the *IS* curve as in Parts a through d. Now assume that the real money supply is 650, and that the demand for money has changed so that it has zero responsiveness to changes in the interest rate. The new equation is $(M/P)^d = 0.25Y$.

What is the equation of the *LM* curve? _____

Plot this *LM* curve in Figure 4I and label it LM_1. What are the initial equilibrium levels of real GDP and the rate of interest (E_0)?

$Y =$ _____

$r =$ _____

After the increase in government expenditure of 120, what are the new equilibrium levels of real GDP and the rate of interest? Label this point E_3.

$Y =$ _____

$r =$ _____

What is the amount of crowding out? _____

Explain this result. _____

_____

f. Assume the same conditions as in Part a above, except that the demand for money now is infinitely responsive to changes in the rate of interest, so that the equation of the *LM* curve is $r = 4$. Plot the *LM* curve and label it LM_2. What are the initial equilibrium levels of real GDP and the rate of interest?

$Y =$ _____

$r =$ _____

After the increase in government spending of 120, what are the equilibrium levels of real GDP and the rate of interest?

$Y =$ _____

$r =$ _____

What is the amount of crowding out? _____

Explain any differences in this result from that obtained in Part a. _____

_____

_____

_____

g. Which form of the *LM* curve, the one in Part e or the one in Part f, do you think is more likely to occur and why?

_____

_____

Question 8

Japan has experienced a decade-long slump in output, which is less severe than the U.S. Great Depression, but worse than anything experienced in the United States since that time. Like the experience of the United States in the 1930s, short-term interest rates have been extremely *low/high*. In this situation, sometimes known as a *money/interest/liquidity* trap, *monetary/fiscal* policy is rendered impotent because this policy cannot be used to *increase/decrease* the interest rate. In the *IS-LM* model, this trap is depicted using a *vertical IS curve/horizontal LM curve*. Japanese policymakers have been hesitant to employ *monetary/fiscal* policy, the only type of policy that will work in this situation, out of concern for the size of the national debt. Under the circumstances, however, using *monetary policy alone/fiscal policy alone/a combined monetary and fiscal policy* would require no *increase/decrease* in the interest rate, and would not result in an increase in the national debt held by the public. This kind of policy, known as *monetizing/selling* debt, is unpopular with central bankers because of fear of inflation, but it might be the right policy to follow at this time.

Question 9

Because of the housing market troubles, the Fed has been strongly criticized by economic analysts. What two reasons contributed to creation of "boom-bust cycle" in the housing market according to these analysts?

a. _____

b. _____

Chapter 5
The Government Budget, Foreign Borrowing, and the Twin Deficits

This chapter takes a closer look at the effects of fiscal policy and the interaction of the government budget with net exports and foreign lending or borrowing. We learn the difference between (and the importance of distinguishing) the actual, structural, and cyclical government budget surpluses and deficits. We examine how the government budget surplus or deficit is related to the economy's output and its choice of fiscal policy.

Question 1

The size of the actual government surplus or deficit depends on the tax structure, the level of government expenditure, and the actual level of real GDP. In this question we examine the interaction among these variables in determining the size of the government surplus or deficit. Answer the questions or fill in the blanks with the correct word or words.

a. In simplest terms, the government budget surplus is defined as _____

   _____

   In the text, tax receipts (T) are set equal to tY. Why? _____

   _____

   _____

b. We can write the surplus equation as $tY - G$. Assume that $t = 0.4$ and $G = 64$.

   What will the surplus be when $Y = 160$? _____

   $Y = 180$? _____

   $Y = 200$? _____

In Figure 5A, draw the budget line associated with these three points, and label the line BB_0.

What are the two key parameters for this line? _____

Identify this line by writing these parameters with subscripts 0 next to BB_0.

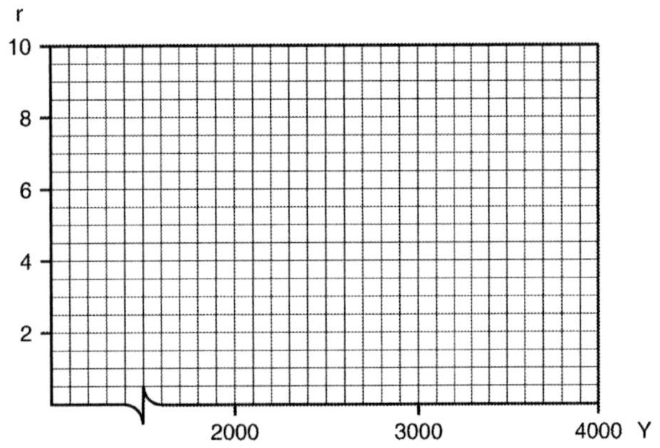

Figure 5A

c. If the government set fiscal policy, that is, tax rates and expenditure levels, as described in BB_0, would it be running a surplus, deficit, or balanced budget?

    _____

    _____

    What does your answer suggest about using the actual budget deficit as a measure of fiscal policy's effect on the economy?

    _____

    _____

    _____

d. For this part of the question, assume that the two parameters have the same values as in Part b. The economy is originally at $Y = 200$.

    What is the surplus? _____

    If there is a fall in investment so that Y falls, what could the government do to stabilize the economy, that is, bring Y back to 200?

    _____

    _____

    Assuming that the government wants to use fiscal policy to bring about this stabilization, what would it have to do to its budget?

    _____

    _____

    _____

If Y fell to 150, what would the government budget surplus be? _____

How would this change in surplus have come about? _____

_____

_____

Since this movement toward deficit helps stabilize the economy and occurs without any overt change in government policy, we refer to it as

_____

e. What would have happened to the economy if there were no built-in stabilization, that is, if the government deficit did not automatically increase when Y fell?

_____

_____

What would be the value of t in this case of no automatic stabilization? _____

_____

f. In Part d we saw that the size of the budget surplus will change automatically as Y changes. The surplus will also change if the government alters the tax rate (t) or government spending (G). Changing the surplus through changes in t and/or G is referred to as

_____

Assume that G remains at 64, but the government decreases the tax rate so that $t_1 = 0.3$. Draw the new budget line. Label it BB_1.

What is the surplus when $Y = 200$? _____

$Y = 180$? _____

At what level of Y will the budget be balanced? _____

Since the tax rate has decreased, the amount of taxes collected at each level of output will decrease. This is an example of *expansionary/restrictive* fiscal policy. Since the surplus is *higher/lower* at each level of income, BB_1 lies *above/below* BB_0.

g. If natural real GDP is 200, what is the natural employment deficit or surplus when $t = 0.4$? _____

$t = 0.3$? _____

h. What is the size of the structural deficit or surplus when $t = 0.4$? _____

$t = 0.3$? _____

How does your answer compare with that for Part g? _____

_____

_____

i.   Assume that $t = 0.3$ and $G = 64$. If $Y = 180$, what is the actual deficit or surplus? _____

What is the cyclical deficit or surplus when $Y = 80$? _____

Question 2

In a closed economy, national saving must always equal domestic investment. For this reason, an increase in government spending is associated with a decrease in domestic investment known as the crowding-out effect. Graphically show that this is true.

Question 3

In a small open economy, an increase in government spending does not crowd out private investment. Graphically show that this is true.

Question 4

This question is concerned with the government budget in historical perspective. Five facts stand out with regard to the relationship between wars, budget deficits, and the growth of government.

a.   What is the impact of wars on the size of government?

_____

_____

b.   What is the impact of wars on tax revenues and on budget deficits? Explain the behavior of budget deficits.

_____

_____

c.   How has the size of government behaved in the decades following World War II?

_____

_____

d.   During the 1980s, how did the budget deficit behave? How much of it was due to a drop in tax revenue?

_____

_____

e.   What was the condition of the budget in the late 1990s, and in most of the first decade of the 21st century?

_____

_____

Question 5

This question is concerned with the phenomenon of "twin deficits" and the possibility of these "twins" being separated and rejoined.

a. Rewrite Equation (5.5) $[S + (T - G)\ \alpha I + NX]$ so that it depicts a government budget deficit where $(G - T)$ on the left side of the equation with a foreign trade deficit $(-NX)$ and all other terms on the right side (i.e., Equation (5.9)).

_____

_____

b. What must be true regarding private domestic saving and domestic investment if there are to be "twin deficits," i.e., $G > T$ and $-NX$?

_____

_____

c. What must be true regarding private domestic saving and domestic investment if the "twin deficits" are to be equal?

_____

_____

d. Your text notes that in the 1990s, there were budget surpluses along with trade deficits. How was that possible?

_____

_____

Chapter 6
International Trade, Exchange Rates, and Macroeconomic Policy

This chapter expands the model to incorporate the international trade. Questions 1–5 familiarize us with some important concepts about the international economy—the balance of payments and foreign exchange rates, and the theory of purchasing power parity as a theory of the long-run adjustment of the exchange rate—and how they relate to aggregate demand and interest rates. Questions 6–9 deal with open-economy *IS-LM* models. In Question 6, we compare effects of fiscal policy in closed-economy and open-economy models. In Question 7, we examine the differences that fixed and flexible exchange rates make to the *IS-LM* model. Finally, in Questions 8 and 9, we introduce the *BP* curve into the *IS-LM* model to deal with the effects of international capital flows and to investigate the effects of monetary and fiscal policy under fixed and flexible exchange rates.

Question 1

In this question we define some important terms and concepts used when choosing policy in an international setting.

a. When discussing economic relations among countries, we often refer to a country's *balance of payments*. What is a country's balance of payments?

_____

_____

What do we mean when we refer to a deficit in the balance of payments? _____

_____

_____

How is a deficit in the balance of payments financed? _____

_____

What are net exports? _____

_____

The bulk of the transactions in a nation's balance of payments can be divided into two categories (excluding the final settlement of accounts). These two categories are the

_____

and the _____

Briefly explain what each of these accounts is.

1. _____

   _____

2. _____

   _____

b. How would you classify the following transactions in the U.S. balance of payments? (For each, write either *capital account* or *current account*.) Also, note whether the transaction represents a *credit* (+) or a *debit* (−) item.

Transaction	Classification	+/−
1. An Alfa Romeo sports car is purchased by a Wall Street investment banker.		
2. A $500 gift is sent by a Swedish couple to their daughter, who is a college student in Minnesota.		
3. A Japanese firm buys a hotel in Tampa.		
4. A Canadian firm buys a U.S.-built Xerox machine.		
5. An American college student buys an aperitif in a Paris sidewalk cafe.		
6. Saudi Arabian oil sheiks buy an additional $10 million of Citibank certificates of deposit.		

c. Explain the role of capital flows in balancing the U.S. balance of payments in the 1980s. _____

_____

As a result of these capital flows, the United States now has a *positive/negative* net international investment position, which gives it a *net debtor/net creditor* position. What real effect will this have on the U.S. economy?

_____

_____

d. Referring to information in your textbook, when did the United States' balance on current account become continually in deficit?

_____

From information in your textbook, in what year did the United States become a net foreign debtor?

e. How does U.S. foreign indebtedness affect the U.S. standard of living?

_____

_____

Question 2

International economic transactions differ from transactions within a country in a very important respect: An international transaction involves the exchange of a country's money for the money of another country. This exchange is normally done through the foreign exchange market at the current foreign exchange rate. In this question we briefly examine exchange rates and exchange-rate policies.

a.   What is the foreign exchange rate? _____

_____

b.   Upon what factors does the demand for foreign exchange depend? Explain. _____

_____

_____

_____

Upon what factors does the supply of foreign exchange depend? Explain. _____

_____

_____

_____

Is the demand curve for foreign exchange negatively sloped? Why or why not? _____

_____

_____

_____

Is the supply curve of foreign exchange positively sloped? Why or why not? _____

_____

_____

_____

c.   If the foreign exchange rate could freely adjust to excess demand or supply, explain how the market would adjust to equilibrate demand and supply in conditions of:

Excess demand _____

_____

Excess supply _____

_____

If, say, the United States wanted to prevent a depreciation of its foreign exchange rate in a situation of excess supply, what action could it take?

_____

_____

d. Find the current spot and 180-day future exchange rates (in U.S. dollars) between the United States and the countries listed on the table below.* (*Note*: As a source for exchange rates, use *The Wall Street Journal* or a similar publication. Be careful to use amounts of foreign currency per dollar, not dollars per unit of foreign currency.)

Foreign Exchange Rate of the U.S. Dollar, Selected Foreign Currencies

United Kingdom (pound)		Canada (dollar)		Japan (yen)		European Union (euro)		Switzerland (franc)	
Spot	180-day	Spot	180-day	Spot	180-day	Spot	180-day	Spot	180-day

What does the difference between the spot and the 180-day exchange rate signify about exchange rate expectations?

_____

_____

_____

e. There are two general types of exchange-rate policies and adjustments to imbalances between foreign receipts and expenditures. These two policies are

1. _____

2. _____

f. Explain how a country adjusts to a balance-of-payments imbalance under each of these policies.

1. _____

   _____

   _____

2. _____

   _____

   _____

g. Which exchange rate policy results in an international "trilemma?" Explain.

_____

Question 3

In this question, we examine some of the determinants of exchange rates in the long run. In particular, we look at the theory of purchasing power parity (PPP). This theory is based on the assumption of "one market, one price." It says that in open economies, the prices of internationally traded goods should be the same everywhere (after adjustments for transportation cost and customs duties are made).

a.   The PPP theory can be written as follows: $e' = P^f/P$, where

$P =$ _____

$P^f =$ _____

$e' =$ _____

b.   If the world price of soybeans is \$7.20 a bushel, and the price in Marseille is 43.20 euros per bushel, then the exchange rate for the euro ought to be:

$e' = \$$ _____

If French inflation pushes the price of soybeans in Marseille to 48.00 euros, then the euro should *appreciate/depreciate* to:

$e' = \$$ _____

c.   It is sometimes more useful to present the above PPP relationship in terms of the rate of change in the exchange rate, $\Delta e'/e'$, and the relative rates of foreign inflation, p^f, and domestic inflation, p. We can write this as follows:

$\Delta e'/e' =$ _____

If the Spanish inflation rate is 7.4 percent per year, while the U.S. inflation rate is 3.6 percent per year, then the annual percentage change in the peseta-dollar exchange rate (in dollars per peseta) should be

_____

Empirical evidence supports PPP as an important factor explaining exchange-rate changes. Other factors can offset PPP, however, and the actual rate of change in exchange rates may differ from what PPP would predict. Gordon discusses three factors that are important qualifications of the PPP theory. Identify them:

1.   _____

2.   _____

3.   _____

d.   If PPP always held, then the real exchange rate would never change. As noted above, however, there are good reasons why PPP does not hold, particularly over short periods. Consequently, through their impact on net exports, changes in the real exchange rate are a major source of instability in aggregate demand.

Show how to calculate the real exchange rate. _____

_____

The rate of change of the real exchange rate, $\Delta e/e$, may be written in terms of the rate of change of the nominal exchange rate and the rates of domestic and foreign inflation as follows: $\Delta e/e = (\Delta e'/e') + p - p^f$. What rate of change in the real exchange rate does the PPP theory predict? Explain.

_____

In the example of Spain given in Part c above, if the actual change in the exchange rate of the peseta is –3.0, what is the change in the Spanish real rate of exchange?

$\Delta e/e =$ _____

What impact, if any, will this have on the Spanish economy? _____

_____

Question 4

In an open economy, changes in the exchange rate can have a significant impact on aggregate demand. In this question we examine how changes in the exchange rate affect net exports, one of the components of aggregate demand.

a. Assume that a dollar can buy 0.76 Euros. A bottle of French wine costs 30 euros when purchased in Paris.

What is the cost, in dollars, of that wine? _____

If the exchange rate appreciates so that each dollar now buys 0.85 euros, what is the dollar price of a bottle of French wine?

_____

In response to this change in exchange rates, the amount of French wine imported into the United States will *increase/decrease*.

b. Once again assume that a dollar can buy 0.76 euros. What is the price in euros of an American computer that costs $1,500 in New York?

_____

If the exchange rate appreciates so that each dollar now buys 0.85 euros, what is the price, in euros, of the American computer?

_____

In response to this change in exchange rates, the number of computers exported from the United States to France will *increase/decrease*.

c. What will happen to the net exports of the United States in response to an appreciation of the exchange rate? Explain why this is so.

_____

d. The relationship described in Part c can be put into algebraic form: $NX = NX_0 - n_0 Y - ue$. If $NX_0 = 840$, $n_0 = 0.15$, and $u = 3$, what will be the level of net exports when real GDP is 3,000 and the exchange rate is 120?

_____

If the exchange rate increases to 140, what will happen to net exports? _____

_____

Question 5

The previous question showed how changes in the exchange rate affect aggregate demand. Now we show how changes in the interest rate can affect the exchange rate and, therefore, aggregate demand.

a. If the interest rate in France remains the same but the interest rate in the United States increases, individuals and firms who have money in interest-earning accounts in France will get a relatively *smaller/larger* return by shifting their money into the United States.

   This shift of money will require the *buying/selling* of euros and the *buying/selling* of American dollars. This activity in the foreign exchange market will tend to *increase/decrease* the demand for American dollars and thus will *increase/decrease* the exchange rate.

b. Based on your answers to Question 4 and Part a of this question, an increase in the interest rate differential between the United States and a foreign country will tend to *increase/decrease* the exchange rate and *increase/decrease* net exports.

Question 6

In this question we examine what happens to the *IS-LM* model when we include the foreign sector. We begin this problem with a short review of how the equation for the *IS* curve is determined in a closed economy. The following equations representing the structure of the economy are the same as those used in Chapter 4. (*Note*: The points addressed in this question are not exposited in Gordon, so you or your instructor may wish to consider this an optional exercise. However, the equations below are used in Questions 8 and 9.)

$$c(Y - T) = 0.8(Y - T)$$
$$a = 300 - 10r$$
$$I_p = 400 - 30r$$
$$G = 180$$
$$T = 250$$
$$(M/P)^d = 0.25Y - 25r$$
$$M^s = 550$$
$$P = 1.$$

a. Review: For the equations given above, respond to the following.

   Define the marginal leakage rate. _____

   _____

   What is the value of the marginal leakage rate? *MLR* = _____

   What is the value of the simple Keynesian multiplier? k = _____

   What is the equation of planned autonomous spending? A_p = _____

What is the equation of the *IS* curve? $Y =$ _____

What is the equation of the *LM* curve? $Y =$ _____

This economy is a *closed/open* economy.

Draw the *IS* curve in Figure 6A, and label it IS_{c_1}. Draw the *LM* curve, and label it LM_0.

The equilibrium levels of real GDP and the interest rate are:

$Y =$ _____

$r =$ _____

Label this point E_1 in Figure 6A.

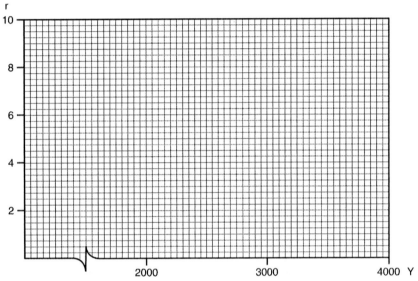

Figure 6A

b. Now assume government spending (G) increases by 120 to a new level of 300. Using the equations given at the beginning of the question, but with the new value of G, respond to the following.

What is the marginal leakage rate? $MLR =$ _____

What is the simple Keynesian multiplier? $k =$ _____

What is the equation of planned autonomous spending? $A_p =$ _____

What is the equation of the *IS* curve? $Y =$ _____

Draw the *IS* curve in Figure 6A, and label it IS_{c_2}.

The equilibrium levels of real GDP and the interest rate are:

$Y =$ _____

$r =$ _____

Label this point E_{c_2}.

What is the value of the government-spending multiplier? $\Delta Y/\Delta G =$ _____

The value of the government-spending multiplier is different from the value of the simple Keynesian multiplier you gave above. Explain why there is this difference.

_____

_____

_____

_____

_____

c.   In this section we add a foreign sector to the economy but otherwise assume the economy is as described by the equations given at the beginning of this question. The following equation describes the foreign sector: $NX = 520 - 0.2Y$.

How does the inclusion of the foreign sector affect the definition of the marginal leakage rate you gave above?

_____

_____

What is the value of the marginal leakage rate? $MLR =$ _____

What is the value of the simple Keynesian multiplier? $k =$ _____

Assume that government spending is at its original value, i.e., $G = 180$.

What is the equation of planned autonomous spending? $A_p =$ _____

What is the equation of the IS curve? $Y =$ _____

Plot the IS curve for the open economy in Figure 6A, and label it IS_{o_1}.

Compare the slope of IS_{c_1} with that of IS_{o_1}. _____

Show mathematically why these slopes differ. _____

_____

_____

The equilibrium value levels of real GDP and the interest rate are:

$Y =$ _____

$r =$ _____

Compare this result to the equilibrium values found in Part a above. _____

_____

d. Assume that government spending (G) increases to 300 in our open economy described in Part c.

What is the value of the marginal leakage rate? $MLR =$ _____

What is the value of the simple Keynesian multiplier? $k =$ _____

What is the equation of planned autonomous spending? $A_p =$ _____

What is the equation of the IS curve? $Y =$ _____

Plot this IS curve in Figure 6A, and label it IS_{o_2}.

The equilibrium value levels of real GDP and the interest rate are:

$Y =$ _____

$r =$ _____

Label this point E_{o_2}.

What is the government-spending multiplier for the open economy? $\Delta Y/\Delta G =$ _____

Is the value for this government-spending multiplier the same as the value of the simple Keynesian multiplier for the open economy that you found in Part c above? _____

Explain your answer. _____

_____

e. In Parts b and d you examined the results of increasing government spending (G) by 120 in a closed economy (Part b) and in an open economy (Part d).

In the closed economy, what is the change in equilibrium output? $\Delta Y =$ _____

In the open economy, what is the change in equilibrium output? $\Delta Y =$ _____

Explain why the results in these two cases differ. _____

_____

Question 7

The previous question compared the effects of a change in government spending in a closed economy and an open economy. Among other things, we learned that the closed economy IS curve slope is flatter and the Y-intercept change is greater in a closed economy than in an open economy. In this question we study the effect on the IS curve of fixed versus flexible foreign exchange rates. (*Note*: The points addressed in this question are not exposited in Gordon, so you or your instructor may wish to consider this an optional exercise.)

a. Let net exports be given by the following equation: $NX = 840 - 0.2Y - 4e$. According to this equation, net exports depend on autonomous exports (840), real GDP, and the foreign exchange rate.

Explain why net exports would change if real GDP changed. _____

_____

_____

Explain why net exports would change if the foreign exchange rate changed. _____

_____

_____

b.   Now consider a fixed exchange-rate system in which the exchange is fixed at 80.

What is the equation for net exports now? $NX =$ _____

Note that this is the same equation used in Question 6, Part c. Assume the values of all other exogenous variables are the same as in Question 6, Part c.

What is the equation of planned autonomous spending? $A_p =$ _____

What is the value of the simple Keynesian multiplier? $k =$ _____

What is the equation of the IS curve? $Y =$ _____

Draw this IS curve in Figure 6B, and label it IS_{fix}.

In the rest of this question, we will compare this fixed-exchange-rate model with one in which the exchange rate can vary, i.e., a flexible-exchange-rate system. We begin with a review of the relationship among changes in the interest rate, exchange rate, and net exports.

c.   In a world in which there is internationally mobile capital, the exchange rate (e) is sensitive to changes in the interest rate. If the interest rate in the United States increases and other interest rates remain the same (increasing the interest rate differential), the exchange rate of the dollar will *increase/decrease*, imports will *increase/decrease*, and exports will *increase/decrease*. These changes in the foreign sector will lead to a(n) *increase/decrease* in net exports.

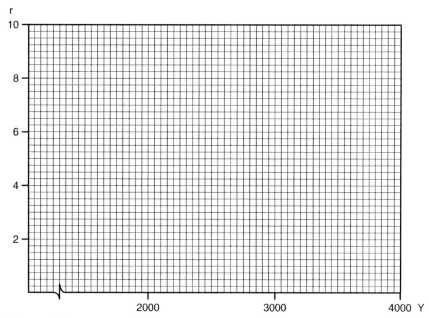

Figure 6B

Assume that the relationship between the exchange rate and the interest rate can be described by the equation $e = 20r$. Recall the equation for net exports written as a function of real GDP and the foreign exchange rate, $NX = 840 - 0.2Y - 4e$.

What is the equation for net exports written in terms of real GDP and the interest rate?

$NX =$ _____

What is the value of A_0 under these assumptions? $A_0 =$ _____

What is the equation of the planned autonomous spending curve? $A_p =$ _____

What is the simple Keynesian multiplier? $k =$ _____

What is the equation of the *IS* curve? $Y =$ _____

Draw this *IS* curve in Figure 6B and label it IS_{flex}.

Earlier we found that using expansionary fiscal policy with a fixed money supply will lead to some crowding out of private autonomous spending. In the next part of this question, we will compare the size of the crowding-out phenomenon in the fixed-exchange-rate model to that of the flexible-exchange-rate model.

d. If the interest rate rises to 6 percent, what will be the new level of A_p in the fixed-exchange-rate model?

$A_p =$ _____

What is the resulting level of Y on IS_{fix}? $Y =$ _____

Explain how you reached these answers. _____

_____

_____

_____

e. If the interest rate rises to 6 percent, what be the value of A_p in the flexible-exchange-rate model?

$A_p =$ _____

What is the resulting level of Y on IS_{flex}? $Y =$ _____

Explain how you reached these answers. _____

_____

_____

_____

f. Assuming that you begin from $Y = 2,600$. In which case is the crowding-out effect larger? Explain your answer.

_____

_____

_____

_____

Question 8

This question considers the effects of an expansionary fiscal policy in a large, open economy under a system of fixed exchange rates. This and the next question use equations from Questions 6 and 7, including the net-export equation, $NX = 840 - 0.2Y - 4e$. (In Question 6c, this equation implicitly assumed an exchange rate of 80.)

a. For purposes of review and easier reference, rewrite the equation of the LM curve from Question 6a and the equation of the IS curve and the equilibrium values of Y and r from Question 6c.

IS: _____

LM: _____

$Y =$ _____

$r =$ _____

In Figure 6C, draw the IS and LM curves given by the above equations, labeling them IS_0 and LM_0, respectively; label the equilibrium point E_0.

b. Assume, as in Questions 6c and 7a, that the foreign exchange rate is 80. What is the value of net exports when the economy is in equilibrium at Point E_0?

_____

What is the value of net foreign investment? _____

The value of capital outflows or inflows is: _____

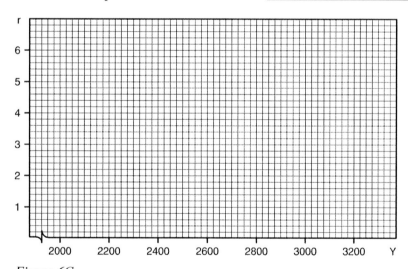

Figure 6C

c.   As in Question 6d, suppose that government spending increases to 300, while the other exogenous variables retain their values from Question 6, including the exchange rate which is fixed at 80. For purposes of review and easier reference, rewrite below from Question 6d the equation of the new *IS* curve and the new equilibrium values of Y and r.

IS: $Y =$ _____

$Y =$ _____

$r =$ _____

Draw in Figure 6C the new *IS* curve, labeling it IS_1; label the new equilibrium point E_0'.

In Question 6 we didn't consider the effects of capital flows on the equilibrium values of real GDP and the interest rate. We want to do that in this question. If the economy described in Figure 6C is a large, open economy, then it has an upward sloping balance-of-payments (*BP*) curve. Let the equation of the *BP* curve be: $r = -9 + 0.005Y$. We shall refer to the economy as the United States.

d.   Draw this curve in Figure 6C, and label it *BP*. At the initial equilibrium (Point E_0), the U.S. balance of payments is in *deficit/equilibrium/surplus*. At the new equilibrium (Point E_0'), the balance of payments is in *deficit/equilibrium/surplus*.

Still assuming the exchange rate is 80, what are net exports now? _____

If the world interest rate were 4 percent, capital would be flowing *into/out of* the United States. This would *increase/decrease* reserves of the U.S. banking system, and the U.S. money supply would *increase/decrease*. This process would continue until the U.S. interest rate *fell/rose* and the balance of payments was in *deficit/equilibrium/surplus*.

e.   Find the interest rate and real GDP level consistent with balance-of-payment equilibrium after the increase in government spending. (*Hint*: Substitute the *BP* equation into the IS_1 equation and solve for Y; then substitute the solution value of Y into either *BP* or IS_1 and solve for r.)

$Y =$ _____

$r =$ _____

Label this point E_1 in Figure 6C.

f.   What is the change in the real money supply that must occur to move the economy from E_0 to E_1?

$\Delta(M^s/P) =$ _____

What is the value of the real money supply after this change? $M^s/P =$ _____

Write the equation of the *LM* curve for that money supply. _____

Draw this *LM* curve in Figure 6C, and label it LM_1.

g.   What is the value of net exports at the new equilibrium point, E_1? _____

Net capital *inflow/outflow* is _____

h. Has the fiscal policy stimulus been more or less effective than in Question 6? Explain.

_____

_____

_____

_____

Question 9

This question considers an expansionary monetary policy in a large, open economy under a system of flexible exchange rates. The economy is described by the same equations as in Questions 6 and 8, and we assume the economy is in initial equilibrium at the same point, E_0. We shall refer to the economy as the United States. Draw IS_0 and LM_0 in Figure 6D and label their intersection E_0.

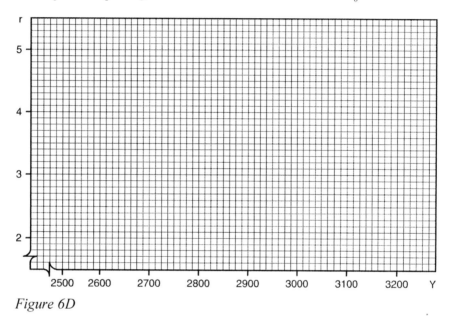

Figure 6D

a. Suppose the Fed decides to follow an expansionary monetary policy, thereby increasing the real money supply to 625. Write the LM curve associated with that real money supply.

_____

Graph this LM curve in Figure 6C and label it LM_1. Given IS_0, solve for the new equilibrium point.

$Y =$ _____

$r =$ _____

Find this point in Figure 6D and label it E_0.

b. Assuming the world interest rate is 4 percent, then in the situation described in Part a of this question, capital will flow *into/out of* the United States. This will *increase/decrease* the supply of dollars on the foreign exchange market, thereby causing the exchange rate of the dollar to *fall/rise*.

c. Suppose the *BP* curve is given by the equation $r = -2.5 + 0.0025Y$. Draw this curve in Figure 6D and label it *BP*. Given this *BP* function, find the levels of real GDP and the interest rate consistent with balance-of-payments equilibrium. (*Hint*: Substitute the equation for *BP* into LM_1 and solve for Y; then substitute the solved value of Y into either LM_1 or *BP* and solve for r.)

Y = _____

r = _____

Label this point E_1. What would bring about this equilibrium point? Explain _____

_____

_____

_____

d. Find the value of A_0 that would shift the *IS* curve through point E_1. _____

Write the equation of the A_p function for this value of A_0. _____

Write the equation of the *IS* curve for this A_p function. _____

Graph this *IS* curve in Figure 6D, and label it IS_1. The point of intersection of IS_1 and LM_1 already should be labeled E_1. (It would be a good idea to solve for equilibrium Y and r with IS_1 and LM_1 to make sure you have obtained the correct *IS* curve.)

In this part of the question, we want to figure out what the exchange rate has to be to produce the new equilibrium at E_1.

e. What is the autonomous component of *NX* in the initial equilibrium? In other words, find $NX_0 - 4e$, where $NX_0 = 840$ and $e = 80$.

_____

Assume that the entire increase in A_0 in Part d is due to a change in the autonomous component of net exports. Then the new value of $NX_0 - 4e$ is the initial value plus ΔA_0.

What is ΔA_0? _____

What, then, is the new value of $NX_0 - 4e$? _____

Solve for the new exchange rate at E_1. (*Hint*: Set the autonomous component of the net-export function, i.e., $NX_0 - 4e$, equal to the value you obtained in the immediately preceding part of this question, and solve for e.)

e = _____

The foreign exchange rate has *appreciated/remained unchanged/depreciated*. Net exports are equal to

_____

so capital *inflows/outflows* are _____

Monetary policy has been *effective/ineffective* in stimulating the economy in this question.

Chapter 7
Aggregate Demand, Aggregate Supply, and the Self-Correcting Economy

Up to this point we have examined the causes and implications of changes in autonomous spending, the real money supply, and real GDP, all under the strict assumption that the price level remains unchanged. In this chapter we drop that unrealistic assumption. When the price level changes, with the nominal money supply constant, there is a change in the real money supply. Since changes in the real money supply affect real output and the interest rate, we find a relationship between the price level and real GDP. That relationship is called the aggregate demand curve (*AD*). Questions 1–3 explore *AD* in some detail.

After developing the aggregate demand curve, our next task is to develop the short-run and long-run aggregate supply curves (denoted *SAS* and *LAS*, respectively). Question 4 introduces the underpinnings of the *SAS* curve. Question 5 considers the impact of changes in the wage rate on the *SAS* curve. Question 6 explores the determination of the equilibrium real wage. Once the short-run aggregate supply curve is developed, it is combined with the aggregate demand curve to give us a model that can explain how changes in aggregate demand or supply affect both output and prices in the short run. This is done in Question 7, where, among other things, the long-run aggregate supply curve (*LAS*) is developed.

In Question 8 we examine the classical model and explore how perfect price flexibility ensures that the economy is always in long-run equilibrium. Question 9 deals with one of the Keynesian objections to the classical model, deflation impotence. Finally, Question 10 treats Pigou's response to deflation impotence, the real-balance effect.

Question 1

In this question we show how flexible prices will change the real money supply when the nominal money supply remains the same. Because changes in the money supply cause changes in demand for goods and services, we have a link between changes in the price level and changes in real GDP. We call this relationship between the price level and real GDP the aggregate demand curve.

Assume that the equation of the *IS* curve is $Y = 4,000 - 200r$ $(A_0 = 800, k = 5)$ and the demand for money is $(M/P)^d = 0.25Y - 50r$, so that the equation for the *LM* curve is $Y = 4(M^s/P) + 200r$. (*Note*: Be sure you know how to derive both the *IS* and *LM* curves.)

a. Explain what is meant by the nominal money supply. _____

_____

Explain what is meant by the real money supply. _____

_____

b. Complete the following table.

Nominal Money Supply (M^s)	Price Index (P)	Real Money Supply (M^s/P)
400	2.0	
400	1.0	
400	0.667	
400	0.5	

c. What is the equation of the *LM* curve when the nominal money supply is 400 and the price level is 1.0?

$Y =$ _____

Given the *IS* curve above, what are the equilibrium levels of real GDP and the rate of interest when the nominal money supply is 400 and the price level is 1.0?

$Y =$ _____

$r =$ _____

Plot the *IS* and *LM* curves in the top part of Figure 7A and label them IS_0 and LM_0.

d. Explain what will happen to the *LM* curve if the price level declines. Why does this happen? _____

_____

_____

_____

Explain what will happen to the *LM* curve if the price level increases. Why does this happen? _____

_____

_____

e. With a fixed nominal money supply, each change in the price level yields a new *LM* curve. Assuming that the nominal money supply still equals 400, complete the following table.

Curve	Price Level	Real Money Supply	Equation of LM Curve	Equilibrium Levels Y	r	Point on Figure 7A
LM_1	2.0		$Y =$			E_1
LM_0	1.0		$Y =$			E_0
LM_2	0.667		$Y =$			E_2
LM_3	0.5		$Y =$			E_3

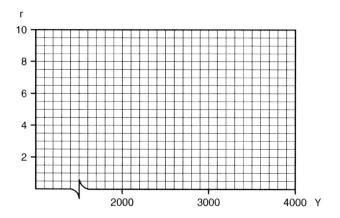

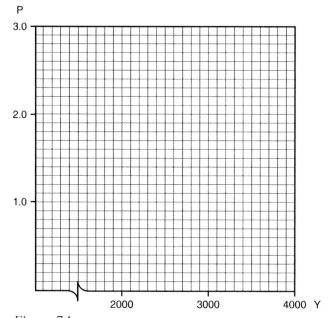

Figure 7A

Plot the new *LM* curves in the top part of Figure 7A and label them LM_1, LM_2, and LM_3. Write the level of the real money supply in parentheses next to each curve. Based on the data in the previous table, plot the aggregate demand curve in Figure 7A, and label it AD_0.

f.   What are the two exogenous variables of the aggregate demand curve? _____

and _____

g.   1.   What is the relationship between the aggregate demand curve and the *IS* and *LM* curves? _____

_____

_____

2.   What markets are in equilibrium for each point on an aggregate demand curve?

_____

3. Why does the aggregate demand curve slope down? _____

_____

4. What factors determine the position of the aggregate demand curve? _____

_____

Question 2

a. Complete the following table.

Price Level	Real Money Supply	Equation of *LM* Curve	Equilibrium Level of	
			Real GDP	Interest Rate
3.0		$Y =$		
2.0		$Y = 1,200 + 200r$		
1.5		$Y =$		
1.0	600	$Y =$		
0.75		$Y =$		

Plot the new aggregate demand curve in the bottom part of Figure 7A. Label the new curve AD_1. Place the parameters of AD_1 in parentheses next to AD_1.

b. If the nominal money supply increases, then for each price level the *LM* curve and the *AD* curve will shift to the

_____

signifying that real GDP has _____

Alternatively, if the nominal money supply increases, then for any given equilibrium level of real GDP and the interest rate, the price level will be

_____

Question 3

Now we show how a change in autonomous planned spending affects the aggregate demand curve.

Assume that the demand-for-money function is the same as in Question 1 and that the nominal money supply is 400. However, autonomous planned spending has increased by 160 at every interest rate (A_0 increases from 800 to 960) so that the new *IS* curve is $Y = 4,800 - 200r$.

a. Complete the following table.

Price Level	Real Money Supply	Equilibrium Levels of	
		Real GDP	Interest Rate
2.0			
1.0			
0.667			
0.5			

b. Plot the original aggregate demand curve from Question 1, Part e, in Figure 7B, and label it AD_0. Plot the aggregate demand curve based on your data in Part a of this question, and label it AD_1.

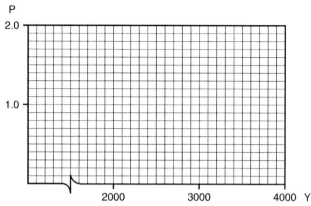

Figure 7B

c. An increase in A_0 will mean that for a given price level, equilibrium GDP will _____

and the equilibrium rate of interest will _____

For any given level of real GDP, the increase A_0 will mean a _____

price level.

Question 4

This question introduces the underpinnings of the aggregate supply curve.

a. The number of extra units of output produced by each succeeding worker declines. This phenomenon is known as

_____

b. Firms maximize profits by hiring additional labor up to the point where the real wage rate (W/P) equals the

_____

Therefore, for the firm, the _____

curve is the same as the marginal product of labor curve.

c. The marginal product of labor and therefore the vertical position of _____ is determined by _____.

d. By combining information about the real wage rate (W/P) and the marginal product of labor, we can determine the _____, and with the use of production we can then determine_____.

e. Given the marginal product of labor curve, the production function, and the nominal wage rate (W), a higher price level will cause the real wage rate to *increase/decrease/remain the same* and real GDP to *increase/decrease/remain the same*. A lower price level will produce the *same/opposite* effect. The resulting relationship between the price level and real GDP is known as the _____.

Question 5

In this question we review the properties of the short-run aggregate supply curve.

a. At every point on the *SAS* curve, firms are maximizing profits and the real wage equals the _____

_____

b. The *SAS* curve slopes upward because _____

_____

_____

c. The position of the *SAS* curve depends on the wage rate (*W*). What will happen to the *SAS* curve
    if the wage rate increases?

_____

_____

d. A decrease in productivity will shift demand for labor to the left. What effect will a decrease in
    productivity have on the *SAS* curve?

_____

_____

_____

Question 6

We have already seen that the wage rate has an important influence on the short-run aggregate supply
curve and therefore will also influence the point of intersection of the short-run aggregate supply curve
(*SAS*) and the aggregate demand curve (*AD*). In this question we look at how the actual wage rate is
determined and introduce the concept of the equilibrium real wage rate.

a. Define the nominal wage rate. _____

_____

Define the real wage rate. _____

_____

If the nominal wage rate increases by 15 percent and the GDP deflator remains the same, what has
happened to real wages?

_____

If nominal wages fall by 10 percent and the GDP deflator falls by 10 percent, what will happen to real
wages?

_____

b. Assume that the subscripts in this problem refer to time periods. Suppose $W_0 < W_1 < W_2$ and $P_0 < P_1 < P_2$ and $W_1/W_0 = P_1/P_0$ but $W_2/W_1 > P_2/P_1$.

What has happened to real wages during the periods 0, 1, and 2? _____

_____

c. We assume that the supply of labor depends on the real wage and that the supply-of-labor curve will slope *upward/downward*. Why would it have this slope?

_____

_____

d. Define the equilibrium real wage rate. _____

_____

If the current real wage rate is below the equilibrium real wage rate, then there will be pressure for the real wage rate to

_____

Why? _____

_____

_____

If there is a fall in the working-age population, there will be a tendency for the equilibrium real wage rate to

_____

Why? _____

_____

Question 7

In this question we examine the effect of an expansionary monetary policy. We distinguish between short-run equilibrium results and long-run equilibrium results.

Assume that the aggregate demand curve is given as AD_0 in Figure 7C. The equation of the aggregate supply curve (SAS_0) is $Y = 800 + 1000[P - (W/100)]$, where W is the nominal wage rate.

a. For $W = 100$, draw this aggregate supply curve in Figure 7C, and label it $SAS_0(W = 100)$.

b. Assume that the nominal wage rate is fixed at $W = 100$ and that the equilibrium real wage (W/P) equals 100. When the actual price level (P) equals 1.00, there is no discrepancy between the actual real wage and the equilibrium real wage, and at that price level, $Y = 800$. What do we call that level of real GDP?

_____

In Figure 7C, draw a vertical line through $Y = 800$, and label it *LAS*.

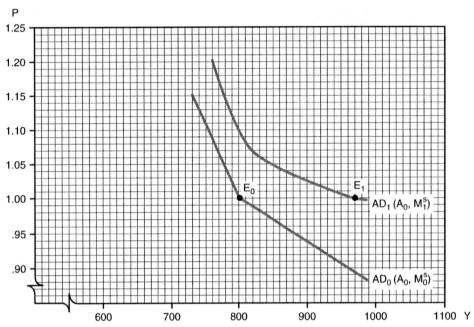

Figure 7C

c. E_0 is the initial equilibrium point because the *AD*, *SAS*, and *LAS* lines all intersect at this point. Explain what each of these curves represents.

AD: _____

SAS: _____

LAS: _____

_____

d. Assume that the Fed expands the nominal money supply such that the new money supply is 10 percent higher than the original level. As a result of this action, there is a new aggregate demand curve, AD_1. AD_1 is to the right of AD_0; that is, for any given price level, there is a greater demand for goods and services because of the increase in the money supply.

Both AD_0 and AD_1 are drawn in Figure 7C. For any level of output, AD_1 is 10 percent higher than AD_0 (for example, compare at $Y = 750$ or $Y = 800$ or $Y = 980$).

Draw *IS-LM* curves in Figure 7D to show why AD_1 has this relationship to AD_0.

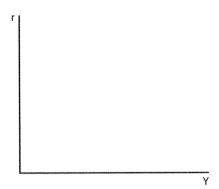

Figure 7D

Use the space below to explain your analysis.

_____

_____

_____

_____

_____

e. Explain the significance of point E_1 in Figure 7C. _____

_____

_____

Under what conditions would the economy move to E_1? Is it likely that these conditions would exist?

_____

_____

_____

_____

f. It is more realistic to assume that prices will increase as output rises (for example, an aggregate supply curve such as SAS_0). Find the new equilibrium level of output and price, given AD_1 and SAS_0. Label this equilibrium point E_2. At E_2,

$P =$ _____

$W =$ _____

$Y =$ _____

$X =$ _____

What has happened to the actual real wage (comparing E_0 and E_2)? _____

_____

Why is E_2 an equilibrium point? _____

_____

_____

In what sense is E_2 not an equilibrium point? _____

_____

_____

g.   Assume that when workers realize that the actual real wage rate does not equal the equilibrium wage rate, they will demand (and receive) a new nominal wage rate, $W = 105$, which brings the workers' real wage rate to the equilibrium level. In Figure 7C draw the new short-run aggregate supply curve associated with this new nominal wage rate and label this curve SAS_1.

At what price level does SAS_1 cross the *LAS* line? _____

Why? _____

_____

_____

In Figure 7C, label the new short-run equilibrium point *K*. At this point,

$P =$ _____

$W/P =$ _____

$Y =$ _____

$X =$ _____

(*Note:* W/P above is the actual real wage.)

Explain the changes that took place in the economy causing the movement from E_2 to *K*.

_____

_____

_____

_____

_____

_____

h.   Assume that once again workers bargain for new nominal wages to bring the real wage back to its equilibrium level.

What will be the new nominal wage rate? _____

In Figure 7C, draw the new *SAS* curve and label it $SAS_2(W = 107)$. Label the new short-run equilibrium point *H*. At this point,

$P =$ _____

$W/P =$ _____

$Y =$ _____

$X =$ _____

i. The shifting of the short-run aggregate supply curve and the changing short-run equilibrium point will continue until the actual real wage equals the equilibrium real wage.

What will the price level be when this occurs? _____

At what level of output will this occur? _____

What do we call this level of output? _____

In Figure 7C, draw the *SAS* curve that intersects AD_1 at this level of output and label it $SAS_3(W = 110)$; label the equilibrium point E_3.

Question 8

In this question we explore how perfect price flexibility keeps real GDP from falling below or rising above the natural level for any length of time.

Assume that prices are perfectly flexible and that the natural level of real GDP is 3,200.

a. When quantity demanded is greater than 3,200, the price level will _____

and the aggregate demand curve will _____

When the demand for output is less than 3,200, the price level will _____

and the aggregate demand curve will _____

Briefly explain your answers. _____

_____

_____

_____

_____

b. In Figure 7E, draw a vertical line at 3,200 (the natural level of real GDP) and label the line *LAS*.

What is the relationship between output and the price level shown by the *LAS* line?

_____

c. Assume that the equation of the *IS* curve is $Y = 4,000 - 200r$ ($A_0 = 800$, $k = 5$). Assume that the equation for the *LM* curve is $Y = 4(M^s/P) + 200r$. If the nominal money supply (M^s) is equal to 400, then the *LM* curve may be written as $Y = (1,600/P) + 200r$. We can solve for the equation of the aggregate demand curve as follows (we'll do this for you the first time so you can see how it's done): Set *IS* equal to *LM* and solve for equilibrium r as a function of P, getting $r = 10 - (4/P)$. Substitute the equation for equilibrium r into either the *IS* or *LM* curve and solve for Y as a function of P, getting $Y = 2,000 + (800/P)$, which is the equation of the aggregate demand curve.

Draw the aggregate demand curve in Figure 7E, and label it AD_0. (*Hint*: Use the equation derived above and find Y for price levels of 0.5, 0.67, 1.0, and 2.0 to generate four points on the *AD* curve.)

Given the aggregate demand curve AD_0, the equilibrium level of $Y =$ _____

and $P =$ _____

Label this point E_0 in Figure 7E. What is nominal GDP at this equilibrium position?

$X =$ _____

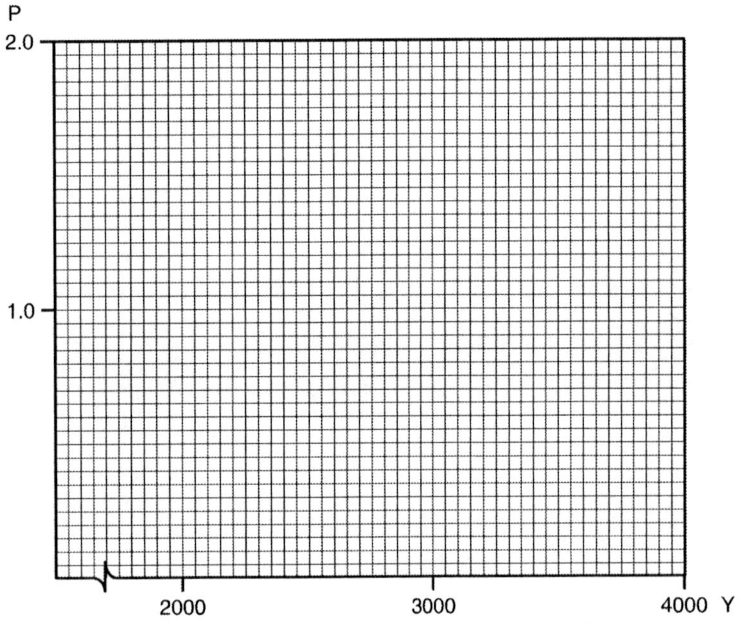

P

2.0

1.0

2000   3000   4000 Y

Figure 7E

d. Now assume an expansionary fiscal policy, specifically, an increase in government expenditure of 160 (A_0 increases from 800 to 960). Solve for the new aggregate demand curve, AD_1.

AD_1: $Y =$ _____

Draw the new AD curve in Figure 7E, and label it AD_1. (*Note:* Use the hint given in Part c above.)

If the price level were fixed at 0.67, real GDP would be $Y =$ _____

Label this point B in Figure 7E.

e. However, prices are not fixed. Since prices are flexible, the economy does not move from E_0 to B, but rather moves to point C where

$Y =$ _____

$P =$ _____

Label this point C on Figure 7E.

What is nominal GDP at Point C? $X =$ _____

f. If, rather than using expansionary fiscal policy, the government used expansionary monetary policy, the nominal money supply would have increased. Would this increase in the nominal money supply raise real GDP above the natural level? Explain.

_____

_____

_____

Question 9

In this question we study the dilemma presented when the economy is in a situation of deflation impotence, i.e., real GDP will not respond to an increase in the real money supply caused by falling prices.

Assume once again that the nominal money supply is 400, so that the equation for the LM curve is $Y = (1,600/P) + 200r$. However, as a result of depressed consumer and business confidence, A_0 has fallen to the very low level of 640; the equation for the IS curve is now $Y = 3,200 - 200r$.

a. The equation for the equilibrium interest rate as a function of the price level is

$r =$ _____

What is the equation for equilibrium real output as a function of the price level? (Solve for this the same way you would solve for the aggregate demand curve. We'll see in a moment that the equation describes only part of the true aggregate demand curve, however.)

$Y =$ _____

b. Using your equations for the equilibrium interest rate and equilibrium real output, calculate the values requested in the last two columns of the following table.

Price Level	Real Money Supply	Equilibrium Levels of	
		Real GDP	Interest Rate
2.0			
1.0			
0.667			
0.5			
0.4			

c. Is it possible to reach the natural level of real GDP if $Y^N = 3,600$? Explain. _____

_____

_____

d. At $r = 0$, a fall in the price level leading to an increase in the real money supply will not be accompanied by an increase in real GDP. Therefore, at $r = 0$, the aggregate demand curve becomes *vertical/horizontal*.

Using the data from Part b above, plot the aggregate demand curve in Figure 7F (remember what happens when $r = 0$), and label it AD_0. Also plot the *LAS* line.

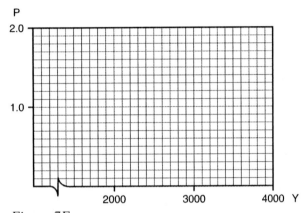

Figure 7F

What is equilibrium real GDP? _____

The price level? _____

What will happen to the price level under these circumstances? _____

_____

e. Suppose the government uses fiscal policy to push A_0 from 640 to 800. How will this policy change the aggregate demand curve? Does this aggregate demand curve look familiar?

_____

_____

Plot this aggregate demand curve in Figure 7F and label it AD_1.

What will be the resulting equilibrium levels of real GDP, the price level, and the rate of interest?

$Y = $ _____

$P = $ _____

$r = $ _____

Question 10

In this question we take up the real balance effect (or the Pigou effect) as a possible solution to the situation of deflation impotence. With the real balance effect, an increase in the real value of the money supply increases autonomous planned spending and shifts the *IS* curve.

Assume once again that the nominal money supply is 400 and the *LM* curve is $Y = 4(M^s/P) + 200\,r$. Natural real GDP (Y^N) is 3,600. The equation for the *IS* curve is $Y = 2,800 + 1.5(M^s/P) - 200\,r$. (This is obtained by letting $A_p = 560 + 0.3(M^s/P) - 40\,r$ and $k = 5$. Real balances (M^s/P) now affect A_p and hence, *IS*.)

a. Solve for the equation of the equilibrium interest rate as a function of the price level.

$r =$ _____

Solve for the equilibrium real GDP as a function of the price level.

$Y =$ _____

What is this last equation called? _____

b. Complete the following table, using the preceding equations to find the equilibrium interest rate and real GDP.

Price Level	Real Money Supply	A_0	Equation of IS Curve	Equilibrium Levels of Real GDP	Interest Rate
2.0			$Y =$		
1.0			$Y =$		
0.667			$Y =$		
0.5			$Y =$		
0.4			$Y =$		

c. Plot the new aggregate demand curve in Figure 7F and label it AD_2. What are equilibrium real GDP and the price level now?

$Y =$ _____

$P =$ _____

d. The real balance effect makes the aggregate demand curve *more/less* elastic.

Chapter 8
Inflation: Its Causes and Cures

In Chapter 7, we concentrated on developing a static equilibrium model that could explain how output and the price level would change from an initial equilibrium in response to a single change in aggregate demand. In this chapter we develop a dynamic model that concentrates on the path that the economy follows as it moves to its new equilibrium. The key variable in this chapter is the rate of inflation (the rate at which the price level changes).

We start with the short-run aggregate supply curve and show how a change in the nominal wage in response to a change in the price level is the key to deriving a short-run relationship between the inflation rate and output. This relationship (the short-run Phillips, or SP, curve) is then examined under alternative hypotheses regarding the expected rate of inflation.

To complete the dynamic model, we must understand the relationship between output and the rate of inflation under alternative assumptions about the rate of growth in aggregate demand. The rate of growth in aggregate demand sets a limit on the size of possible changes in inflation and real GDP growth. Toward the end of this chapter we use our new model to analyze the economy's response to continuous changes in the level of aggregate demand.

Up to this point, we have examined the dynamics of the inflationary process when the change in the inflation rate resulted from a change in the rate of growth of nominal GDP (x). These changes in x result from changes in the growth of aggregate demand, which in turn come from changes in either autonomous spending (ΔA_0) or the nominal money supply (ΔM^s). In the last part of this chapter, we extend our study of the dynamics of inflation to the case in which the rate of inflation and the level of real GDP are affected by changes that originate on the supply side of the economy. Such changes cause a shift in the short-run Phillips curve without initially changing people's expected rates of inflation. This concentration on the supply side complements our earlier emphasis on demand-induced inflation. Furthermore, the examination of the supply-side inflation process (the role of supply shocks) yields a more complete understanding of the inflationary process occurring from the 1970s to the year 2007.

Finally, we analyze the relationship between the real-output ratio, Y/Y^N, and the unemployment rate known as Okun's law.

Question 1

In this question, we examine the initial effects on the price level caused by a change in demand. We find that a continuously shifting demand curve, along with the shifting aggregate supply curves (because of changing expectations), generates a short-run Phillips curve.

Assume an aggregate supply curve with the equation $Y = 100 + 80[P - (W/100)]$. The supply curve for $W = 100$ is drawn in Figure 8A and is labeled SAS_0. (*Note*: In Chapter 8 of the textbook, Gordon defines W as an index of the wage rate. In this study guide, in contrast, we have used an absolute value for the wage rate. The nominal wage index used by Gordon is equivalent to our absolute value divided by 100.) Assume an aggregate demand curve with the equation $Y = 140 - 40P$. This demand curve is shown in Figure 8A as AD_0. The initial equilibrium position ($Y = 100$, $P = 1.00$) is shown as E_0 in Figure 8A. (*Note*: To simplify the diagrams, we use linear equations to represent aggregate demand curves.)

a.   The point E_0 represents the situation at the beginning of Period 1. Assume that the economy takes one period to move from one equilibrium to the next equilibrium. In Period 1, there are two alternative policies that could be followed. Policy A would leave the demand curve at its current position, i.e., AD_0. Policy B would shift the demand curve to the right as shown by AD_1 in Figure 8A.

Locate the new equilibrium situation under Policy B, and label it E_1.

Complete the following table.

Alternative Policies in Period 1

Policy	Beginning Price Level	Point	End-of-Period Values			
			Y	P	p	W/P
A: AD_0	1.00	E_0				
B: AD_1	1.00	E_1				

In the bottom part of Figure 8A, we place the rate of inflation (the percentage change in the price level) on the vertical axis. (*Note*: A lowercase letter represents the rate of change of its corresponding uppercase letter; for example, p represents the rate of change of P.)

In the bottom part of Figure 8A, plot the points that correspond to the results for Policies A and B. Label these points E_0 and E_1. Label the resulting curve SP.

Explain why E_1 is a short-run equilibrium but not a long-run equilibrium. _____

_____

_____

What would you expect to happen once the economy reached E_1? _____

_____

_____

b. Now we study the economy's behavior in the second period. Assume that in the first period the government moved the demand curve to AD_1 and the economy ended up at E_1. Also, assume that when people have the chance to renegotiate contracts, they expect the price level to remain at the new higher level ($P = 1.05$). They therefore demand nominal wages of 105 to bring them back to the equilibrium real wage of 100.

In Figure 8A, draw the short-run supply curve based on these assumptions, and label it SAS_1.

If people expect the price level to be 1.05, how much inflation are they expecting? Why?

_____

_____

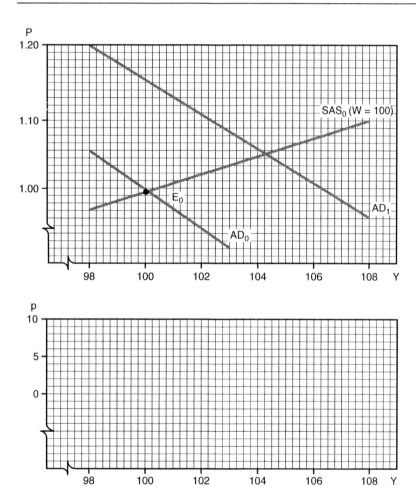

Figure 8A

For the actual real wage rate to equal the equilibrium real wage rate, actual output must be equal to the natural level of output ($Y = 100$). Label the point E_0 along the new aggregate supply curve, SAS_1, where output equals 100. What would the government have to do to bring about this level of output?

_____

_____

If the aggregate demand curve did not change (that is, remained at AD_1), real output would be _____, the price level would be _____, and the actual real wage would be _____. Label this point E_2.

If the government wanted to keep real output at 104, what would it have to do? _____

_____

Find the point along SAS_1 where $Y = 104$. What is the price level associated with this point?

_____

Label this point E_1.

c. Complete the following table, using the data you generated in Part b of this question.

Alternative Policies in Period 2

Policy	Beginning Price Level	Point	End-of-Period Values			
			Y	P	P	W/P
C: Shift AD to left of AD_1	1.05	E_0		1.05		
D: AD_1	1.05	E_2				
E: Shift AD to right of AD_1	1.05	E_1				

(*Note:* When computing p, ignore compounding effects. For example, assume that a steady 4-percent inflation rate would result in price levels of 1.00, 1.04, 1.08, 1.12, and so on.)

Plot the points in the bottom of Figure 8A that correspond to the results for Policies C, D, and E.

d. The short-run Phillips curve generated in Part c of this question should be identical to the Phillips curve generated in Part a. Why?

_____

_____

_____

Question 2

In Question 1, we generated a short-run Phillips curve by assuming the nominal wage adjusted upward whenever the actual real wage fell below the equilibrium real wage. In that question, workers expected zero inflation. In this question, we assume that workers anticipate inflation. To prevent a fall in the real wage, workers insist on a nominal wage high enough to achieve the equilibrium real wage if the expected inflation actually takes place.

a.   We assume the same aggregate demand and supply functions as in Question 1. These curves are drawn in Figure 8B. The initial equilibrium point is labeled E_0.

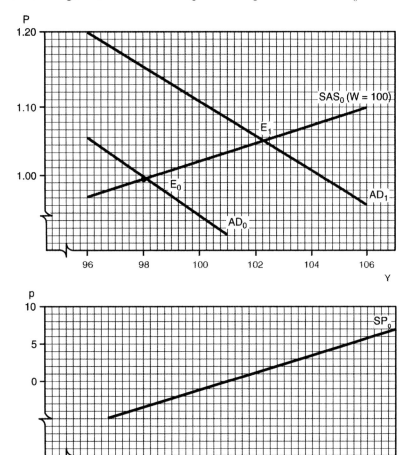

Figure 8B

Again we assume that aggregate demand shifts because of expansionary policy. With this new demand function (AD_1), the economy reaches E_1. The movement from E_0 to E_1 takes place along a given aggregate supply curve.

What is the key parameter for the short-run Phillips curve? _____

What is the value of that parameter for SP_0? _____

Write the parameter for SP_0 in Figure 8B.

b. Now we change our assumptions about the way people react to inflation. We assume they anticipate inflation and base their inflation expectations on the previous period's rate of inflation. Consequently, to prevent a decline in their actual real wage, workers will base their wage demands on the expected rate of inflation.

If the economy ended up at E_1 in Period 1, what was the price level at the end of Period 1?

_____

Assuming the economy began at E_0, what was the inflation rate during Period 1? _____

What is the inflation rate expected during the current period? _____

What is the expected price level? _____

What is the new level of nominal wages?_____

Draw a new aggregate supply curve, SAS_1, corresponding to this new nominal wage.

c. For people's expectations to be met and for the actual real wage to equal the equilibrium real wage, output must equal Y^N. Label the point E_0 along SAS_1 where $Y = Y^N$. What would the government have to do to bring about this level of output?

_____

_____

If the government wanted to keep real GDP equal to 104, what would it have to do? _____

_____

Find the point along SAS_1 where $Y = 104$ and label it E_1.

Assume the government wanted to bring the inflation rate to zero during this period. What would the price level have to be?

_____

What level of real GDP would give this result? _____

Find this point on SAS_1 and label it E_3.

d. Complete the following table, using the data you generated in Part c above.

Beginning Price Level	End-of-Period Values				
	Point	Y	P	p	W/P
1.05	E_0				
1.05	E_1				
1.05	E_3				

Using your results from this table, plot a short-run Phillips curve in the bottom of Figure 8B. Label it SP_1.

Why does this Phillips curve (SP_1) lie above the original curve (SP_0)? _____

_____

e.   If we assume that workers set their wage demands by adjusting their earlier demand by the previous rate of inflation, what will happen to the current rate of inflation if the government persists in maintaining Y above Y^N (for example, if the government keeps real GDP at 104)?

_____

_____

f.   If the economy moved to E_0, what would the aggregate supply curve for the next period look like? Explain.

_____

_____

_____

What would the *SP* curve look like? _____

_____

g.   If the economy moved to E_1, what would the aggregate supply curve for the next period look like? Explain.

_____

_____

_____

What would the *SP* curve look like? _____

_____

h.   In Questions 1 and 2, we have assumed that the equilibrium real wage is constant, so that an increase in actual real GDP above natural real GDP requires *an increase/a decrease* in the actual real wage relative to the equilibrium real wage, so that labor is *on/off* the labor supply curve, the labor market is in *equilibrium/disequilibrium*, and there is *no pressure/pressure* for the nominal wage to *rise/fall/remain the same*.

In practice, the equilibrium real wage will *increase/decrease* over time. Why? _____

_____

What effect will this have on natural real GDP? _____

i.   Review:

Why does the *SP* curve slope upward? _____

_____

_____

_____

_____

What determines the rate at which output changes as the inflation rate changes? That is, what determines the slope of the *SP* curve?

_____

_____

_____

What determines the position of the *SP* curve? _____

_____

Question 3

The *SP* curve gives the alternative combinations of real output (Y) and inflation (p) for the economy in the short run, assuming a given expected inflation rate. As will be studied thoroughly later, to find out which of these possible combinations will actually occur, we need to know the relationship among real and nominal GDP growth and the inflation rate. In this question, we see that a given nominal GDP growth rate is divided between inflation and real GDP growth.

a. We begin our analysis with the following identity: nominal GDP (X) is equal to real GDP (Y) multiplied by the GDP deflator (P), that is, $X = PY$.

    If the price level (P) is equal to 1.0 and real GDP (Y) equals 2,000, what is nominal GDP (X)?

    _____

    If real GDP increases by 4 percent and the price level remains the same, what is the new level of nominal GDP?

    _____

    If real GDP remains the same and the price level increases by 4 percent, what is nominal GDP?

    _____

    In each of the last two cases, the percentage increase in X is equal to _____

    which equals the sum of the percentage increases in P and Y.

    Recalling that lowercase letters represents percentage rates of change, we can write this result in the following way: $x = p + y$.

    This formula can also be applied to cases in which *both* P and Y are changing. For example, starting from $P = 1.0$ and $Y = 2,000$, if P and Y both increase by 2 percent, the new level of X is

    _____

    which is equal to a percentage increase of _____

b. Using the approach described above, complete the following table.

Period	X	Y	P	x	y	p
Alternative A: Zero Inflation						
0	2,000	2,000	1.00	—	—	—
1	2,080					0
Alternative B: 2-Percent Inflation						
0	2,000	2,000	1.00	—	—	—
1	2,080					2
Alternative C: 6-Percent Inflation						
0	2,000	2,000	1.00	—	—	—
1	2,080					6

c. In Figure 8C, draw and label $SP(p^e = 0)$, given by $p = p^e + 0.33(Y - 100)$.

What are the three conditions for a long-run equilibrium?

1. _____

2. _____

3. _____

Find the long-run equilibrium point when $x = 0$. Label this point E_0 in Figure 8C.

d. If a stimulus during Period 1 increases nominal GDP growth from $x = 0$ to $x = 4$, will real GDP increase to 104? Explain your answer.

_____

_____

Label the new equilibrium point F. What is real GDP at F? $Y = $ _____

What is inflation? $p = $ _____

Is F a long-run equilibrium point? Explain. _____

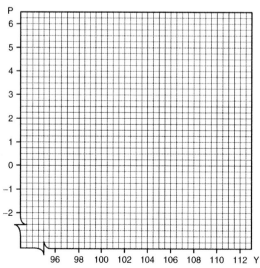

Figure 8C

e. In Period 1, real output rose by 3 percent (from 100 to 103). If the expected inflation rate remains equal to zero and in Period 2 the nominal GDP growth is once again 4, will real output once again rise by 3 percent; that is, will the new equilibrium output be equal to 106? Explain why or why not.

_____

_____

_____

Identify the new equilibrium point for Period 2, and label it G in Figure 8C.

At Point G, $Y =$ _____

$p =$ _____

f. In each time period, GDP and inflation have risen above the previous levels. Identify the point in Figure 8C at which output and inflation will remain constant with $x = 4$ and $p^e = 0$? Label that point E_2.

Is point E_2 a long-run equilibrium? Explain. _____

_____

Question 4

Workers and firms will be concerned with the expected inflation rate during the period in which they receive their wages and pay or receive the prices for their goods. If contract negotiators are making long-run agreements today that will last for the coming period (for example, three years), they have to base their agreements on some expected rate of inflation. This question studies how these expectations might be formed and the implications of alternative formations.

a. One approach to setting expectations is to predict the future behavior of the inflation rate using an economic model that specifies the relationship of the inflation rate to other economic variables. For example, if negotiators believe that an increase in the nominal growth rate of GDP will lead to more inflation in the future, they might change their current expectations. This approach is known as the

_____

approach.

b. An alternative approach does not attempt to calculate the implications of economic disturbances in advance but simply adjusts to what has already happened. This approach is known as the

_____

approach.

Why might it be rational for workers and firms to form their expectations by looking backward rather than forward?

_____

_____

_____

c. The most popular form of backward-looking expectations assumes that when people find that actual events do not turn out as they expected, they adjust their expectations to bring them closer to reality. This hypothesis is known as the

_____

model.

A general model for this approach is as follows: $p^e = p_1^{\epsilon} + j(p_{-1} - p_1^{\epsilon})$. Assume that $j = 1$ and $p^{\theta} = 1$. Fill in columns 3 and 4 in Table 8A below.

Table 8A

Time	p	(3) p^e $(j = 1)$	(4) $p - p^e$	(5) p^e $(j = 0.6)$	(6) $p - p^e$
0	1.0				
1	1.5				
2	1.5				
3	1.5				
4	2.0				
5	2.5				
6	2.5				

Describe the relationship between p and p^e if inflation increases to a new level and then remains at that higher level (see Periods 1–3 and 5–6).

_____

_____

d. Assume $j = 0.6$ and $p^{\theta} = 1$. Fill in columns 5 and 6 in Table 8A.

Describe the relationship between p and p^e if inflation increases to a new level and then remains at that higher level (See Periods 1–3 and 5–6).

_____

_____

e. Compare your answers for Parts c and d. Explain why they differ. _____

_____

_____

_____

Question 5

In Question 3, we saw that the location of the economy depends on both the *SP* curve and the rate of nominal GDP growth in the economy. In that question, the *SP* curve did not shift over time. Now we allow the *SP* curve to shift as people change their expectations regarding inflation.

a.   Assume that people adapt their expectations concerning the inflation rate according to the following equation (from Question 4): $p^e = p_1^e + j(p_{-1} - p_1^e)$.

Question 3 assumed that expected inflation was zero in the first period and remained at this level. What value for *j* was implied by this assumption?

_____

Is this a realistic assumption? Explain. _____

_____

For the rest of this question, assume that $j = 1$. If $j = 1$, then $p^e = $ _____

b. SP_0 ($p^e = 0$) in Figure 8D is reproduced from Figure 8C. The equation for the *SP* curve is $p = p^e + 0.33(Y - Y^N)$, with $Y^N = 100$. The initial equilibrium point, E_0, is identified at $p = 0$ and $Y = 100$.

As in Question 3, assume that the economy receives a stimulus that causes the rate of growth of nominal GDP (*x*) to increase from $x = 0$ to $x = 4$ in Period 1.

The *SP* curve for Period 1 is the same as for the initial period, even though *x* has increased. Why?

_____

_____

Label the equilibrium point in Period 1 *F'*. At this point,

$Y = $ _____

$p = $ _____

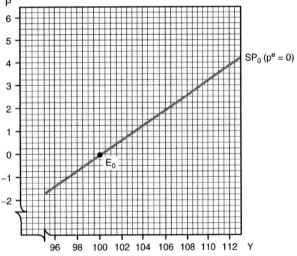

Figure 8D

c. During Period 2, x is once again equal to 4.

Why is the *SP* curve for Period 2 different from the *SP* curve for Periods 0 and 1? _____

_____

_____

Draw the *SP* curve for Period 2 and label it SP_2. (*Hint*: Refer to the equation for the *SP* curve given in Part b of this question.)

Find the equilibrium point for Period 2 and label it G'. At G',

$Y =$ _____

$p =$ _____

d. Draw the *SP* curve for Period 3 and label it SP_3. What is the key parameter for SP_3? _____

Find the equilibrium point for Period 3 and label it H'. At this point,

$Y =$ _____

$p =$ _____

e. Draw the *SP* curve for Period 4. Describe its relationship to SP_3. _____

_____

Find the equilibrium point for Period 4 and label it I'. At this point,

$Y =$ _____

$p =$ _____

f. Explain why the path followed in this question ($E_0F'G'H'I'$ in Figure 8D) differs from that in Figure 8C (E_0FG).

_____

_____

_____

_____

g. Describe the point at which the economy will finally reach long-run equilibrium if the government continues its policy of setting $x = 4$. Find this point in Figure 8D and label it E_3.

_____

_____

_____

h. Describe what will happen to the economy between Period 4 (Point I') and the eventual period when the economy reaches E_3.

_____

_____

_____

_____

_____

Question 6

Questions 6 and 7 examine the response of the economy to a decrease in nominal GDP growth. We will see that the slope of the *SP* curve plays the key role in determining the rate at which the economy moves toward its new long-run equilibrium.

Assume the economy is in long-run equilibrium with expected inflation of 8 percent ($p^e = 8$). This initial position is shown as E_0 in Figure 8E. Also, assume that price expectations are set following the adaptive expectations model with $j = 1$.

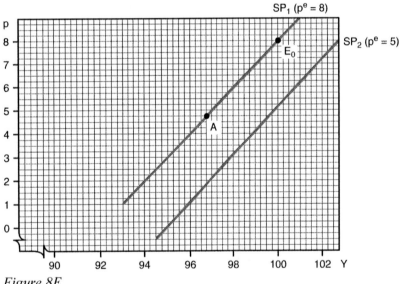

Figure 8E

a. What is the rate of nominal GDP growth? $x =$ _____

    How did you reach that answer? _____

    _____

    Now assume that nominal GDP growth is permanently lowered so that $x = 2$.

b. Remembering that nominal GDP growth must be "used up" by the inflation rate (p) and real GDP growth (y), complete the following table.

x	p	y
2	7	
2	6	
2	5	
2	4	
2	3	
2	2	
2	1	
2	0	

c. In the first period after the decline in nominal GDP growth, the position of the economy will be found along SP_1.

Explain why $p = 6$, $Y = 98$ is not the new equilibrium position. _____

_____

Explain why $p = 5$, $Y = 97$ (Point A) *is* the new equilibrium position. _____

_____

d. To determine the position of the economy in the second period, we must find the point along the appropriate SP curve. Why is SP_1 *not* the appropriate SP curve for the second period?

_____

_____

The appropriate curve for Period 2, SP_2, is drawn in Figure 8F. Why does this curve go through the point $p = 5$, $Y = 100$?

_____

_____

e. To determine where the economy will be in the second period, we must find that point along SP_2 consistent with $x = 2$ and the fact that we are starting from $Y = 97$. Using the table in Part b as a guide, fill in the following table, which shows some of the alternative positions that are possible given that $x = 2$ and that the economy is currently at $Y = 97$.

p	y	Y
3		96
2		
1		

The new equilibrium for the economy in Period 2 is $p =$ _____

$Y =$ _____

Label this point B.

f. For Period 3, the *SP* curve will once again shift. What is the parameter for this new curve?

$p^e = $ _____

Draw this new curve in Figure 8E and label it SP_3. Write the new parameter next to the label.

The new equilibrium in Period 3 will be $p = $ _____

$Y = $ _____

Label this point *C*.

To see the path taken by the economy, connect the points E_0, *A*, *B*, *C*.

Question 7

Question 6 examined the path that the economy would follow when nominal GDP growth decreased permanently from 8 percent to 2 percent. Now we continue this examination, but we use an alternative *SP* curve. At the end of the question, we study the implications of alternative *SP* curves.

Once again you will be using Figure 8E and will begin at the long-run equilibrium, point E_0. However, for this question, the *SP* curve has a slope of 0.5; that is, there is a one percentage point increase in the inflation rate for every increase of 2 units of real output. The equation for this new *SP* curve is $p = p^e + 0.5(Y - Y^N)$, with $Y^N = 100$.

a. Draw the *SP* curve with $p^e = 8$. Label that curve SP_1.

Now assume that nominal GDP growth falls permanently from 8 percent to 2 percent; that is, now $x = 2$.

b. What is the equilibrium for the economy at the end of Period 1? $p = $ _____

$Y = $ _____

Label this point A' in Figure 8E.

c. What is the parameter for the *SP* curve in Period 2? _____

Draw the *SP* curve for Period 2 and label it SP_2.

To help you find the new equilibrium, fill in the following table showing some of the alternative positions for the economy in Period 2 given that $x = 2$ and the level of output in Period 1 = 96.

p	*y*	*Y*
4		94
3		
2		

The new equilibrium output is $Y = $ _____

and the new rate of inflation is $p = $ _____

Label this point B'.

d. Again the *SP* curve must shift; the parameter for the *SP* curve in Period 3 is_____

Draw the new *SP* curve and label it SP_3. Write the value of the parameter next to the label. Fill in the following table showing alternative positions for the economy in Period 3.

p	y	Y
2		94.8
1		
0		

The new equilibrium output is $Y =$ _____

and the new rate of inflation is $p =$ _____

Label this point *C'*.

Connect the points indicating the path followed by the economy in response to the change in nominal GDP growth ($E_0A'B'C'$).

e. In both Questions 6 and 7, the decrease in nominal GDP growth from 8 percent to 2 percent leads eventually to the same long-run equilibrium. In each case,

$Y =$ _____

$p =$ _____

The cases examined in these two questions, in which nominal GDP is permanently reduced to a new desired level, is an example of the

_____

approach to curing inflation.

f. In which question is the economy more sensitive to changes in the inflation rate? Explain.

_____

_____

The flatter *SP* curve in *Question 6/Question 7* results in a flatter loop in Figure 8E with a *deeper/shallower* recession and a *longer/shorter* recession. The flatter the *SP* curve, the *more/less* long-lasting and painful will be the cold-turkey approach to curing inflation.

g. An alternative to the cold-turkey approach to curing inflation is the _____ approach. How would this approach be implemented?

_____

Compare the results of following this latter approach with that of the cold-turkey approach.

_____

_____

_____

Which of these approaches is the preferred way of curing inflation? _____

_____

_____

_____

Question 8

Before we study the effects of supply shocks on inflation, we shall review some of the terms associated with supply shocks.

a. An economic model analyzes the response of *endogenous/exogenous* variables to *endogenous/ exogenous* disturbances. A supply shock is an example of an

_____

disturbance.

b. A(n)_____

supply shock is one that makes inflation worse while causing real GDP to fall. Give some examples of this type of supply shock.

_____

c. A(n)_____

supply shock is one that makes inflation better while causing real GDP to rise. Give some examples of this type of supply shock.

_____

d. An adverse supply shock can have both *direct* and *indirect* effects on the economy.

What is the *direct* effect? _____

Why is this called a direct effect? _____

_____

_____

What is the *indirect* effect? _____

_____

Question 9

Now, we examine the effect of an adverse supply shock on the inflation rate. We begin by distinguishing between temporary and permanent supply shocks.

a. What is a temporary supply shock? Describe the likely behavior of prices and expected inflation because of a temporary supply shock.

_____

_____

_____

_____

What is a permanent supply shock? Describe the likely behavior of prices and expected inflation because of a permanent supply shock.

_____

_____

_____

_____

b. Suppose that in Period 1 there is an unusually intense heat wave, causing a tremendous loss of life among livestock, especially chickens. As a result, there is a temporary increase in the relative price of poultry and other meats. However, in Period 2 the weather improves and the *relative prices* return to their original positions.

Complete the following table (in this simple example, we ignore the effect of compounding on the rate of inflation). To simplify further, assume no change in Y^N.

Variable	Period				
	−1	0	1	2	3
Price level	95	100	107		
Inflation rate	5		5		

c. Suppose that in Period 1 the International Cartel of Climate Controllers and Water Producers (ICCCWP) drastically reduces the world's usable water supply and pushes up the international price of water. The ICCCWP is able to keep its members faithful to its goals, and the increase in the price of water relative to other goods lasts for the entire three-year period.

Complete the following table. Once again, assume no change in Y^N.

Variable	Period				
	−1	0	1	2	3
Price level	95	100	107		
Inflation rate	5		5		

d. Review:

If the shock is temporary, there *will/will not* be a revision of inflationary expectations, since the increased relative prices of the goods in short supply are expected to *fall back to their original position/remain at the higher level.* If the shock is permanent, there *must be/may not be* a significant revision of inflationary expectations if the increase in relative prices is believed to be a one-time change.

Question 10

In this question, we examine the effect on the rate of inflation and the level of real GDP of an adverse supply shock. We will find that the actual effect will depend on the policymaker's response to the initial shock.

a. Assume the economy is initially in the position illustrated by point A in Figure 8F. The rate of inflation is 5 percent, and the economy is currently at the natural level of real GDP ($Y/Y^N = 1.00$). The current rate of growth of nominal GDP (x) is 5 percent. The general equation for the SP curve is as follows: $p = p^e + 100[(Y/Y^N) - 1] + z$, where z represents the impact of the supply shock on the rate of inflation. For SP_0 in Figure 8F, $p^e = 5$ and $z = 0$.

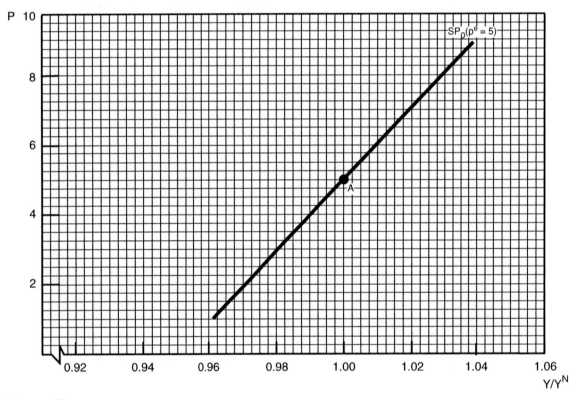

Figure 8F

At Point A in Figure 8F, the economy is in *disequilibrium/a temporary equilibrium/long-run equilibrium.* Explain.

_____

_____

Suppose that the ICCCWP (see Question 9c) pushes up the international price of water. Although the United States is a major producer of water, its consumption is so great that it also imports much of its water from the Pacific Basin, Canada, and other international producers, so that the domestic price of water rises sharply. Soon the price of products that use water in the production process also begin to rise. The impact of the ICCCWP water cartel is to shift the short-run Phillips curve upward so that the rate of inflation is four percentage points higher at each level of real GDP, but without any change in the expected rate of inflation.

What is the equation of the new *SP* curve? _____

Draw the new short-run Phillips curve in Figure 8F and label it SP_1.

If the government does not change *x*, the growth rate of nominal GDP, what are the new output ratio and inflation rate?

$Y/Y^N =$ _____

$p =$ _____

This represents a *short-run/long-run* equilibrium.

Explain how you reached your answer. _____

_____

Label this new equilibrium point in Figure 8F with a *B*.

b. Three general policy options are available to the government in response to the supply shock described in Part a above. If the government maintains a fixed growth rate of nominal GDP (*x*), it is following a(n)

_____

policy. If the government attempts to maintain the same output ratio as in the original equilibrium position ($Y/Y^N = 1.00$), it is following a(n)

_____

policy. If the government attempts to eliminate entirely the extra inflation caused by the supply shock, it is following a(n)

_____

policy. Which of these policies is illustrated by point *B* in Figure 8F? _____

As a result of this policy, the output ratio *rose/fell/remained unchanged* and the rate of inflation *rose/fell/remain unchanged*.

c. Assume that the government attempts to prevent the output ratio from changing. As the supply shock shifts the *SP* curve upward, the government adjusts the growth of nominal GDP (*x*) to keep Y/Y^N from changing. At what level must *x* be set?

$x =$ _____

Label the new equilibrium point C in Figure 8F. The equilibrium real GDP ratio and the rate of inflation at point C are

$Y/Y^N =$ _____

$p =$ _____

This is a *short-run/long-run* equilibrium solution. Explain. _____

_____

_____

d. Alternatively, the government could respond to the supply shock by attempting to prevent an increase in the rate of inflation. To do this, the government must adjust the rate of growth of nominal GDP (x) to keep the inflation rate (p) at the same level as at point A in Figure 8F. At what level must the government set the growth of nominal GDP?

$x =$ _____

Find the equilibrium point associated with this policy, and label it D.

At point D, $Y/Y^N =$ _____

$p =$ _____

This is a *short-run/long-run* equilibrium solution. Explain. _____

_____

_____

e. If the supply shock lasted for only one period, what would be the equation of the SP curve in the second period?

$p =$ _____

Under what conditions would the SP curve return to its original position (SP_0)? _____

_____

Explain why it might be difficult to bring the SP curve back to SP_0 if labor contracts include COLAs (assuming no government policy action).

_____

_____

_____

What could the Fed do, if COLAs exist, to keep the expected inflation rate from rising in response to the supply shock?

_____

_____

_____

What are the costs of following a policy such as that outlined above? _____

_____

_____

Question 11

The analysis of a beneficial supply shock is merely the reverse of the analysis of an adverse supply shock. Just as an adverse supply shock causes the *SP* curve to shift upward without any immediate change in the expected rate of inflation, a beneficial supply shock causes a downward shift in the *SP* curve without any immediate change in the expected rate of inflation. The response of the rate of inflation and the level of real GDP to a beneficial supply shock depends on the government's policy adjustment to the supply shock.

a.   Give some examples of events that can cause beneficial supply shocks. _____

_____

_____

b.   Assume that the initial position of the economy with respect to the output ratio (Y/Y^N) and the rate of inflation (p) is depicted in Figure 8G at point E.

What is x? _____

What is p^e? _____

The output ratio and the rate of inflation at point E are $Y/Y^N =$ _____

and $p =$ _____

This situation is a *temporary/long-run* equilibrium. Explain. _____

_____

c. Suppose that because of the emergence of double-digit inflation, the president imposes (with approval of Congress) price and wage controls that lower the rate of inflation by four percentage points for each level of real GDP. This imposition of controls will shift the *SP* curve *upward/downward*.

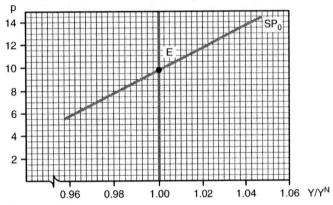

Figure 8G

Draw the new *SP* curve in Figure 8G and label it SP_1.

d. If the government decides to follow a neutral policy with respect to the favorable supply shock, how would it adjust the rate of growth of nominal GDP?

_____

This policy would result in $Y/Y^N =$ _____

and $p =$ _____

Label this point *A* in Figure 8G.

e. If the government chose to follow an accommodating policy with respect to the favorable supply shock, how would it adjust the rate of growth of nominal GDP?

_____

This policy would result in $Y/Y^N =$ _____

and $p =$ _____

Label this point *B* in Figure 8G.

f. If the government chose to follow an extinguishing policy with respect to the favorable supply shock, how would it adjust the rate of growth of nominal GDP?

_____

This policy would result in $Y/Y^X =$ _____

and $p =$ _____

Label this point *C* in Figure 8G.

g. Which of the policies best describes the policy followed in the United States in the 1971–73 price-control experience? Explain.

_____

_____

_____

h. The levels of p and Y/Y^N in subsequent periods will depend on how society adjusts its inflationary expectations. If there is a downward adjustment of expectations in response to the actual reduction in inflation, the SP curve will shift *upward/downward* relative to SP_0, and the new long-run equilibrium will be *at/above/below* point E in Figure 8G. This result is most likely to occur if the government follows a(n)

_____

policy.

i. If the government follows a neutral policy, and if people think that the price controls are merely temporary, it is likely that they *will/will not* adjust their expectations when the controls are lifted. In this case, the SP curve will

_____

when the controls are lifted, and the economy will end up at point _____

in Figure 8G.

j. What do you think might be the impact of price controls if the government followed an accommodating policy?

_____

_____

_____

Question 12

The relationship between Y/Y^N and the unemployment rate can be approximated by Okun's law. In this question, we examine some of the underlying interactions that lead to the existence of Okun's law.

a. The total amount of output produced depends on the number of workers employed and on the amount each worker can produce. For arithmetic simplicity, we will define Y (that is, real GDP) as output produced in one day.

Complete the following table. (Assume that $U^N = 5$ percent; therefore, $Y^N = 15,200$.)

Labor Force (000s)	Number of Unemployed (000s)	Number of Employed (000s)	Unemployment Rate (%)	Average Hours/ Employee	Productivity (Y/hr.)	Output (000s)	Y/Y^N
100			8	8	20		
100			7	8	20		
100			6	8	20		
100	5	95	5	8	20	15,200	1.000
100			4	8	20		

When the unemployment rate changes by one percentage point, what happens to Y/Y^N? _____

_____

_____

b. As shown in the text, Okun's law can also be written as the following equation: $U = U^N - h$ $[100(Y/Y^N) - 100]$. Using the value for the parameter h given in the text (0.5), complete the following table.

Year	Y/Y^N	$U(U^N = 5)$	$U(U^N = 6)$	$U(U^N = 7)$
1	1.060	2.0		
2	1.025		4.75	
3	0.920			11.0
4	0.960			

c. What is the percentage change for Y/Y^N for the last two-year period for which data are available?* _____

By how many percentage points did the unemployment rate change during this same period?*

_____

(*Note*: Annual values for Y and Y^N from 1875 to 2000 are given in Appendix A, Table A-1, of the text. After 2000, you can find Y in *Economic Indicators* or the *Survey of Current Business*. To determine Y^N after 2000, use the 2000 growth rate of 3.2 percent and assume that growth rate continues through the period you are using.)

Is your estimate of Okun's law consistent with the value for Okun's law given in the text? If not, why do you think the difference exists?*

_____

_____

Chapter 9
The Goals of Stabilization Policy: Low Inflation and Low Unemployment

In Chapter 8, we developed a model of inflation, explored its effects on real GDP, and considered some policy options. We did not study all of the effects associated with inflation, however, nor any of its costs other than those implied by the implicit relationship between the level of real GDP and the unemployment rate. In this chapter, we begin in Question 1 by examining, in a general way, the costs of inflation versus those of unemployment. Question 2 defines hyperinflation. In Question 3, we examine in detail the relationship between the growth in nominal GDP and the nominal money supply on inflation. Question 4 distinguishes between real and nominal interest rates and explores the importance of that distinction for the understanding of the effects of inflation. In Questions 5 and 6, we study the redistributional effects of unanticipated inflation. Question 7 examines how the government can create inflation through its budgetary actions. Question 8 examines the efficiency costs of inflation.

This chapter continues with an analysis of the causes of unemployment, the costs unemployment imposes on society, and policy options to reduce unemployment. The distinction is made between natural unemployment, which persists even when the economy is at its natural real GDP, and cyclical unemployment, which is related to the business cycle. Next, two types of natural unemployment are distinguished: mismatch or structural, the unemployment that is associated with a mismatch between the characteristics of the job and the characteristics of the job-seeker, and turnover or frictional, the unemployment associated with the transition between jobs. These are treated in Questions 9 and 10.

Question 1

This question deals in general terms with the costs of inflation versus the costs of unemployment.

a. What is the misery index? _____

   What does the misery index imply about the social costs of inflation and unemployment?

   _____

   _____

b. We learned that to reduce the rate of inflation by restrictive monetary or fiscal policy will *increase/ decrease/leave unchanged* real GDP. A change in real GDP is *directly related/inversely related/unrelated* to the unemployment rate.

c. As an implication of your answers to Part b, those economists and others who contend that inflation is not a serious problem either implicitly or explicitly regard

   _____

   as a greater problem.

Question 2

This question distinguishes between hyperinflation and moderate inflation.

a. How does Gordon define *hyperinflation*? _____

_____

b. List some countries that suffered from hyperinflation, so defined, from the late 1980s to the 1990s.

_____

c. What happened to inflation rates in these countries after year 2000?

_____

Question 3

This question explores the relation among the money supply, the velocity of money, inflation, and output.

a. Write the quantity equation and define its terms. _____

_____

_____

b. Rewrite the quantity equation in terms of rates of change in the variables, rather than in terms of the levels of the variables.

_____

c. Gordon says that in the long run, inflation equals (1) the excess growth rate of nominal GDP and (2) the excess growth rate of the money supply. We want to explore these assertions in this question.

Write the equation relating the price level (P), real GDP (Y), and nominal GDP (X).

_____

Convert this expression to growth rates, with the inflation rate on the left-hand side of the equation.

_____

d. Now, subtract the growth rate of natural real GDP (y^N) from both nominal GDP growth and real GDP growth in your preceding equation, and write the result below.

_____

e. In Chapter 8, we learned that in long-run equilibrium real GDP equaled nominal GDP. Converting this equilibrium condition to growth rates gives

_____

f. Rewrite the equation you wrote in Part b, taking into consideration the result in Part c.

_____

Does this confirm the first part of Gordon's assertion? Explain _____

_____

g.   We know that the quantity equation can be written as $x = m^s + v$. Substitute the right-hand side of this expression into the equation you wrote in Part d.

_____

Assuming that the velocity of money is constant in the long run, then $v =$ _____

Substitute this value into the above equation, getting: _____

Does this confirm the second part of Gordon's assertion? Explain. _____

_____

Question 4

To make proper investment and saving decisions, businesses and savers must consider the real interest rate that they will earn on investment or be paid on savings. Businesses should be aware of the effect of inflation on the expected revenue from new capital goods and the fall in the real value of the funds they borrow to purchase the capital goods. Savers should be aware of the loss in the purchasing power of the funds they have placed in interest-yielding financial assets. What is important for investment and saving decisions is not the nominal rate of interest but the expected real rate of interest.

a.   Briefly define:

the nominal rate of interest (i): _____

_____

the expected real rate of interest (r^e): _____

_____

The formula relating the expected real rate of interest to the nominal interest rate and the expected rate of inflation is:

$r^e =$ _____

If the nominal rate of interest is 8 percent and the expected rate of inflation is 5 percent, then the expected real rate of interest is

_____

If the expected real rate of interest is 4 percent and the nominal rate of interest is 12 percent, what is the expected rate of inflation?

_____

If the expected real rate of interest is 4 percent and people expect a 2 percent rate of deflation, the nominal rate of interest would be

_____

b. The expected real rate of interest depends on the expected rate of inflation. If people are mistaken in their inflationary expectations, then the actual real rate will differ from the expected real rate. While the actual real rate is relatively constant, the expected real rate depends on the accuracy of expectations about the rate of inflation.

The formula relating the actual real rate of interest to the nominal interest rate and the actual rate of inflation is

$r =$ _____

If the nominal rate of interest is 11 percent and the expected rate of inflation is 6 percent, the expected real rate of interest is

_____

However, if the actual rate of inflation turns out to be 4 percent, then the actual real rate of interest is

_____

Question 5

This question is designed to illustrate the different effects on the distribution of wealth of fully anticipated inflation and unanticipated inflation.

a. *Case 1*. Tom Thrifty and Steve Spender both want to buy new compact disk players costing $300. Their mutual rich uncle gave each of them a $300 one-year savings certificate that pays a 4-percent annual interest rate. However, they are not allowed to touch the certificate for one year. Tom decides that he will patiently wait a year before he buys his CD player, but Steve can't do without it, so he borrows $300 at a 4-percent interest rate to buy the system now (the borrowing and lending rate are the same in this example). Both the actual and the expected rate of inflation during the year are equal to zero. Complete the following table. (*Note*: Not every blank requires an entry.)

Event	Tom	Steve
1. Tom and Steve each receives a $300 savings certificate.	$300	$300
2. Steve borrows $300 and buys a CD player.		
3. The savings certificates mature.		
4. Steve repays the loan including 4-percent interest.		
5. Tom buys a CD player.		
Balance at year's end (line 3 minus lines 4 and 5)		

b. *Case 2*. Tom and Steve once again are given $300 savings certificates which they cannot redeem for a year, but this time a 7-percent fully anticipated inflation occurs during the year. Consequently, if the real rate of interest is again 4 percent (on the savings certificate and the loan), then the nominal rate of interest is

_____

Complete the following table. (*Note*: Not every blank requires an entry.)

Event	Tom	Steve
1. Tom and Steve each receives a $300 savings certificate.	$300	$300
2. Steve borrows $300 and buys a CD player.		
3. The savings certificates mature.		
4. Steve repays the loan including 11-percent interest.		
5. Tom buys a CD player.		
Balance at year's end (line 3 minus lines 4 and 5)		

c. Is either Tom or Steve better or worse off in Case 2 as compared to Case 1? Explain. _____

_____

_____

_____

d. The two cases in Parts a and b illustrate situations of a zero inflation (Case 1) and a fully anticipated positive rate of inflation (Case 2). They compare the effects of these alternative situations on the relative well-being of different individuals. The problems are highly simplified and make several important assumptions about economic behavior and institutional constraints. Listed below are five subjects about which simplifying assumptions were made. In the space provided, write the assumption used in the two cases.

1. Inflationary expectations _____

_____

2. The interest rate on financial assets, including money balances _____

_____

3. The taxation of interest income and the tax deduction of interest paid _____

_____

_____

4. The effect of anticipated inflation on lending and borrowing rates _____

_____

_____

5. Relative prices_____

_____

Which of the assumptions a through e are accurate? Inaccurate? _____

_____

e. *Case 3*. This case has the same particulars as Cases 1 and 2 except there is a completely unexpected inflation of 7 percent during the year. The interest rate on the savings certificate and the borrowing rate both remain at 4 percent. In this case, the real rate of interest is

_____

Complete the following table. (*Note*: Not every blank requires an entry.)

Event	Tom	Steve
1. Tom and Steve each receives a $300 savings certificate.	$300	$300
2. Steve borrows $300 and buys a CD player.		
3. The savings certificates mature.		
4. Steve repays the loan including 4-percent interest.		
5. Tom buys a CD player.		
Balance at year's end (line 3 minus lines 4 and 5)		

f. Is Tom better or worse off as compared with his positions in Cases 1 and 2? Explain. _____

_____

_____

g. Is Steve better or worse off as compared with his positions in Cases 1 and 2? Explain. _____

_____

_____

Question 6

We found in the previous exercise that surprise inflation hurts savers and other creditors whose financial assets earn less than the expected real rate of interest. This is particularly true when the nominal rate of interest ends up being less than the actual rate of inflation so that the actual real return on financial assets is negative. But who gains from surprise inflation? Unlike the net creditors, who lose, those persons and institutions with large debts and few, if any, financial assets gain during an unanticipated inflation.

a. Let us consider Sidney Trend, who, on January 1, purchases a $250,000 house in suburban Serial, California, with a 10-percent down payment and a $225,000 mortgage. (We ignore the repayment of the mortgage debt in this example.) During the year, a surprise inflation occurs and increases the value of Sidney's house by 7 percent. Complete the following table, which represents Sidney Trend's statement of net worth for the year.

Item	January 1	December 31
Assets: House	$250,000	
Liabilities: Mortgage debt	225,000	
Net worth: Assets – liabilities		
Real net worth: Net worth/price index	25,000	

What is Sidney's nominal *gain/loss* in net worth during the year? _____

What is Sidney's real *gain/loss* in net worth during the year? _____

b. Suppose that Phil Pharmer purchases farmland on January 1 for $80,000 with a 10-percent down payment. During the year there is an unexpected deflation reducing the value of the farmland (and the prices Phil receives for crops) by 5 percent. Complete Phil's net-worth statement for the year.

Item	January 1	December 31
Assets: Farm	$80,000	
Liabilities: Mortgage debt		
Net worth: Assets – liabilities		
Real net worth: Net worth/price index		

What is Phil's nominal *gain/loss* in net worth during the year? _____

What is Phil's real *gain/loss* in net worth during the year? _____

c. In an unanticipated inflation, those with net financial *assets/liabilities* gain, and those with net financial *assets/liabilities* lose. In a deflation, those with net financial *assets/liabilities* gain, and those with net financial *assets/liabilities* lose.

Question 7

When the government makes expenditures, it must collect funds to pay for them. Its two sources of funds are taxation and debt. In this question, we identify the alternative sources of debt and examine how these types of debt affect the economy.

a. The difference between government spending on goods and services (G) and net tax revenues (T) is known as the

_____

There is one other type of expenditure the government must make. This expenditure is for

_____

and is represented by the symbol _____

If government expenditures exceed tax revenue, the deficit *increases/decreases*. This change in the deficit must be financed by new bond sales. If bonds are sold to the public, there will be an increase in

_____

which is represented by the symbol _____

If the bonds are sold (indirectly, through open-market operations) to the Federal Reserve, there will be an increase in

_____

which is represented by the symbol _____

Government expenditure minus current tax revenue plus interest payments must equal the issuance of new debt and high-powered money,

or

$$G - T + (iB/P) = (\Delta B/P) + (\Delta H/P).$$

This equation is referred to as the_____

As we have seen, the government deficit can be financed by selling bonds to either the public or the Fed. In Part b of this question, we examine the advantages and disadvantages of these two alternatives of financing a deficit. Assume that the deficit has increased due to an increase in government spending.

b. In terms of *IS-LM* analysis, an increase in government spending will cause a shift to the *right/left* of the *IS/LM* curve. If the government is financing the deficit by selling bonds to the Fed, there will be an increase

_____

This effect will be shown as a shift to the *right/left* of the *IS/LM* curve.

c. Alternatively, if the government finances the deficit by selling bonds to the public, there is no change in the money supply and the *LM* curve will

_____

At the new equilibrium, there will be a *higher/lower* interest rate. This change in the interest rate is referred to as part of the

_____

effect. We can also see this change in the interest rate by examining what is happening in the financial markets. If the increased deficit is financed by selling bonds to the public, there will be an increase in the *demand for/supply of* bonds. This change will cause the price of bonds to *increase/decrease* and yields on existing bonds to *increase/decrease*. As a result of these actions, the interest rate will *increase/decrease*.

d. Review:

Faced with a deficit, the government can sell bonds to either the public or the Fed. In which of the two alternatives would the deficit have the bigger impact on aggregate demand? Explain your answer.

_____

_____

_____

Based on your answer above, which alternative would be preferred if the economy were currently below its natural level of output?

_____

There is one danger with financing the deficit by selling to the Fed: If the economy is close to its natural level of output, there will be a tendency for

_____

e. In what way does inflation aggravate government debt financing? _____

_____

In what way does inflation increase the revenue of the government? _____

_____

_____

What is this called? _____

Inflation may also reduce the cost of servicing the government debt. Explain how this works.

_____

_____

_____

Question 8

If actual inflation closely approximates expected inflation and if all contracts are written in real terms, then the redistributive effects of inflation disappear. However, as long as money balances pay less than the market rate of interest, even a fully anticipated inflation will result in a real loss to holders of money balances. This loss is called the *shoe-leather costs of inflation.*

a. What are the three reasons that money balances earn less than the market rate of interest, even in a fully anticipated inflation?

1. _____

2. _____

3. _____

_____

_____

b. Assume that the equation for the demand for money with respect to the market rate of interest (i) is $(M/P)^d = 0.25Y - 25i$; the nominal money supply (M^s) is 300; the price level (P) is 1.00; the level of real GDP is 1,800 and constant; and the expected and actual rates of inflation are zero ($p = p^e = 0$). In Figure 9A draw the demand for money with respect to the market interest rate given the level of real GDP. Add the real money supply as a vertical line and label it $M^s/P = 300$.

At what real rate of interest does $M^s/P = (M/P)^d$? _____

Label as A_0 the point at which the supply and demand for money are equal.

c. Suppose the Federal Reserve adopts a policy of increasing the money supply by 4 percent per period and this leads people to anticipate a 4-percent inflation rate. To maintain the real rate of interest found in Part b, the nominal rate of interest will have to move to

_____

For the supply and demand for money to be equal at that market rate of interest, the real money supply will have to *shrink/expand* to

$M^s/P =$ _____

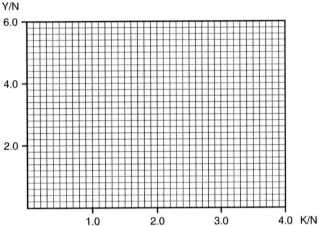

Figure 9A

Draw the new real money supply in Figure 9A, and label it appropriately. At what nominal rate of interest are the demand and supply of money equal?

_____

_____

Label the new equilibrium of demand and supply A_1.

d.   Even if people correctly anticipate inflation, there can still be a loss in people's welfare due to the inflation. Now we show one way of measuring this shoe-leather cost of inflation.

People hold real money balances because of the services that money gives them. To get these services, people must give up the income (measured by the interest rate) that other financial assets could give them. The interest rate at which the real supply and demand for money are equal measures the value of the services received for the last dollar held in money balances. For example, if the interest rate is 4 percent, then the value of the additional services that people are getting from the last dollar held in money balances is 4 cents.

These services are called _____

At Point A_0 in Figure 9A, ECS = _____

and at Point A_1, ECS = _____

The move from A_0 to A_1 represents a *gain/loss/no change* in the total ECS due to anticipated inflation.

e.   Assuming that the money supply is measured in billions of dollars, what is the total value of the ECS lost as a result of the 4-percent anticipated inflation?

_____

_____

Show this amount in Figure 9A by shading the appropriate area, and label it "Loss of ECS."

f.   Why is this net loss to society referred to as the shoe-leather cost of inflation? _____

_____

_____

g.   What would have to be done to remove this cost? _____

_____

_____

_____

_____

_____

Question 9

We have already learned how the government can use policy tools to stimulate aggregate demand, increase production, and create new jobs in the economy. Whether these new jobs solve the unemployment problem depends on the match between the types of jobs created and the types of workers who are unemployed at the time the jobs are created.

a.   Assume there are 1,000 workers in the economy. Each worker is trained to do only one kind of job. The workers can be grouped in the following way: 500 factory workers, 300 engineers, and 200 teachers. The current level of output requires 925 workers (that is, there are 925 available jobs). What is the unemployment rate for this economy?

_____

If the structure of the economy is such that 50 percent of the available jobs are for factory workers, 30 percent are for engineers, and 20 percent are for teachers, what is the rate of unemployment for each of the three types of workers when the unemployment rate for the economy is 7.5 percent?

_____

What is the unemployment rate for each type of worker if output in the economy increases and the overall unemployment rate falls to 5 percent?

_____

b.   Assume the structure of the economy remains the same as in Part a. The same proportions of different workers are needed, but some engineers are trained to become factory workers. The labor force is now segmented as shown in the table below. Complete the table.

Describe the situation in the market for engineers. _____

_____

_____

	Overall $U = 7.5\%$			Overall $U = 5\%$		
Worker Type	Workers Required	Workers Available	$U(\%)$	Workers Required	Workers Available	$U(\%)$
Factory workers	462.5	510	9.3		510	
Engineers		290		285	290	
Teachers		200			200	
Total	925.0	1,000	7.5		1,000	5.0

Compare the effects of the economic expansion in Part b with the effects in Part a. _____

_____

_____

_____

c. Assume that the supply of workers in the labor force is the same as in Part a but that there has been a change in the demand for different kinds of labor. Now, 31 percent of the workers are demanded as engineers and only 19 percent as teachers (with 50 percent demanded as factory workers). Complete the following table.

	Overall $U = 7.5\%$			Overall $U = 5\%$		
Worker Type	Workers Required	Workers Available	$U(\%)$	Workers Required	Workers Available	$U(\%)$
Factory workers		500		475	500	
Engineers	286.75	300			300	
Teachers		200			200	
Total	925.00	1,000	7.5		1,000	5.0

Describe the situation in the markets for engineers and teachers. _____

_____

_____

Compare the effects of the economic expansion in Part c with the effects in Parts a and b.

_____

_____

d. In Parts b and c, an economic expansion led to a lowered overall unemployment rate, with concurrent shortages (unemployment) in some labor markets and surpluses (vacancies) in other markets. Economists consider this situation a partial explanation of why the natural rate of unemployment is so high. What is the name that economists give to this view of unemployment?

_____

Question 10

The previous question examined the mismatch or structural component of unemployment. Another explanation for the relatively high natural rate of unemployment is turnover, or frictional, unemployment. This question studies some of the similarities and dissimilarities between the two explanations.

a.   Why doesn't the economy react to shortages and surpluses in the labor market; that is, why does the mismatch occur?

_____

_____

_____

_____

b.   What are some solutions to this problem? _____

_____

_____

_____

_____

c.   Briefly describe the meaning of turnover or frictional unemployment. _____

_____

_____

_____

d.   In what ways are the mismatch and the turnover explanations of unemployment complementary?

_____

_____

_____

e.   In what ways do the two differ in explaining the high rate of natural unemployment? _____

_____

_____

_____

f.   In the 1990s, the natural rate of unemployment has declined. Give four reasons for this decline:

_____

_____

_____

Chapter 10
The Theory of Economic Growth

In previous chapters, we were concerned with the determinants of actual real GDP and with the causes of fluctuations in actual real GDP and the price level. In this chapter, we are concerned with the determinants of natural real GDP. This is typically called growth theory in economics.

In Question 1, we learn how to measure economic growth, and we develop an appreciation for the importance that small differences in growth rates can make for economic well-being. Question 2 studies the properties of the aggregate production function used in growth theory. The next topic is Robert Solow's growth model, to which we devote Question 3. Solow's model, although providing much insight into why countries grow, appears inconsistent with the historical record. Question 4 shows one way to modify Solow's model to remove this inconsistency. In Question 5, we examine some empirical aspects of economic growth. Question 6 examines some other shortcomings of the Solow model and introduces "human capital" as a factor of production to better explain the differences in per capita output between rich and poor countries. Finally, because the improved model leaves the "immigration puzzle" unresolved, Question 7 examines the new endogenous growth theory.

Question 1

In this question, we learn how growth is defined and how small differences in growth rates can become very significant in a relatively short time.

a. How is economic growth defined? _____

_____

_____

b. Complete the following table. Assume that Y^N grows at 3 percent per year.

Table 10A

Year	Y	Y^N	Y/Y^N	$\%\Delta Y$
0	100	100.0	1.00	
1	106	103.0		6.0
2	108		1.02	
3	105			
4	112			
5	116			

If the economy had grown at 3 percent per year, what would the yearly levels of Y have been?

_____

In Year 2, the ratio Y/Y^N is *greater/less* than Y/Y^N in Year 1. The growth rate of actual Y is *greater/less* than the growth rate of Y^N.

In Year 4, the ratio Y/Y^N is *greater/less* than Y/Y^N in Year 3. The growth rate of actual Y is *greater/less* than the growth rate of Y^N.

We can conclude from these statements that there are two components of the observed growth rate: The first depends on the rate of change in Y^N; the second depends on the degree of utilization of Y^N, that is Y/Y^N.

The subject of _____

is concerned with this first component. The subject of _____

is concerned with this second component.

c. Because growth rates are compounded over time, seemingly small differences in growth rates can become very significant when they persist over a period of time. Complete the following table.

Table 10B

Value of $1 Compounded Annually		
Rate of Interest		
Year	2%	5%	8%
1	1.0200	1.0500	1.0800
2			
3		1.1576	
4			1.3605
5			

d. Each of the countries—Upper Pandora, Middle Pandora, and Lower Pandora—has a real GDP (Y) of 300 in the initial period, but the growth rates for the countries differ. Complete Table 10C below. (*Note*: Your results from Part c will be helpful.)

After only five years, the real GDP of Upper Pandora is _____ percent higher than that of Lower Pandora.

e. If real GDP for Lower Pandora were 700 in 1990 and for Upper Pandora, 600 in 1990, then Lower Pandora's GDP in 1990 would be

_____

percent higher than Upper Pandora's.

Table 10C

Item	Upper Pandora	Middle Pandora	Lower Pandora
1990 Y	300.0	300.0	300.0
Growth rate	8%	5%	2%
1995 Y			
1995 Y ÷ 1995 Y of Lower Pandora			1.00

If the countries grew at the rates in the preceding table, how many years would it take for Upper Pandora's real GDP to exceed that of Lower Pandora?

_____

f. Even for the very short time frame in the above examples (five years), the impact of compounding is quite dramatic. How many years would it take for Y to double if the growth rate were:

2 percent? _____

3 percent? _____

5 percent? _____

7 percent? _____

Question 2

The aggregate production function is a major tool of economic growth theory, and this question investigates its properties.

a. We begin with a simple agricultural example. Assume that the yield of a plot of land can be estimated by the following equation: $Y = 4F + 0.02W + 6C$, where Y = yield, in bushels of wheat per day; F = fertilizer, in pounds per day; W = water, in gallons per day; and C = cultivation, in hours per day.

If a farmer uses 3 pounds of fertilizer, 200 gallons of water, and spends 2 hours cultivating, what will the yield be?

$Y =$ _____

If the farmer increases the use of fertilizer by 1 more pound (holding the other inputs constant), what will the yield be?

$Y =$ _____

If the farmer doubles (from the original values) the use of all inputs, what will the yield be?

$Y =$ _____

We could write this equation in a more general form: $Y = b_1F + b_2W + b_3C$, where the bs represent the numerical coefficients given above. The equation can be written even more generally as $Y = f(F, W, C)$.

A relationship between inputs and output that specifies the maximum output that can be obtained with any given combination of inputs is called

_____

b. We can develop a production function for the overall economy. There are two types of aggregate inputs: Capital stock (K) and labor (N). To develop a usable production function, we must specify how these inputs are related to the output produced. One such specification is:

$$Y = AK^b N^{1-b}.$$

The exponents (b, $1 - b$) determine how much Y changes as K and N change (later, we'll see that each exponent can be interpreted as the percentage change in output per one-percent change in the associated input). Output obviously depends on the amount of inputs utilized. It also depends on a host of other variables that are represented in the multiplicative term, A. If A increases, even if K and N don't change, Y will increase (later, we'll discuss the meaning of this term in more detail). For this question, assume that $b = 0.5$ and $A = 3$.

Note: When calculating rates of change between two observations in this question's Parts b and d, use the average of the two observations for the base; for example, the percentage change between 120 and 160 equals $40/140 = 0.286$, or 28.6 percent.

If $K = 100$ and $N = 256$, what is output? $Y =$ _____

If K increases to 121 while N and A remain the same, what is the new output?

$Y =$ _____

By what percent did real GDP increase? $\%\Delta Y =$ _____

By what percent did the capital stock increase? $\%\Delta K =$ _____

The ratio of the percentage change in Y to the percentage of change in K is called _____

_____

and in this case equals _____

If $K = 100$ and $A = 3$, their original values, and if N increases to 324, what is output?

$Y =$ _____

By what percent did real GDP increase? $\%\Delta Y =$ _____

By what percent did the labor force increase? $\%\Delta L =$ _____

The elasticity of real GDP with respect to labor is _____

Note that the elasticity of output with respect to a given input is equal to the exponent on the relevant input in the production function. This is not generally true but is a feature of the production function we are using.

c. Assume that K and N are at their original levels ($K = 100$ and $N = 256$) and that A increases from 3 to 4 (28.6 percent).

What is Y? _____

By what percent has Y increased? _____

Is this *larger than/smaller than/equal to* the percentage increase in A?

d. What if both K and N increase from their initial levels by 20 percent?

The new level of K is _____

The new level of N is _____

What is the new level of Y? _____

By what percent has Y increased from its initial level? _____

This characteristic of a production function (an equal percentage increase in each input causing the same percentage increase in real GDP) is called

_____

Parts e and f use the production function of Part a with $A = 3$ and $b = 0.5$, i.e., $Y = 3K^{0.5}N^{0.5}$.

e. Calculate Y for the alternative values of N and K given in Table 10D. Write your answers in Column 3 of Table 10D (the other columns will be used later). Round calculation in Column 3 to the nearest whole number and those in columns four and five to two decimal places.

f. Convert the production function given above into one with Y/N as the dependent variable.

$Y/N =$ _____

Use this formulation to complete the last two columns in Table 10D.

Table 10D

N	K	Y	K/N	Y/N
100	256			
100	400			
100	100			
256	144			
256	256			

How do your answers for Y/N found in this question compare to those implied by your answers in Part e?

_____

_____

In Figure 10A, draw the production function.

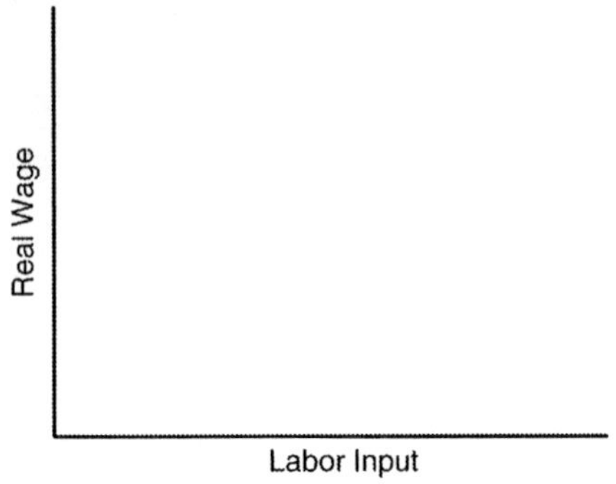

Figure 10A

g.   What happened to Y when K and N both increased from 100 to 256? _____

_____

What happened to Y/N when K and N both increased from 100 to 256? _____

_____

Production will increase when either of two variables increases. Those variables are:

_____

_____

However, there is only one variable that can cause a change in Y/N. That variable is

_____

If that variable is unchanged, Y/N will _____

Question 3

This question deals with Robert Solow's model of economic growth, the basis for most modern theories of economic growth.

Recall the national income accounting identity, $S_P + T = I + G + NX$, which says that leakages from the economy must equal injections into the economy. If we assume there is no foreign trade deficit ($NX = 0$), then the identity can be rewritten as $S = I$, where S, total national saving, equals S_P, total private saving, plus $T - G$, total government saving.

Gross investment may also be written as $\Delta K + dK$.

a.   What is ΔK? _____

What is dK? _____

Explain why $I = \Delta K + dK$. _____

_____

b. Define the term *steady state* as it is used in growth theory. _____

_____

Throughout this question we assume there is no change in the parameter A. If that is the case, the ratio Y/N is

_____

in the steady state. In this case, what is happening to K/N in the steady state? (*Hint*: Review your answer to Part g in the previous question.)

_____

If K/N is constant in the steady state, then K must grow *at the same rate as/faster than/slower than N*. Using k as the symbol for the growth rate of K and n as the symbol for the growth rate of N, we can conclude that in the steady state, k is *greater than/equal to/less than n*.

c. Combining the results from Parts a and b, we can write the level of saving in the steady state as:

$$S = (n + d)K.$$

With some algebraic manipulation, this steady state condition can be rewritten as:

$s(Y/N) = (n + d)K/N$. Derive this steady-state condition. _____

_____

_____

What does the left-hand side of this equation represent? _____

_____

What does the right-hand side of this equation represent? _____

_____

Describe what will happen in the economy if the left-hand side of the equation is greater than the right-hand side.

_____

_____

If the parameters of the production function (A and b) remain constant, the ratio (Y/K) *increases/decreases/remains constant* as new capital is accumulated. Why is this so?

_____

In the next section of this question, we will examine that happens to an economy when it leaves the steady state. For this section, assume that following:

$$Y = 0.25K^{0.5}N^{0.5}, k = 0.03, n = 0.03, s = 0.20, d = 0.02.$$

d. In Table 10E complete the lines for Periods 0 and 1.

Is this economy in a steady state? Explain. _____

_____

_____

Table 10E

Period	K	N	K/N	Y	Y/N	Y/K	k	n
0	100.00	100.00	1.00					
1	103.00	103.00						
2	108.15	106.09						
Steady state	—	—		—				0.03

e. Start with the equation in Part a, $S = \Delta K + dK$, and derive the following equation:

$(k - n) = s(Y/K) - (n + d)$.

_____

_____

_____

In the steady state, the value of k is *equal to/greater than/less than* the value of n.

Verify your answer by substituting the values you found for Period 1 in Table 10E into the equation you derived above.

_____

f. Now, assume that in Year 2 the saving rate in the economy increases from 0.20 to 0.28. As a result, the capital stock, K, in Year 2 increases to 108.15. Verify that this is the case. (*Hint*: Find ΔK based on Period 1 values, then add that to K for Period 1.)

_____

_____

Using this information, complete Table 10E for Year 2.

Describe what will happen in subsequent years if the saving rate remains at 0.28.

_____

_____

_____

Complete Table 10E for the steady state. (*Note*: In the steady state, $k = n$, so the left-hand side of the equation in Part e equals zero in the steady state. Y/N is determined from the production function. You cannot calculate the steady-state values of K, N, and Y).

g. One of the most important conclusions of Solow's analysis is that the economy's steady-state growth rate depends only on the

_____

An increase in the saving rate *will/will not* increase the steady state growth rate, however it *will/will not* raise the standard of living, measured as Y/N from one level to a higher new level.

What happens to the growth rate of real output in the period when the economy is moving from one steady state to another?

_____

_____

Question 4

Solow's growth model implies that an economy's long-run output growth rate is the same as its population growth rate and that the standard of living, as measured by Y/N, is constant. This implication is inconsistent with the historical record of industrialized countries. In this question, we modify the model to make it more consistent with reality.

a. What has been the behavior of Y/N over the last 100 years in the major industrialized nations?

_____

The Solow model can be made consistent with this historical fact through the introduction of

_____

into the model.

b. When technological change takes place, workers become more efficient. One technique to include this effect in the growth model is to assume that it is the *effective* labor input, not the actual number of workers, that determines the level of output.

Assume the same production function as in the last question. Now, however, define N as the effective labor input. Each year the labor force (which we'll equate with the population) rises by 1 percent, but the productivity of each worker rises by an additional 2 percent.

Under these conditions, the level of effective labor input rises by _____ percent each year.

Complete Table 10F.

Table 10F

Period	K	Population	N	K/N	Y	Y/N	Y/K	Y/Population
0	100	100	100	1.0	25.00	0.25	0.25	0.2500
1	103	101	103					
2								

c. During Periods 1 and 2, *K*/*N* remains unchanged, thus *Y*/*N* _____

However, output per capita *rises/falls* because population rises *faster/slower* than the effective labor force.

The type of technological change used in this example is called _____

d. The type of technological change studied in Part b assumes that the only effect of technology is to make workers more efficient.

However, technology can also make _____
more efficient.

The type of technological change that makes both labor and capital more efficient is called

_____

If both inputs became more productive, then output would *increase/remain the same* when inputs remain at the same level.

How could this change in output be incorporated into the production function? _____

_____

e. Assume the production function can be described by the equation:

$$Y = AN^{0.5}K^{0.5}.$$

This is identical to the function we have been using except that now we shall assume that the technology factor (*A*) is variable. Complete Table 10G.

Table 10G

Period	K	N	A	K/N	Y	Y/N	Y/K
0	100.0	100.0	0.2500	1.00	25.00	0.2500	0.25
1	106.0	103.0	0.2536				
2	112.4	106.1	0.2576				
3	119.3	109.1	0.2610				

f. In Parts b and c, we worked through several periods leading up to a steady state. What happened to *Y*/*N* and *K*/*N* during these periods?

_____

In Parts d and e, we also have a steady-state growth path. What is happening to *Y*/*N* and *K*/*N* in this example?

_____

In these two cases, the behavior of *Y*/*N* and *K*/*N* is different and yet each is a steady-state growth path. Explain what these two examples have in common that makes them both examples of a steady state?

_____

_____

Question 5

The previous questions examined the Solow model and some extensions from a theoretical perspective. In this question, we consider the results of some empirical studies of the determinants of economic growth.

a. Based on the results of the last question, we conclude that there are three variables that can lead to growth of output. They are:

    _____

    _____

    _____

b. Assume a production function of the form:

    $$Y = AK^b N^{1-b}.$$

    This can be written in terms of growth rate as follows:

    $$y = a + bk + (1 - b)n.$$

    What does Gordon call a? _____

    What type of economic conditions are summarized by the variable a? _____

    _____

    _____

    According to Solow, how significant was a in U.S. economic growth in the first half of the twentieth century? _____

Question 6

This question examines how the introduction of "human capital" as a factor of production enables the Solow model to better explain the differences in per capita output between rich and poor countries.

a. Gordon says that problems with Solow's model include technological change, which is assumed to be *exogenous*, and an implied *convergence*, which has not occurred. Explain.

    _____

    _____

    _____

    _____

b. On the basis of the per-person production function, $Y/N = A(K/N)^b$, what are the determinants of per-capita growth in real GDP?

_____

_____

Consider two countries, one poor and one rich. If they both have access to the same technology and both have the same share of real GDP going to capital, then any differences in their standards of living must be due to differences in their

_____

Suppose the rich country has per-capita GDP ten times greater than that of the poor country, that $A = 1$ for both countries, and that $b = 0.25$ for both countries, then how much must the two countries' capital-labor ratios differ? Explain.

_____

_____

_____

c. The production function, $Y = AK^bN^{1-b}$, is the total-output version of the per-capita production function given above. For this production function, the equation of the marginal product of capital is $MP_K = Ab(K/N)^{b-1}$. (Students who know some calculus can derive this by taking the partial derivative of the production function with respect to K.) Let the capital-labor ratio of the poor country be 1 and, as before, let $A = 1$ and $b = 0.25$. What is the marginal product of capital for the poor country?

_____

If the rich country's capital-labor ratio is 10,000 times that of the poor country, but that A and b are the same for both countries, what is the marginal product of capital in the rich country?

_____

What do your last two answers imply about investment opportunities in the poor versus the rich country?

_____

Given your answer, in what direction would we predict capital to flow between these two countries?

_____

Is it generally the case that capital flows from rich countries to poor countries?

_____

_____

Your response to this set of questions would seem to imply a problem with the Solow model. The implausibility of the responses suggests that there is a "missing" factor of production. That factor is "human capital." The introduction of human capital to the model provides a partial remedy. Even so, it leaves the "immigration puzzle" unresolved. That will be dealt with in Question 7.

d.   Distinguish between human capital and physical capital. _____

_____

_____

_____

How does an economy accumulate physical capital? _____

_____

_____

How does an economy accumulate human capital? _____

_____

_____

_____

Which type of capital is an economy more likely to accumulate faster? Why? _____

_____

_____

_____

How might these considerations help explain the persistence of differential standards of living between rich and poor countries?

_____

_____

_____

_____

e.   Write a per-person production function representing both physical capital per person (K/N) and human capital per person (H/N).

_____

Use b as the exponent for physical capital, and c as the exponent for human capital. Assume that $b = 0.25$ and $c = 0.60$. Further assume that per-person income of a rich country is 10 times that of a poor country. Find the value of the exponent for labor (1-b-c), and give the approximate value of the multiple of combined physical and human capital that the rich country must have in order to produce 10 times the output per person of the poor country.

_____

_____

Question 7

Does the income of immigrants who have moved from poor to rich countries behave in a way that is consistent with this view of the role of human capital in economic growth?

_____

_____

_____

How does endogenous growth theory help to resolve this "immigration puzzle?"

_____

_____

Chapter 11
The Big Questions of Economic Growth

In the previous chapter, we were concerned with the determinants of natural real GDP or growth theory. In this chapter we are concerned with expanding the Solow neoclassical growth model to try to explain why the convergence predicted by the model has or has not taken place in various countries. We will also address the apparent slowdown in productivity growth in the last decades of the 20th century, and the revival of productivity growth that began in 1995.

Question 1 reviews the two concepts of productivity as they relate to economic growth. It also examines the relationship between labor productivity and the real wage. Question 2 addresses the issue of convergence, which was raised in the previous chapter as a predicted outcome of the Solow neoclassical growth model. Further refinements of the growth model are introduced. Question 3 focuses on rich countries and examines some of possible causes of the apparent productivity slowdown, and the possibility that the slowdown in productivity is an illusion. Question 4 is concerned with explaining how productivity shocks and labor supply shocks cause lower real wage growth. Question 5 considers the relationship between the productivity revival after 1995 and the possible emergence of the "New Economy."

Question 1

Gordon makes a distinction between labor productivity and the standard of living, and then uses this distinction to understand the European experience of the past several decades.

a. What ratio defines productivity? _____

What ratio defines the standard of living? _____

Write these ratios as growth rates. _____

Use these growth rates to explain how the standard of living can rise at a slower pace than labor productivity.

_____

_____

What has happened in the European experience of the past few decades to produce this result?

_____

_____

Gordon notes that the concept of multifactor productivity (MFP) and labor productivity differ, and then demonstrates that changes in the K/L ratio in an economy will affect the relative growth of MFP and labor productivity.

b. Write the production function $Y = AK^b N^{1-b}$ in terms of growth rates. _____

Solve this equation for a and rearrange the equation so that the first term represents growth in labor productivity, i.e., $(y - n)$.

_____

What does Gordon call a? _____

What type of economic conditions are summarized by the variable a? _____

_____

Look at the second term of the equation for a and use it to explain how changes in the K/L ratio in an economy will affect the relative growth of multifactor productivity and labor productivity.

_____

_____

In the previous chapter we learned that b is the elasticity of output with respect to capital and $1 - b$ is the elasticity of output with respect to labor. In this chapter, $1 - b$ is also defined as labor's contribution to output. That is $1 - b = WN/PY$ where W is the nominal wage rate, N is the quantity of labor input, and PY is total income in nominal terms.

c. Use the equation given above to demonstrate that if labor's share of national income is constant, then the real wage must grow at the same rate as labor productivity.

_____

_____

_____

According to Gordon, labor's share of income has remained the same over the past 25 years because labor productivity has increased *less rapidly than/more rapidly than/at the same rate as* the real wage rate.

Question 2

The Solow model predicts that the standard of living in poorer nations will converge on that of richer nations through rapid capital formation that raises output per person. The introduction of technological change to the model *does/does not* change this prediction because technology is assumed to be freely available to all countries. The key prediction of the Solow model adapted to include technological change *has/has not* been borne out, i.e., with a few exceptions convergence *is/is not* a reality.

One of the shortcomings of the Solow model is that it treats technological change as freely available to all countries. Gordon notes the inherent problem in this assumption, and repeats a theme from the previous chapter concerning the importance of human capital formation to economic growth. Gordon discusses the importance of human capital formation to the introduction of new technology to a poor country. He then points to three methods by which a poor country might import technological change without having to incur the heavy expense of research and development (not to mention human and physical capital formation) out of its own saving.

a.   What are the three methods Gordon identifies?

_____

b.   Noting that even these options might be impossible for countries caught in a "poverty trap," Gordon turns to exogenous factors affecting economic growth. These factors include:

_____

_____

c.   How are these factors integrated into the production function for an economy? Why is the production function adapted in that specific way?

_____

_____

Question 3

Gordon notes the substantial slowdown in the growth of labor productivity in the United States from an annul rate of 2.9 percent for the period 1948–73 to 1.6 percent for the period 1973–95.

What are the six possible causes of the slowdown identified by Gordon?

_____

_____

_____

Question 4

Gordon notes that along with slow labor productivity growth in the period 1973–95, real wages also grew slowly. In this question we examine how productivity shocks and labor supply shocks cause lower real wage growth.

a.   What sort of productivity shocks are consistent with this explanation of the link between real wage growth and the growth of labor productivity? Explain.

_____

_____

_____

b.   Are there productivity shocks that could change the direction of causation so that lower real wage growth generated lower growth in labor productivity? Explain.

_____

_____

_____

c. Graphically illustrate in Figure 11A the impact of the type of productivity shock described in Part a.
    In Figure 11B, illustrate the impact of the type of productivity shock describe in Part b.

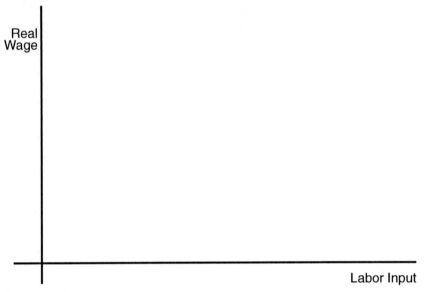

Figure 11A

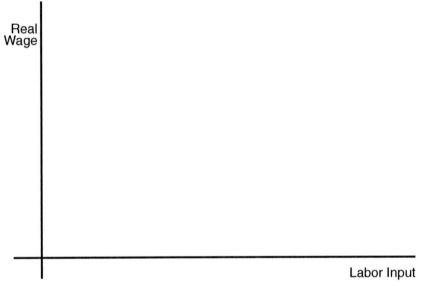

Figure 11B

d. How could the changes that have occurred in the labor force and the capital stock in the United States
    since 1973 have caused a productivity slowdown?

_____

_____

Question 5

This question considers the relationship between the labor productivity revival after 1995 and the possible emergence of the "New Economy."

a.   What were the trends in labor productivity growth rates for the following years: 1960, 1980, 1990–95, 1999–2004, 2006–07?

b.   How did the resurgent labor productivity in the late 1990s resolve "Solow's Paradox?"

c.   The idea of a "New Economy" driven by hi-tech equipment such as computers, cell phones, and the World Wide Web was rooted in part in the apparent simultaneous reversal of four economic problems. Name them.

d.   Skeptics maintain that there were several reasons to doubt the idea of "New Economy." What were those reasons? Did they prove to be true?

Chapter 12
The Government Budget, the Public Debt, and Social Security

Chapter 10 stressed the importance of the saving rate as a key to economic growth. In this chapter, we begin, in Question 1, with a study of the role played by fiscal policy in determining national saving. In the 1980s and much of the 1990s, national saving fell dramatically; only the increased borrowing from the foreign sector allowed investment to continue to grow. Federal budget surpluses during 1998–2001 were offset by a collapse of the household saving rate. Foreign borrowing continued to play a significant role in financing domestic investment. These developments are explored in Question 2.

After our examination of national saving, we discuss, in Question 3, the advantages and disadvantages of alternative rates of economic growth. Question 4 examines the issues of the appropriate size of the government deficit and national debt. Finally, in Question 5, we discuss the historical record of the national debt.

Question 1

As we learned in Chapters 4 and 5, various combinations of fiscal policy and monetary policy can be used to reach any given level of real output. In this question we review these results and compare the implications of the alternative combinations of policies.

Assume that the economy can be described by the following equations: $C = 0.8(Y - T)$, $T = 500$, $I_p = 500 - 40r$, and $G = 560$. The equation for the IS curve is $Y = 5(660 - 40r)$. It is drawn in Figure 12A, labeled IS_0. The current LM curve is also drawn, labeled LM_0. The equilibrium for the economy is shown as Point A. The economy is at its natural level of real GDP ($Y^N = 1,500$).

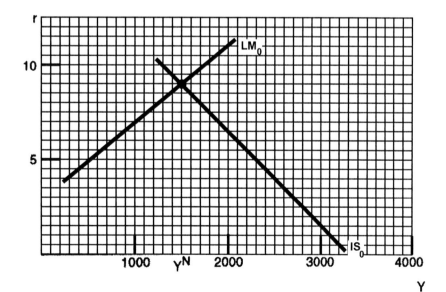

Figure 12A

a.   Fill in the top half of the first column of Table 12A indicating the levels of planned expenditure at Point *A*.

The level of planned expenditures must equal real output for the economy to be in equilibrium. Is the economy in equilibrium at Point *A*?

Table 12A

Variable	$Y = 1{,}500, G = 560,$ $T = 500$	$Y = 1{,}500, G = 400,$ $T = 500$	$Y = 1{,}500, G = 320,$ $T = 400$
	1	2	3
Consumption			
Investment			
Government expenditure			
Planned expenditure			
Private saving			
Government budget surplus			
National saving			

b.   Assume that policymakers want to increase private investment. According to this model, what would increase investment to 300?

_____

Is it possible for policymakers to use only one policy tool (fiscal or monetary) and reach the desired level of investment while output remains at 1,500? Explain.

_____

_____

_____

If policymakers decide to choose whatever monetary policy is necessary to reach Y^N, then the fiscal policy chosen (as indicated by the location of the *IS* curve) will be the primary determinant of the

_____

Since investment is a critical determinant of the rate of economic growth and the interest rate is a key determinant of investment,

_____

policy becomes the major determinant of the rate of economic growth in the economy.

c.   We can clearly see the importance of fiscal policy for investment and growth by rewriting the identity that leakages equal injections: $S + (T - G) = I$, where *S* is *private* saving. (This symbol was used for total national saving in Chapter 10.)

What does the left side of the equation represent? _____

_____

In equilibrium, national saving must equal planned investment. Complete the bottom half of Column 1 in Table 12A. Does the level of national saving equal planned investment?

_____

We can see from this equation that if policymakers want to increase investment there must be an associated increase in either of two types of saving:

1. _____

2. _____

The next part of the question examines two alternative fiscal policies that might allow the economy to reach an investment level of 300. In each case, assume that the Fed has set monetary policy so that LM_1 is now the appropriate LM curve.

d. Assume that policymakers choose to decrease government spending to 400 while keeping taxes equal to 500.

Draw the new IS curve and label it IS_1. Label the new equilibrium Point B. Complete the second column in Table 12A.

In this case, investment has risen by _____

This increase in investment is funded by an increase in *private/government/both private and government* saving equal to

_____

e. Alternatively, assume that policymakers decrease government spending to 320 and lower taxes to 400.

How would the IS curve for this compare to IS_1? Explain your answer. _____

_____

Complete the third column in Table 12A. Compared to the initial situation (Column 1), investment has risen by

_____

This increase in investment is funded by an increase in private saving of _____

and government saving of _____

f. Moving from Points A to B is an example of shifting to a(n) *tight/easy* fiscal policy and a(n) *tight/easy* monetary policy.

g. In each of the three cases examined, output remained at the natural rate of output. In which of the three cases will the rate of future economic growth be the largest? Explain your answer.

_____

_____

_____

_____

_____

_____

Question 2

In the last question, we saw the importance of national saving as a determinant of investment. In this question, we broaden our model to include the foreign sector, and we examine the historical behavior of national saving and investment.

We can include the foreign sector into our model by returning to the identity that leakages equal injections and by adding net exports (NX): $S + T = I + G + NX$. Rearranging, we get:

$$I = S + (T - G) - NX.$$

a. As used in this equation, when net exports are positive, they can be interpreted as a source of *lending to/borrowing from* foreigners. Explain why this is so.

_____

_____

_____

b. Use Figure 5-10 in Chapter 5 of your text to answer the following question.

Investment was lower during the 1980s and mid 1990s as compared to the pre-1980 period. What would have happened to the level of private investment if the foreign trade balance had not been in deficit during the 1980s and mid 1990s? Explain your answer.

_____

_____

_____

c. In 1998, there was a federal budget surplus. What would have happened to the level of private investment if the foreign trade balance had not been in deficit during 1998? Explain your answer.

_____

_____

_____

Question 3

At this point, we analyze the very important economic question: What is the optimal rate of economic growth? The benefits from faster economic growth come only if society pays the cost of increased growth. After a discussion of these costs, we review some of the options available to the government if it pursues a policy of stimulating economic growth.

a. To grow faster, the economy must increase the saving ratio and channel these added savings into productive investment. If the saving ratio increases, what happens to the consumption ratio?

_____

Assume that the economy is growing at a 4-percent annual rate and that the consumption function for the economy is $C = 0.95Y$. Calculate Y and C for the next seven years, and enter your results in the table below under the heading *Alternative 1*.

As an alternative to this growth policy, suppose that in Year 1 the government initiates a program that increases the saving ratio from 0.05 to 0.10. Assume that the decreased consumption is replaced by investment so that the economy continues to grow at 4 percent per year for the first and second years. Then, because of the increased capital stock, assume that the economy grows at 7 percent per year from Year 3 through Year 7. Calculate Y and C for the economy for the seven-year period, and enter the results under the heading *Alternative 2* in the following table.

What is the *total* consumption for the seven-year period (Years 1–7) if Alternative 1 is followed?

_____

Alternative 2? _____

From the standpoint of consumers, which alternative is more desirable? Explain. _____

_____

_____

Year	Alternative 1		Alternative 2	
	Y	C	Y	C
0	100.0	95.0	100.0	95.0
1				
2				
3				
4				
5				
6				
7				

b. If the rate of time preference in society were 6 percent, what would we know about that society?

_____

_____

_____

How could we obtain a rough approximation of the actual rate of time preference for an economy?

_____

_____

c. What does the rate of return on capital measure? _____

_____

_____

What could we conclude about the rate of investment (and capital formation) in an economy if the national rate of return on private investment is greater than the society's rate of time preference? Explain your answer.

_____

_____

d. Based on information about current rates of return on investment and rates of time preference, what can we conclude about the amount of saving in the United States? Explain your answer.

_____

_____

_____

e. In general, policymakers could stimulate national saving either by creating incentives to raise

_____

or to run a *larger/smaller* government surplus. Such a change in the government surplus would be an example of a shift toward *tighter/looser* fiscal policy. If the government follows this policy, what must it do with its monetary policy?

_____

_____

Explain the consequences of not following the correct monetary policy. _____

_____

_____

The fiscal shift discussed in this section will be greater if it reduces private

_____

rather than private saving. With this statement in mind, what type of tax policy would best induce private investment?

_____

_____

f. The second way to stimulate private investment is to stimulate private saving. What types of reforms to stimulate private business saving have been suggested?

_____

_____

One suggested reform to stimulate private household saving is to distinguish between real and nominal returns when establishing taxes. Explain why that distinction is important.

_____

_____

g. Complete the following table showing the private saving rate in the United States for the last six quarters.* Express saving as a percent of national income.

Table 12B

Period	Saving Rate
20:Q	
20:Q	
20:Q	
20:Q	
20:Q	
20:Q	

Question 4

This question deals with the appropriate size of the deficit.

a. The correct deficit size depends on considerations related to two types of economic goals: short-term stabilization goals and long-term economic growth goals. Explain how society's concern for each of these goals would affect the deficit size.

Stabilization: _____

Economic Growth: _____

_____

Since the existence of a deficit implies a change in the magnitude of the total debt, another way to view the question of the proper size of the deficit is to ask: What is the appropriate size for the national debt?

b. One aspect of this question relates to the burdens associated with the debt. If the government goes into debt today, when will it pay off the debt?

_____

Explain how the type of government expenditure made by the government affects its ability to pay off (service) the debt?

_____

_____

Some economists argue that if the government is spending on public investment (e.g., roads, sewer systems, housing), the question of public debt is very similar to the case of private debt, where a corporation services its debt through its higher earnings from the investment. In what ways are the private and public cases different, however?

_____

_____

_____

_____

c. One possibility for raising funds to pay the annual interest charges on the debt would be to issue new debt equal to the interest payments. Consider the following situation: At the start of 2004, real GDP equals $1,000 billion, the real government debt held by the public equals $225 billion, the real growth rate of the economy is 4 percent, and the real interest rate is 3 percent. (The government pays the real rate of interest on its debt.) The ratio of debt to GDP is

_____

The annual interest cost of the debt is $ _____

If the government raises the funds to pay the interest charge on the debt by selling more bonds to the public, then at the end of the year

the real debt equals $ _____

the real GDP equals $ _____

and the ratio of debt to GDP equals _____

The ratio of debt to GDP has *risen/fallen/remained the same*.

d. Consider the following alternative situation for 2004: Initial real GDP and the real debt are the same as in Part c above, $1,000 billion and $225 billion, but now the real rate of growth is 2.5 percent and the real rate of interest is 4 percent.

The annual interest cost of the debt is $ _____

If the government raises the funds to pay the interest by selling bonds to the public, then at the end of the year

the real debt equals $ _____

real GDP equals $ _____

and the ratio of debt to GDP equals _____

The ratio of debt to GDP has *risen/fallen/remained the same*.

To prevent the ratio of real government debt to real GDP from rising, the government can meet its interest bill by issuing more bonds only if

_____

_____

Question 5

This question examines the historical record of the national debt.

a. There are two primary explanations for increases in the debt/GDP ratio for the period prior to the 1980s. They are:

1. _____

2. _____

_____

b. How did the behavior of the debt/GDP ratio from 1981 to 1992 differ from this historical pattern?

_____

_____

c. How did the debt/GDP ratio behave from 1994 till 2005? _____

_____

_____

_____

Chapter 13
Money and Financial Markets

We begin our study of money and financial markets in Question 1, which examines how money is defined, conceptually and in practice. Since the key to effective monetary policy (regardless of the strategy chosen) is control of the money supply, Questions 2 and 3 examine the process of bank expansion and the creation of money, and Question 4 surveys the three instruments that the Fed uses to affect the money-creation process. Question 5 deals with how well the Fed is able to meet its own monetary growth targets. In Questions 6–8, we review several alternative theories of the demand for money: the quantity theory of money, the Keynesian theory, and the Baumol-Tobin theory. In Question 9, we examine the effect deregulation has had on the demand for money, and we use the *IS-LM* model to study how deregulation affects activist monetary policy. Finally, in Question 10 we consider the reasoning behind the Fed's choice of an interest rate target contrasted with the arguments for money supply and nominal GDP targets.

Question 1

We begin our study of money and financial markets by examining the functions of money and the official measures of the U.S. money supply.

a.   In this chapter, two of the traditional functions of money are mentioned. List them below.

　　1. _____

　　2. _____

b.   Which of these two functions is most closely related to each of the following types of assets?

　　Checking deposits in a bank: _____

　　Money market deposit accounts: _____

　　Traveler's checks: _____

c.   There are two major measures of the money stock used in the United States: M_1 and M_2. In this part of the question, we examine what kind of asset is included in each of these definitions of the money supply.

In the table below, write "yes" or "no" in the column or columns that indicates which of the following items are contained in M_1 or M_2.

Item	M_1	M_2
Transactions (checking) accounts		
Time deposits (under $100,000)		
Gold		
Money-market mutual funds		
Currency		
Treasury bills		
Traveler's checks		
Savings deposits		
Commercial paper		
Money-market deposit accounts		

Which function of money applies primarily to M_1? _____

Which function of money applies to M_2? _____

Which would you expect to show more instability, the demand for M_1 or the demand for M_2? Why?

_____

_____

Financial deregulation during the last two decades has had an important bearing on the debate over the proper conduct of monetary policy. It has undermined the argument for a constant growth-rate rule (CGRR) and at times has forced the Federal Reserve to abandon M_1 as a policy target.

d.   What effect did the development of interest-bearing checking accounts have on the M_1 demand for money?

_____

What effect did the development of money-market mutual funds, which allow limited check writing, have on the M_1 demand for money?

_____

e.   Complete the following table. Record the values of the listed variables for the most recent four quarters for which data are available.*

Period	M_1	$1/V_1$	M_2	$1/V_2$
20:Q				
20:Q				
20:Q				
20:Q				

Question 2

This question develops a simple example of bank expansion and the money-creation process. This process occurs because people prefer bank liabilities to other forms of money for use as their primary medium of exchange. Under a fractional reserve banking system, banks will continue to purchase earning assets (the public's IOUs) by issuing, in return, checking deposits (the bank's IOUs) until all of the bank's excess cash reserves have been converted into required reserves.

Suppose that the starship "Trecky" lands in a fertile valley on the planet Htrae and a hardy group of planetary settlers organizes a colony. The activity of the settlers that especially concerns us is their decision to continue to use their "star credit" coins and currency as a legal medium of exchange. The settlers have 5,000 units of star credit coins and currency; for reasons of both convenience and safety, they decide to keep all 5,000 units in the newly organized first world bank (FWB).

This is the T-account for the newly formed FWB.

First World Bank

Assets		Liabilities	
Star coins and currency	5,000	Deposits owed to settlers	5,000
Total assets	5,000	Total liabilities	5,000

a. The new colonists initially handle their economic transactions by withdrawing star currency from the bank and paying the correct amount of cash to the store owners. However, the settlers soon realize that this process might lead to their money being lost or stolen by aliens that have infiltrated the settlement. As a means of protection (and as a way of improving record keeping), the colonists begin to make payments by transferring their bank deposits at the FWB through the use of a written order to the FWB. The written order is called a check. One day the colony's logician points out to the bankers that since the FWB is now a fully functioning bank, it must follow the rules for banks set down by the federation bank board (FBB). The Board of Governors of the FBB has ruled that all banks must keep a cash reserve (in star credits) equal to at least 10 percent of the total deposits of the bank.

Complete the following T-account for the bank, showing its position after it has complied with this reserve requirement.

First World Bank

Assets		Liabilities	
Star coins and currency		Deposits owed to settlers	_____
Required reserves	_____		_____
Excess reserves	_____		_____
	_____		_____
Total assets		Total liabilities	

b. The FWB Committee realizes that it has a non-earning asset, the

_____

in excess cash reserves, which it is not required to hold. It decides to use these excess reserves to purchase an earning asset. Soon afterward, the colony's vintner comes to the bank bemoaning the fact that he does not have enough cooperage to properly age the wine needed to satisfy the community's growing thirst. The FWB's manager quickly suggests that the vintner borrow the FWB's excess reserves to finance the purchase of new barrels for aging the wine. The bank gives the vintner a check in the amount of

_____

which is equal to the total excess reserves. The vintner purchases new barrels and endorses the bank's check over to the cooper. (The vintner could have withdrawn the proceeds of the loan in coin and currency and paid the cooper in cash, but it is more likely that he would want to use a bank draft.) The cooper, like the rest of the community, prefers to use bank money, so he deposits the check into his account at the FWB.

Complete the following T-account, which shows the bank's position after this transaction between the vintner and the cooper.

First World Bank

Assets		Liabilities	
Star coins and currency		Original deposits owed to settlers	_____
Required reserves	_____	New deposit owed to cooper	_____
Excess reserves	_____		_____
Loan owed by vintner	_____		_____
Total assets		Total liabilities	

When this entire transaction is over, the bank manager finds that although she has loaned out the entire amount of excess reserves, she still has excess reserves. Explain how this happened.

_____

_____

_____

_____

c. The colony's logician comes into the office of the FWB and tells the manager, "I can solve your problem and get rid of your excess reserves in exchange for earning assets. Just loan me

_____

star credits to buy software for my new computer installation and your problems are over." The manager loans this amount to the logician, which the logician spends on software for Galactic Systems, Inc. The owners of Galactic Systems redeposit the star credits in their account at the FWB.

Complete the following T-account, which shows the bank's position after this transaction between the logician and Galactic Systems, Inc.

First World Bank

Assets		Liabilities	
Star coins and currency		Original deposits owed to settlers	_____
Required reserves	_____	Deposits owed to cooper	_____
Excess reserves	0	New deposit owed to Galactic Systems	_____
Loans			
Owed by vintner	_____		
Owed by logician	_____		
Total assets		Total liabilities	_____

d. After the above transaction between the logician and Galactic Systems, is any further bank expansion possible? Explain.

_____

_____

For every unit of original deposit of star coin and currency, the FWB ended up with _____ units of bank money (transferable deposits).

e. Five conditions are necessary for the bank expansion in this question to take place. List these five assumptions and briefly explain them.

1. _____

   _____

2. _____

   _____

3. _____

   _____

4. _____

   _____

5. _____

   _____

Question 3

In this question, we develop a simple equation that generalizes the bank expansion process described in Question 2. Let D stand for the total deposits after complete expansion has occurred and there are no excess reserves. Let e represent the fraction of deposits (D) that banks must hold as cash reserves, and let H stand for high-powered money.

a.   What determines the reserve requirement (e)? _____

_____

_____

Define high-powered money (H). _____

_____

_____

In Part c of Question 2,

$H =$ _____

$e =$ _____

Give the general and numerical form of the equation for total deposits (the five assumptions listed in Question 2, Part e, still hold).

General form:

$D =$ _____

Numerical form:

$50,000 =$ _____

b.   If the reserve requirement (e) were raised to 15 percent of deposits, then total deposits (D) would equal

_____

and the money creation multiplier would be equal to _____

We conclude that if e increases, the money multiplier _____

and if e decreases, the money multiplier _____

c.   We now relax the assumption in Question 2, Part e, that requires a seller who receives the proceeds of a loan to redeposit the funds in the same bank. Instead, we assume that the seller redeposits the full amount in another bank. Will the level of deposits estimated in Part a above change? Explain why or why not.

_____

d. Now let us assume that people want to hold coin and currency as well as bank deposits as money, and that the amount of cash (coin and currency) they wish to hold is a given fraction (c) of demand deposits. The general form for the equations of the demand and supply of high-powered money are:

Demand = _____

Supply = _____

If we set these equations equal to each other and solve them for deposits, we have:

$D =$ _____

If we assume total high-powered money is 5,000, the reserve requirement is 15 percent, and the amount of cash that people want to hold is 5 percent of their demand deposits, then:

$D =$ _____

e. Now that we have equations for both cash and bank deposits, we can develop an equation for the money supply. The money supply (M) is equal to cash plus transaction deposits. Since cash (coin and currency) is equal to

_____

and D is equal to _____

then $M =$ _____

f. If $c = 0.05$, $e = 0.15$, and $H = 5{,}000$, what is the total money supply?

$M =$ _____

Given these values for c, e, and H, the components of the money supply are:

$D =$ _____

and cash = _____

g. The money-creation multiplier (the ratio of total money supply to high-powered money) is equal to:

General form:

$M/H =$ _____

Numerical form:

_____ = _____

Question 4

To set the money supply at some predetermined level, policymakers must be able to control the money supply or to predict those factors on which the money supply depends. We now turn to the subject of the instruments of Federal Reserve control.

a. In Question 3, we found that the money supply depended on the quantity of high-powered money (H), the bank reserve ratio (e), and the desired ratio of publicly held cash to deposits (c). Which of the following are under the control of the Federal Reserve Bank? If the factor is not controlled by the Fed, what economic unit does control it?

   1. H is controlled by _____

   _____

   2. e is controlled by _____

   _____

   3. c is controlled by _____

   _____

b. The Federal Reserve has three main policy tools (instruments) that it uses to control the money supply. List these tools, and indicate which of the above factors (H, e, or c) in the money-supply equation each tool influences.

Tool (Instrument)	Factor Influenced (H, e, or c)
1.	
2.	
3.	

c. The most important of the Federal Reserve's three instruments of monetary policy is

   _____

   To use this tool, the Federal Reserve buys or sells _____

   If the Fed buys, *H/e/c increase/decreases*. If the Fed sells, *H/e/c increases/decreases*. The Federal Reserve policy for this instrument is decided at a monthly meeting in Washington D.C. of

   _____

d. Suppose that following the monthly meeting, the manager of the System Open Market Account at the trading desk in the Federal Reserve Bank of New York is directed to buy $25 million of government securities for the Federal Reserve System from a government securities dealer in New York. The dealer would take the check drawn on the Federal Reserve Bank (used to pay for the securities) and deposit it immediately in his or her commercial bank, which in turn would forward it to the Fed for deposit in its reserve account.

Complete the following T-accounts showing the initial impact on the banking system of this transaction. (Assume that $e = 10\%$ and $c = 0$; all amounts are in millions of dollars.)

Federal Reserve Banks		Commercial Banks	
Assets	**Liabilities**	**Assets**	**Liabilities**
Government securities	Commercial bank reserve deposits	Reserve deposits at Federal Reserve banks	Deposits owed to securities dealers

e. Complete the following T-account for commercial banks, assuming that the simple expansion described in Question 3 takes place (and the five conditions in Part e still hold).

Commercial Banks

Assets		Liabilities	
Reserve deposits at Federal Reserve banks		Original deposits of government securities dealers	_____
Required	_____		
Excess	_____		
New loans	_____	New deposits	_____
	_____		_____
Total assets		Total liabilities	

f. Explain what would happen to high-powered money, bank deposits, and the money supply if instead of buying government securities, the manager of the System Open Market Account was instructed to sell $8 million of securities.

_____

_____

_____

g. The second policy instrument of the Federal Reserve is the _____

which is the interest rate charged to commercial banks (and, since early 1980, to other depository financial institutions) who borrow from the Fed. When this rate is high relative to other short-term market rates of interest, it tends to *encourage/discourage* banks and other financial institutions from borrowing at the Fed. When this rate is low relative to other short-term market rates, it tends to *encourage/discourage* borrowing from the Fed and to *increase/decrease H/e/c.*

h. Complete the following table for the latest six months for which data are available.*

Month and Year	Treasury Bill Rate (3-month)	Prime Rate	Federal Funds Rate	Discount Rate	Amount of Borrowing from Fed
, 20					
, 20					
, 20					
, 20					
, 20					
, 20					

Do you think the discount rate has affected the level of high-powered money during the period covered in the table? Explain.*

_____

_____

_____

i. Why have many economists and other Fed watchers criticized the Federal Reserve's past discount rate policy?

_____

_____

j. The third of the Federal Reserve's monetary policy tools is _____

This policy tool works through changes in $H/e/c$; an increase in this rate will tend to _____

the money supply, while a decrease in this rate will tend to _____

the money supply.

Until recently, only commercial banks that were members of the Federal Reserve System were required to hold reserves with the Federal Reserve banks. Since passage of the Monetary Control Act of 1980, all depository institutions (commercial banks, savings and loan associations, mutual savings banks, savings banks, and credit unions) that offer transaction accounts (that is, deposits subject to transfer by check) must hold a required reserve either with the Federal Reserve Bank or in the form of vault cash.

k. Will this change tend to increase or decrease the Fed's control of the money supply? Explain.

_____

Question 5

The Fed's money-supply growth target zones are established by the Federal Open Market Committee (FOMC) and are presented in congressional hearings by the chairman of the Board of Governors. At times, the Fed may revise these targets or change the base date for the targets. This change results in *base drift*. As a result, the growth of M_1 (or M_2) may be quite different from the target growth rate.

a.   The Fed starts its target period in November of Year 1. The original value for the M_1 money supply on that date is 200 (billion). The Fed chairman announces that the Fed's M_1 growth target zone for the next twelve months is between 4 and 8 percent.

What is the minimum target-zone value of M_1 for the end of the period (November of Year 2)?

_____

What is the maximum target-zone value of M_1 for the end of the period? _____

In Figure 13A, draw the monetary cone for the twelve-month period starting in November of Year 1.

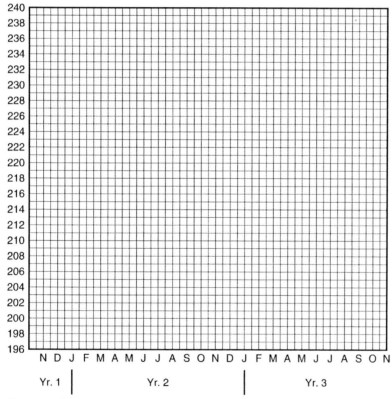

Figure 13A

b. In the early months of Year 2, the popularization of interest-bearing checking accounts and the growing use of point-of-scale (POS) terminals in grocery stores cause M_1 to grow first at the upper limit of the target zone and then at a rate above the target range. The values are as follows:

Year	Month	M_1 (billions)
1	December	201
2	January	202
	February	204
	March	207
	April	209
	May	212

In Figure 13A, draw a line showing the growth of M_1 for the period from November of Year 1 to May of Year 2.

Rather than restrict the growth of M_1 to bring it back into the target zone, the Fed decides to abandon the original target zone and establish a new target zone (with the same upper and lower growth rates) for the remaining part of the period. The starting point of the new monetary cone is at the value of M_1 in May of Year 2. Draw the new monetary cone in Figure 13A. (Remember that the original growth rates were for a year, so that for the six-month period they would be 2 and 4 percent.)

What is the new minimum target-zone value of M_1 for the end of the period (November of Year 2)?

_____

What is the new maximum target-zone value of M_1 for the end of the period? _____

_____

During the rest of the first period, the actual growth of M_1 is:

Month	M_1 (billions)
June	214
July	215
August	217
September	218
October	219
November	220

In Figure 13A, draw the rest of the line showing the growth of M_1 during the rest of the first target period. Is M_1 at the end of the first period (November of Year 2) within the new target zone?

_____

c. At the end of Year 2, the Fed chairman announces that the target zone for the second period, ending in November of Year 3, also has an acceptable growth range for M_1 of between 4 and 8 percent.

What is the minimum target-value of M_1 for the end of the second period? _____

What is the maximum target-value of M_1 for the end of the second period? _____

In Figure 13A, draw the monetary cone for the second period, using the M_1 value in November of Year 2 as the base.

The values for M_1 in the second period are:

Year	Month	M_1 (billions)
2	December	221
3	January	223
3	February	224
3	March	226
3	April	227
3	May	228
3	June	229
3	July	230
3	August	231
3	September	233
3	October	235
3	November	236

In Figure 13A, draw the remaining part of the growth line of M_1.

d.   If the money supply had grown at the maximum target rate from November of Year 1, the money supply in November of Year 3 would have been

_____

What is the actual money supply in November of Year 3? _____

Is the final figure within the second target zone? _____

How can this money supply be within the second target zone and yet be higher than the maximum target level announced in November of Year 1?

_____

_____

Question 6

One of the main elements of pre-Keynesian macroeconomic theory was the assumption of a stable demand for money. Although the influence of the interest rate on the demand for money was occasionally discussed, it was never formally integrated into the analysis. To a certain extent, the same can be said regarding the influence of wealth on the demand for money. In this question, we examine that dominant element in pre-Keynesian macroeconomics: the quantity theory of money.

a.   Describe the shape of the LM curve if the demand for money is not influenced by the interest rate.

_____

If the LM curve is as described above, a shift in the IS curve will cause real GDP to

_____

b. An important part of the development of the quantity theory of money is the famous equation of exchange: $MV \equiv PY$. This equation is true by definition; mathematically, it is a(n)

_____

Define the terms in the equation of exchange:

1. M: _____

2. V: _____

3. P: _____

4. Y: _____

According to the quantity theory of money, why do economic units hold money?

_____

_____

c. To move from a mere *identity* (the equation of exchange) to a *theory,* we must postulate some form of economic behavior. If we assume that people want to hold a *constant/variable* fraction ($1/V$) of their nominal income (PY) in the form of money (M), then we can rewrite the original equation as $M = (1/V^*)PY$, where V^* represents a constant velocity of money. Using the quantity theory of money, explain what will happen if the money supply is increased when the economy is initially in an equilibrium position.

_____

_____

_____

_____

d. The original pre-Keynesian version of the quantity theory usually assumed that prices were relatively flexible, so that almost all of the effect of a change in M on nominal income would take place on

_____

and almost none of the effect on _____

Distinguish between the *weak version* and the *strong version* of the quantity theory of money.

1. Weak version: _____

    _____

2. Strong version: _____

    _____

e. The economists who developed the quantity theory did not believe that $(1/V^*)$ was necessarily constant in the long run (although they did assume it was constant in the short run). Some of them, particularly economist Irving Fisher (1867–1947), extensively discussed the determinants of the velocity of money and what might account for secular movement in its value. Write the effects (*increase, decrease, no change*) on $(1/V^*)$ of each of the following:

1. A general increase in the use of credit cards. _____

2. A shift in the frequency of wage payments from weekly to monthly. _____

3. An increase in the time it takes to clear checks. _____

4. A balance-of-payments deficit that causes a loss of gold reserves and a decline in the money supply (as in Irving Fisher's time).

_____

Question 7

In the *General Theory*, John Maynard Keynes divided the demand for money into two parts: the transactions motive and the speculative notice. This question examines the characteristics of these two motives for holding money.

a. Define Keynes's transactions motive for holding money. _____

_____

_____

The amount of money the individual desires to hold to satisfy this transactions motive varies

_____

with the individual's income; thus, the total amount of money desired in the economy for transactions purposes depends on

_____

What notation did Keynes use for the transactions motive? _____

b. The second part of Keynes's demand for money was called the *speculative motive for holding money.* In this aspect of the demand for money, Keynes emphasized the role of the speculator who was very sensitive to changes in the interest rate. Keynes assumed that individuals had a choice of two financial assets as a way of holding their financial wealth (long-term bonds and money) and that they would switch between bonds and money to maximize the return from their wealth. If the speculator thought that the interest rate was higher than normal, then he or she expected that the interest rate would

_____

and bond price would _____

In this case, if the speculator bought bonds, now he or she would receive a _____

yield than if he or she waited until interest rates fell. As the price of the bonds _____

the speculator would receive a capital _____

Conversely, if the speculator thought the current interest rate was lower than normal, then he or she expected the interest rate would

_____

In this case, if the speculator held bonds, he or she would find that when the interest rate rose, the price of bonds would

_____

and he or she would have a capital _____

on the bonds. To avoid losses and to maximize gains, the speculator would hold _____

when the interest rate was high and hold _____

when the interest rate was low. (High and low were relative to the speculator's perception of the normal rate of interest.)

c. Suppose we have a bond that pays $1.00 per year forever. The price of the bond would be equal to $(1/r)$ where r is the interest rate. If the normal interest rate were 3 percent, the normal price of bonds would be

_____

If the interest rate were to increase to a high value of 5 percent, the price of the bond would be

_____

If the interest rate were to fall to a low level of 1 percent, the price of the bond would be

_____

If an individual bought bonds at a high rate of 5 percent and the interest rate fell to the normal rate, he or she would make a capital

_____

equal to _____

on each bond. If the individual bought bonds at a low rate of 1 percent and the interest rate returned to normal, he or she would make a capital

_____

equal to _____

on each bond.

d. What notation did Keynes use for the speculative motive? _____

e. The expression for the total demand for money as found in Keynes's *General Theory* is

    $M =$ _____

f.   In the nearly seventy years since the *General Theory* was published, the above formulation of the demand for money has been criticized along several lines. Briefly identify the criticism given by Gordon.

_____

_____

_____

Question 8

In this question, we study some of the post-Keynesian approaches to interest responsiveness of the transaction demand for money. In his discussion of the speculative motive for holding money, Keynes emphasized the chance of capital gains or losses (as a result of changes in the interest rate and the price of bonds) when an individual held bonds as opposed to money. By holding money, the speculator could avoid capital loss, but would lose income since money balances did not pay interest. In this theory, Keynes assumed that the individual had a choice between only money and bonds. However, once we allow for the existence of other financial assets that have a fixed capital value but still earn interest, the significance of the speculative motive is greatly diminished since the individual need not hold money to avoid capital losses.

a.   What financial assets other than money (M_1) will satisfy the speculative motive? _____

_____

_____

Abandoning the speculative motive for holding money does not mean the demand for money is not responsive to changes in the rate of interest. Early in the post-World War II period, William Baumol and James Tobin each independently demonstrated that by using capital theory to explain the demand for money, it could be shown that the transaction demand for money was sensitive to changes in the interest rate. (In this question, we will follow Baumol's version of the theory.)

b.   Each individual compares the benefits of holding money balances (demand deposits plus currency) with the benefits of holding savings deposits or other liquid assets that earn interest (r). The benefit of holding money (M) is the avoidance of broker's fees. Explain the nature of the broker's fees.

_____

_____

_____

The number of transactions (T) is the number of times that a broker's fee is incurred; it is equal to the individual's original paycheck (Y) divided by the average amount of cash obtained in each transaction (C). Suppose a woman receives a paycheck for $2,000 each month; she initially puts half of it in her savings account and half in her checking account. On the fifteenth of the month, she transfers the amount that is in her savings account into her checking account. In this case,

$Y =$ _____

$T =$ _____

$C =$ _____

If the individual transfers only $250 into her checking account each transaction, the broker's fee is incurred

_____

times. The total cost to the individual of maintaining her average cash balance is the combination of the cost of the broker's fees (bT) plus the interest forgone by holding money instead of savings deposits ($rC/2$), so that the cost function is:

$$\text{Cost} = bT + (rC/2) = b(Y/C) + (rC/2).$$

The optimal amount of cash obtained in each transaction is the level of C that minimizes the above cost function (and thus maximizes the net interest return). That level of C is:

$$C = (2bY/r)^{0.5}.$$

c. Using the above formula for the average amount of cash obtained, determine the optimal C in each of the following cases. Assume that the individual receives a paycheck (Y) of $2,000 each month and intends to spend the entire amount during the month. (*Note*: A calculator would be useful in solving this problem.)

1. The interest rate is 5 percent per annum (thus, on a monthly basis,

   $r =$ _____

   percent) and the broker's fee (b) equals $1.00.

   $C =$ _____

   The average number of trips to the bank per month is _____

2. The interest rate increases to 8 percent per annum (or

   _____

   percent per month) and the broker's fee (b) equals $1.00.

   $C =$ _____

   The average number of trips to the bank per month is _____

3. The interest rate is again 5 percent per annum, but the broker's fee (b) decreases to $0.50.

   $C =$ _____

   The average number of trips to the bank per month is _____

4. The interest rate rises to 8 percent per annum, and the broker's fee remains at $0.50.

   $C =$ _____

   The average number of trips to the bank per month is _____

d.   We can conclude from the above examples that an increase in the interest rate will _____

the demand for money. A decrease in the broker's fee will _____

the demand for money. What impact should telephone transfer accounts and automatic transfer accounts at commercial banks and savings and loans have on the demand for money? Explain.

_____

_____

_____

Question 9

One of the major changes in the U.S. economy in the late 1970s and early 1980s was the deregulation of financial markets. In this question we study the effect that deregulation had on the shape of the *IS-LM* curves and ultimately on the stability of interest rates and real output.

a.   What does the slope of the *IS* curve measure? _____

_____

If the same size change in the interest rate leads to a smaller change in real output, the *IS* curve has become *steeper/flatter*. In such a situation, the commodity market in the economy has become *more/less* interest sensitive.

For several reasons, deregulation of the financial markets has made the commodity market less interest sensitive (*IS* curve steeper). List four of these reasons and briefly explain how they affect the slope of the *IS* curve.

1.   _____

_____

2.   _____

_____

3.   _____

_____

4.   _____

_____

Let the before-deregulation *IS* curve be $Y = 4{,}000 - 300r$. Draw it on the left-hand side of Figure 13B, and label it *IS*. Let the after-deregulation *IS* curve be $Y = 3{,}000 - 100r$. Draw this *IS* curve in the right-hand side of Figure 13B, and label it *IS'*.

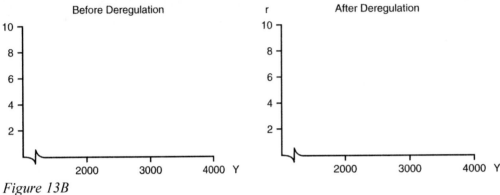

Figure 13B

b. Before deregulation, the demand for money had the equation: $(M/P)^d = 0.5Y - 150r$. When the money supply equals 500, what is the equation for the *LM* curve?

$Y = $ _____

Draw this *LM* curve in the left-hand side of Figure 13B and label it LM_0. Deregulation of the financial markets has made the *LM* curve *steeper/flatter* relative to the situation before deregulation. Explain why this is so.

_____

_____

_____

After deregulation, the equation describing the demand for money for this economy is $(M/P)^d = 0.5Y - 50r$. When the money supply equals 1,000, what is the equation of the *LM* curve?

$Y = $ _____

Draw this *LM* curve in the right-hand side of Figure 13B and, label it LM_0.

c. Locate the equilibrium point in the before-deregulation case, and label it *A*. The equilibrium real output and interest rate are:

$Y = $ _____

$r = $ _____

Locate the equilibrium point in the after-deregulation case, and label it A'. The equilibrium real output and interest rate are:

$Y =$ _____

$r =$ _____

In this section, we compare the effect of activist monetary policy on the economy before and after deregulation. Assume that policymakers want to reduce the level of real GDP. They therefore decrease the money supply by 300.

d.   What is the new money supply in the before-deregulation case? _____

What is the equation for the new *LM* curve?

$Y =$ _____

Draw this *LM* curve in the left-hand side of Figure 13B, and label that curve LM_1. Label the new equilibrium point B. After the reduction in the money supply, the new equilibrium real GDP and interest rate are:

$Y =$ _____

$r =$ _____

e.   What is the new money supply in the after-deregulation case? _____

What is the equation for the new *LM* curve?

$Y =$ _____

Draw this *LM* curve in the right-hand side of Figure 13B, and label that curve LM_1. Label the new equilibrium point B'. After the reduction in the money supply, the new equilibrium real GDP and interest rate are:

$Y =$ _____

$r =$ _____

f.   Review:

As a result of the deregulation of the monetary sector, the *IS* curve for the economy will be *steeper/ flatter* and the *LM* curve for the economy will become *steeper/flatter*. After deregulation, a given change in the money supply will lead to a *larger/smaller* change in the interest rate. A major part of the explanation for why interest rates in the United States were much more volatile in the 1980s than in earlier periods is the

_____

_____

Question 10

In this question, we examine the use of alternative instruments for the conduct of monetary policy. The central question is whether policymakers can better stabilize the economy by holding the money supply constant (in a dynamic situation, a constant growth rate of the money supply) or by maintaining a constant interest rate. We also investigate an alternative target, that of stabilizing nominal GDP, which may be superior to either of these two choices.

a. The initial position of the economy is described by the following *IS* and *LM* curves:

$$IS_0: Y = 3,800 - 200r \ (A_p = 950 - 50r; \ k = 4)$$
$$LM_0: Y = 2,000 + 100r \ [(M^s/P) = 500; \ (M/P)^d = 0.25Y - 25r].$$

We assume throughout this problem that as a result of long-term wage and price contracts, the price level remains constant, with $P = 1.0$, and that $Y^N = 2,600$.

Draw the *IS* and *LM* curves in Figure 13C, label them IS_0 and LM_0, and label the point of intersection A.

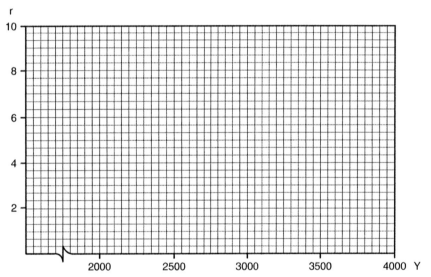

Figure 13C

What are the equilibrium levels of real GDP and the interest rate?

$Y =$ _____

$r =$ _____

In the next section we examine what happens to the economy when commodity demand is unstable, monetary demand is stable, and policymakers follow a constant growth-rate policy.

b. Since money demand is stable, if the monetary authority follows a constant growth-rate rule (CGRR) with a zero growth rate in the money supply, what happens to the *LM* curve?

_____

c. Suppose that autonomous private spending increases by 75 so that the IS curve becomes IS_1: $Y = 4,100 - 200r$. Draw the new IS curve in Figure 13C and label it IS_1. Label the new equilibrium Position B.

The new equilibrium levels of real GDP and the interest rate are:

$Y =$ _____

$r =$ _____

Compared to the situation in Part a, by how much has Y changed? _____

By how many percentage points has r changed? _____

d. Alternatively, assume that the level of autonomous private spending fell from its initial level by 75 so that the new IS curve has the equation: $Y = 3,500 - 200r$. Draw the new IS curve in Figure 13C and label it IS_2. Label the new equilibrium Position C.

The new equilibrium levels of real GDP and the interest rate are:

$Y =$ _____

$r =$ _____

Compared to the situation in Part a, by how much has Y changed? _____

By how many percentage points has r changed? _____

Because there is often a recognition lag in the economy, policymakers may not be aware of the shift in the commodity market; however, since financial markets are relatively sensitive to changes in the demand for funds, an increase in private spending might lead to an increase in the interest rate. Unaware of the commodity shift, but observing the change in interest rates, policymakers might keep financial markets from tightening and seek to keep interest rates constant.

e. Assume that private autonomous spending has increased and the IS curve has shifted from IS_0 to IS_1. To keep the interest rate constant, the monetary authorities increase the real money supply from 500 to 575. The equation for the new LM curve is $Y = 2,300 + 100r$.

Draw the new LM curve in Figure 13C and label it LM_1. Label the new equilibrium Position D.

The new equilibrium levels of real GDP and the interest rates are:

$Y =$ _____

$r =$ _____

Compared to the situation in Part a, by how much has Y changed? _____

By how many percentage points has r changed? _____

f. Assume that private autonomous spending has decreased and the *IS* curve has shifted from IS_0 to IS_2. Seeing the interest rate begin to fall, the monetary authorities decrease the real money supply by 75 so that the *LM* now has the equation: $Y = 1,700 + 100r$.

Draw the new *LM* curve in Figure 13C and label it LM_2. Label the new equilibrium Position *E*.

The new equilibrium levels of real GDP and the interest rates are:

$Y = $ _____

$r = $ _____

Compared to the situation in Part a, by how much has *Y* changed? _____

By how many percentage points has *r* changed? _____

g. On the basis of the above examples, we can conclude that if spending in the commodity market is unstable (*IS* curve shifts) and the demand for money is stable (*LM* curve remains constant), then to stabilize the level of real GDP, monetary policymakers will do better to follow a policy of constant

_____

than a policy of constant _____

Finally, we examine what happens in the economy with an unstable commodity demand and a stable demand for money when policymakers choose to target real GDP; that is, they attempt to keep real GDP constant. We assume that policymakers can quickly recognize changes in private spending and provide a countercyclical adjustment in the money supply.

h. Assume that autonomous spending increases by 75 so that IS_1 is the new *IS* curve. The monetary authorities respond by reducing the real money supply by 37.5 so that the new *LM* curve is $Y = 1,850 + 100r$. (*Note*: To keep Figure 13C from becoming too complicated, do not draw this new *LM* curve.)

The new equilibrium levels of real GDP and the interest rates are:

$Y = $ _____

$r = $ _____

Compared to the situation in Part a, by how much has *Y* changed? _____

By how many percentage points has *r* changed? _____

i. Now, assume that autonomous spending decreases by 75 so that IS_2 is now the *IS* curve. The monetary authorities respond by increasing the real money supply by 37.5 so that the new *LM* curve is $Y = 2,150 + 100r$. (*Note*: Do not draw this new *LM* curve.)

The new equilibrium levels of real GDP and the interest rates are:

$Y = $ _____

$r = $ _____

Compared to the situation in Part a, by how much has *Y* changed? _____

By how many percentage points has *r* changed? _____

j. When commodity demand is unstable and money demand is stable, the policy of stabilizing real GDP by countercyclical changes in the money supply is *better/worse* than the constant money-supply policy.

When commodity demand is unstable and money demand is stable, the policy of stabilizing real GDP by countercyclical changes in the money supply is *better/worse* than the constant interest-rate policy.

What is the major disadvantage of using a policy of offsetting (countercyclical) changes in the money supply?

_____

_____

Until now, we assumed that instability in the economy comes from the commodity sector. Now, we assume that commodity demand is stable (*IS* remains at IS_0) but there is instability in the demand for money.

k. If the money supply is held constant (CGRR), what will happen to the *LM* curve when the demand for money increases?

_____

When the demand for money decreases? _____

l. Assume that the instability in money demand (with CGRR) can be shown as a fluctuation between LM_1 and LM_2 in Figure 13C. In this circumstance, equilibrium real GDP will fluctuate between a low and a high of

_____

and the interest rate will fluctuate between a high and a low of _____

If the monetary authorities wish to keep the interest rate constant when the demand for money increases (tending to cause *LM* to shift to LM_1/LM_2), they will *increase/decrease* the money supply. When the demand for money decreases (tending to cause *LM* to shift to LM_1/LM_2), they will *increase/decrease* the money supply.

If the policymakers are successful in keeping the interest rate constant, what will happen to real GDP?

_____

m. Under conditions of a stable commodity demand and an unstable money demand, an interest-rate target will be *better than/worse than/the same as* a money-supply target (CGRR) in stabilizing real GDP.

Under these conditions, what is the difference between an interest-rate target and a real-GDP target?

_____

n. What monetary policy is best when there is instability in both commodity demand and the demand for money?

_____

_____

Chapter 14
Stabilization Policy in the Closed and Open Economy

In earlier chapters, we derived the aggregate demand and supply curves. Using these tools, we examined the effect on the equilibrium levels of prices and output of changes in aggregate demand or supply. After developing the short-run Phillips curve, we constructed a model that could explain the relationship between the rate of inflation and the level of real GDP. Up to this point, we have assumed that nominal GDP growth could be set precisely at a predetermined desirable level. This is unrealistic because it is not possible for policymakers to control nominal GDP either precisely or immediately. The economy is not like a Porsche that hugs the turns on a Grand Prix track, but rather, as Gordon points out in Chapter 14 of the text, the economy is more like a supertanker that must plan a change of course well in advance.

In this chapter, we question whether there should be an attempt to adjust nominal GDP through discretionary monetary and fiscal policy. We begin by examining the key points in the debate between two groups of economists: rules advocates and policy activists. Rules advocates believe that government attempts to stabilize the economy through changes in nominal GDP tend to be ineffective at best and probably destabilizing. The policy activists, conversely, believe that the economy is inherently unstable and active manipulation of nominal GDP is necessary.

Question 1

This question discusses the contrasting views of policy activists and rules advocates concerning the business cycle. The question also examines the relationship between policy instruments and targets.

a. In what ways do the views on the business cycle of the rules advocates agree with those of the policy activists?

_____

_____

In what way do they disagree? _____

_____

_____

b. The activist position is that private spending is a source of instability in the economy, and that therefore, government countercyclical policy should be actively used to achieve economic stability. The activist pursuit of economic stability requires the use of policy instruments that can be set to achieve target levels of major economic variables associated with the desired situation.

Fill in the blanks to complete the following statements.

Each target requires at least _____

policy instrument(s). For example, a money-supply change cannot simultaneously achieve a target level of

_____

and a target _____

Both _____

and _____

policies must be used together to achieve a given combination of _____

and _____

Long-run real output is limited to what the economy can produce at _____

because any higher real GDP achieved through monetary and fiscal policy will result in

_____

A permanent reduction of unemployment requires a permanent fall in _____

_____

which in turn can be achieved only through _____

c. *Policy instruments* are connected to *target variables* by way of *structural relations*. The structural relations are the equations of the model, e.g., *IS* and *LM* curves. Target variables can be influenced by exogenous non-policy variables included in the structural relations. In addition, both policy instruments and non-policy variables may have economically irrelevant side effects. Figure 14A presents a schematic version of these interactions.

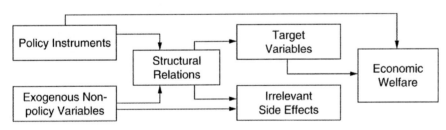

Figure 14A

In the space provided, indicate whether each of the following is a policy instrument (I), a structural relation (S), a target variable (T), an exogenous non-policy variable (E), or an irrelevant side effect (R).

1. Demand for money	14. Unemployment rate
2. Inflation rate	15. Consumer optimism
3. Interest ceilings	16. The money supply
4. Foreign demand	17. Short-run Phillips curve
5. Distribution of income	18. Foreign exchange rates
6. National debt	19. Government expenditure
7. Tax rates	20. Growth rate of natural real GDP
8. Investment function	21. Business confidence
9. Wars	22. International policy
10. Balance of payments	23 Consumption function
11. Manpower programs	24. Share of public vs. private spending
12. Nominal GDP	25. Long-run Phillips curve
13. Supply shocks	26. Price and wage controls

d. Rules advocates oppose activist countercyclical changes in the money supply and believe that such a policy may do more harm than good. What kind of monetary policy do rules advocates propose?

_____

Rules advocates claim that economists who favor an activist stabilization policy "require a utopian set of assumptions about the economy." What are the five main characteristics of this utopian "activists' Paradise"?

1. _____

_____

2. _____

_____

3. _____

_____

4. _____

_____

5. _____

Question 2

Answer this question on the views of rules advocates and the activist response to those views by completing the blanks with the correct word or words.

a. Most rules advocates would agree with the following propositions.

1. Without the interference of _____

    introduced by _____

    private spending would be _____

2. Not only is private spending relatively _____

    but so is the_____

3. Even if_____

    spending and the_____

    are not_____

    an activist _____

    is likely to do _____

4. Even if prices are _____

    so that the economy can _____

    from _____

    in the_____

    there can be no dispute regarding the_____

    of the price level, the _____

    the period of time allowed for adjustment.

b. Relate each of the following arguments to the rules advocates' points that it supports, if any. Write 1, 2, 3, 4 or *none* in the space provided.

_____ 1. All policy changes affect the economy with a long and uncertain lag.

_____ 2. The *IS* curve is relatively flat because of the broad range of assets whose demand depends on the interest rate.

_____ 3. Because business finances most of its investment from retained earnings, the *IS* curve is nearly vertical.

_____ 4. Rules advocates have a relatively low rate of time preference.

_____ 5. The velocity of money is perfectly constant.

_____   6. Demand shocks are transitory, and price flexibility quickly neutralizes them.

_____   7. Flexible prices will quickly guide the economy back to the natural level of real GDP (Y^N).

_____   8. Personal consumption expenditures are very stable because they depend on permanent income rather than current disposable income.

_____   9. The velocity of money is predictable, and the growth of the money supply should be a steady rate to give a steady growth of nominal GDP.

_____ 10. Since monetary policy is relatively ineffective, variations in tax rates should be used for short-run stabilization of the economy.

_____ 11. Economic forecasting is not accurate enough to offset the lag in the effects of discretionary monetary and fiscal policy.

_____ 12. The destabilizing effects of instability in the demand for money disappear before stabilizing government policy can be put into effect.

c. Listed below are the responses to the rules advocates' views. Indicate to which view each statement refers.

_____   1. Although there is no denying that monetary and fiscal policy have been destabilizing at times in the past, economic knowledge is now advanced enough so that we can use monetary and fiscal policy to offset the economic effects of destabilizing swings in private spending.

_____   2. The time period needed for price flexibility automatically to bring the economy back to the natural level of real GDP is long, and there is no reason for the government to allow the higher unemployment and GDP gap that would exist during this lengthy adjustment period.

_____   3. Given the instability of the velocity of money during the past decade, a CGRR would have destabilized the growth of nominal GDP.

_____   4. Discretionary monetary and fiscal policy is needed to offset the instability in private spending caused by changes in consumer and business attitudes and expectations.

Question 3

Much of the controversy between rules advocates and policy activists concerns the degree of inherent stability of autonomous private planned spending. Rules advocates argue that private spending is inherently stable, while activists respond that such spending is inherently unstable. This question surveys the recent movements in private and government expenditures to see if there are any immediately apparent signs of stability or instability.

a. Find the levels of real (1996 dollars) federal government expenditure, fixed investment (nonresidential fixed investment plus residential fixed investment) expenditure, and personal consumption expenditure for the most recent six quarters for which data are available. Calculate the quarter-to-quarter percentage change in each series.*

	Government		Fixed Investment		Consumption	
Period	Amount	Percentage Change	Amount	Percentage Change	Amount	Percentage Change
20: Q						
20: Q						
20: Q						
20: Q						
20: Q						
20: Q						

b. Which types of spending show the greatest stability?* _____

_____

Which types of spending show the greatest instability?* _____

_____

In the period above, did government expenditures offset swings in private planned spending? Explain.*

_____

_____

c. Does the above period support the rules advocates' position or the activist position? Explain.*

_____

Question 4

In Chapter 13 we showed that a properly timed, activist countercyclical monetary policy could stabilize real GDP better than a constant growth-rate rule (CGRR) for the money supply. In this question, we study some of the limitations of this type of policy.

a. What are the two major objections to an activist countercyclical monetary policy?

1. _____

2. _____

Are both objections accepted by rules advocates? _____

In Chapter 13, we found that nominal GDP targeting by the Fed was as good as or better than a policy of targeting either the money supply or interest rates. Whether the above objections to an activist policy are relevant to a policy of targeting nominal GDP depends on the nature of the main source of instability in the economy. Explain why.

_____

_____

_____

b. There are five sources of lags between an initial change in the economy and the time that monetary policy can influence spending: transmission lag, legislative lag, effectiveness lag, data lag, and recognition lag. Arrange these lags in the proper chronological sequence, and briefly explain each one.

1. _____

    _____

2. _____

    _____

3. _____

    _____

4. _____

    _____

5. _____

    _____

What is David and Christina Romer's estimate of the length (in months) of the total lag in monetary policy?

_____

Question 5

The multipliers in Chapters 3–5 (summarized in the *IS-LM* curves) indicate the size of the change in real GDP that results from a given change in a policy tool such as government spending, tax rates, or the money supply. But the *IS-LM* curves are a static model that ignores both the path the economy takes toward the new equilibrium and the time lag between use of the policy tool and the resulting effect on the level of real GDP. In this question, we use three of the better-known econometric models (the Federal Reserve Bank of St. Louis model (FRB), the MIT-Penn-Social Science Research Council model (MPS), and the Brookings Institution model) to estimate the government-spending multiplier. We examine both the magnitude of the resulting change in real GDP and the distribution of that change over time.

a. Below are given the effects on real GDP of a permanent $1 billion increase in government expenditure over a twelve-quarter time span. The effects are listed for each of the three econometric models. Plot and label these changes in real GDP in Figure 14B.

Table 14A: Effects on Real GDP of a $1 Billion Increase in Real Government Expenditure

	Model and Effects ($billions)		
Quarter	Brookings	MPS	St. Louis FRB
1	1.8	1.2	0.5
2	2.4	1.5	1.0
3	2.7	1.9	1.0
4	2.8	2.2	0.5
5	2.8	2.3	−0.1
6	2.8	2.4	−0.2
7	2.8	2.4	−0.2
8	2.7	2.2	−0.2
9	2.625	1.825	−0.2
10	2.55	1.45	−0.2
11	2.475	1.025	−0.2
12	2.4	0.7	−0.2

b. After a sustained four-quarter $20 billion increase in real government expenditure, what would be the change in real GDP according to each of the above econometric models?

Brookings: _____

MPS: _____

St. Louis FRB: _____

After eight quarters?

Brookings: _____

MPS: _____

St. Louis FRB: _____

After twelve quarters?

Brookings: _____

MPS: _____

St. Louis FRB: _____

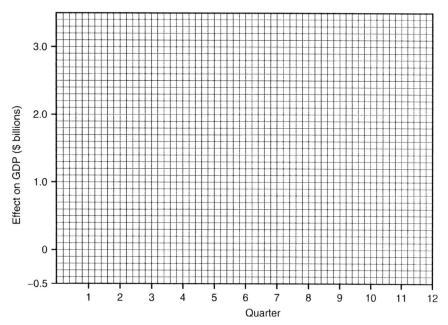

Figure 14B

c. Which of the above econometric models do you think is the most supportive of the rules advocates' viewpoint? Why?

_____

_____

_____

Which of the models best supports the activist case? Why?

_____

_____

Question 6

Recently, additional reasons to question the efficacy of policy activism have been advanced. These considerations involve time inconsistency, credibility, and reputation.

One of the arguments in favor of policy rules is that under such rules consumers, workers, and firms will be able to form accurate expectations of future policy actions. The policy activists' counterargument is that any good rule could be adopted by a discretionary policymaker. We begin by examining the merits of these arguments.

a. What are feedback policy rules? _____

_____

_____

b. In Chapter 17 of the textbook, we studied the Lucas-Friedman supply function: $Y = Y^N + h(p - p^e)$. It states that real GDP (Y) is equal to natural real GDP (Y^N) plus an amount equal to a coefficient times the excess of the actual price level over the expected price level. What is the value of the term $h(p - p^e)$ if there is a CGRR policy?

_____

Explain why this is so. _____

_____

_____

c. What is the value of $h(p - p^e)$ if there are feedback policy rules in effect? _____

Does the feedback policy rule have to be announced in advance for this effect to take place? Explain.

_____

d. What light does this exercise shed on the debate raised in the paragraph preceding Part a?

_____

We now turn to a problem with the preceding analysis, time inconsistency.

e. What is the problem of time inconsistency in macroeconomic policy? _____

_____

What kind of policy rule is best, given the possibility of time inconsistency? _____

_____

f. What does it mean for a central bank to "invest in its reputation"? _____

_____

What implications does investment in reputation have for the ability of the Fed to reduce the rate of inflation?

_____

_____

Question 7

This question extends the debate over rules versus activism in monetary policy to include the question of foreign exchange rate policy.

a. If a country chooses a fixed exchange rate target, will it be more or less able to use monetary policy to stimulate output. Explain.

_____

_____

_____

b. A fixed exchange rate policy may be expected to *lower/raise* the inflation rate in an economy over time. Such a policy will *lower/raise* inflationary expectations and consequently *lower/raise* the inflation rate that the central bank can achieve at the natural rate of output.

c. What does the evidence from developing countries suggest about the impact of fixed exchange rates on the average inflation rate in the future?

_____

_____

Chapter 15
The Economics of Consumption Behavior

A major belief of rules advocates is that the private economy would be basically stable if government would leave it alone. In this chapter, we investigate this belief as it applies to personal consumption behavior. The key question is: Does personal consumption spending contribute to economic stability by damping down instability in other forms of spending, or does consumption add extra instability of its own?

We begin this chapter with a review of the simple consumption function introduced in Chapter 3. We find that this function is not consistent with empirical findings regarding time-series and cross-section consumption behavior. To fit a consumption function to the empirical observations, economists have developed a number of alternatives to the simple function. In this chapter we take a close look at two of these alternatives: the permanent-income hypothesis (PIH) and the life-cycle hypothesis (LCH). The PIH and the LCH explain why consumption spending (especially for nondurable goods and services) is relatively stable, thus lending support to the position of rules advocates. However, there are several qualifications of the simple PIH and LCH theories, especially the inclusion of consumer durable spending, which may reintroduce an element of instability in consumption spending behavior.

Question 1

This question reviews some of the characteristics of the consumption function introduced in Chapter 3. The emphasis in this question is on the behavior of consumption and saving under alternative assumptions about the structure of the consumption function.

a. What economic relationship is explained by a consumption function? _____

_____

What is the marginal propensity to consume? _____

_____

What is the average propensity to consume? _____

_____

What is the relationship between the average propensity to consume and the average propensity to save?

_____

b.   In the following table, we compare two alternative specifications for a consumption function. Complete the following table.

Quarter	Y – T	Alternative A $C = 0.9(Y - T)$			Alternative B $C = 20 + 0.7(Y - T)$		
		C	APC	APS	C	APC	APS
1	100						
2	120						
3	140						
4	130						
5	110						
6	90						
7	100						

The data above summarize the behavior of consumption and the average propensities to consume and save during a rather simplified business cycle.

During what quarters is the economy experiencing an expansion? _____

During what quarters is the economy experiencing a recession? _____

Describe the behavior of the APC and APS for Alternative A during the cycle. _____

_____

Describe the behavior of the APC and APS for Alternative B during the cycle. _____

_____

_____

Alternative A is sometimes referred to as a proportionate consumption function, and Alternative B is referred to as a nonproportionate function. Can you explain why?

_____

_____

_____

c.   What is a cross-section consumption function? _____

_____

_____

According to the studies of the U.S. economy (summarized in Gordon), the cross-section consumption function is a *proportionate/nonproportionate* function.

d. What is a time-series consumption function? _____

_____

_____

A consumption function that relates C and $(Y - T)$ over a long period of time is referred to as a long-run consumption function. If we observe the average saving ratio, $S/(Y - T)$, that occurred during each of the major business cycles of the twentieth century, we find that the ratio has *increased/decreased/ remained relatively constant* over time. Thus, we conclude that the long-run consumption function is *proportionate/nonproportionate*.

Question 2

The previous question showed that the behavior of the saving ratio as income changes is different in cross-section data from the behavior observed for time-series data. One of the hypotheses advanced to resolve this apparent conflict is the permanent-income hypothesis (PIH). This question examines how permanent income is estimated and studies the relationship between consumption and income (permanent and actual) under the PIH.

a. Assume that at the beginning of a year, a woman estimates her permanent income. If, during the year, her actual income is greater (less) than her permanent income, we would expect her to revise her estimated permanent income upward (downward). In the text, the following equation is given to describe this adaptive behavior:

$Y^P = Y^P_{-1} + j(Y - Y^P_{-1})$, where Y is current income.

Explain this equation. _____

_____

_____

Explain the situation when $j = 0$. _____

_____

_____

Explain the situation when $j = 1$. _____

_____

_____

Which value of j do you think is most likely? Why? _____

_____

_____

The equation can be rewritten as follows: $Y^P_{-1} = jY + (1-j)\ Y^P_{-1}$.

Explain this equation. _____

_____

_____

b. Assume that the estimate of Y^P for the initial period is $20,000. If $j = 0.4$, what will be the permanent income in Period 1 (Y^P_{-1}) if the actual income in Period 1 (Y_1) equals $28,000?

_____

If the actual income for the next three years also equals $28,000, what will be:

Y^P_2 ? _____

Y^P_3 ? _____

Y^P_4 ? _____

Explain the movement in Y^P over the four years? _____

_____

_____

c. One of the assumptions of the PIH is that a person's consumption is a constant fraction of permanent income, that is, $C = kY^P$. Derive this consumption function (using the first equation for permanent income given in Part a above).

$C =$ _____

Rewrite this equation for the special case when $k = 0.8$ and $j = 0.4$.

$C =$ _____

If actual income turns out to be equal to permanent income, what does consumption equal?

$C =$ _____

d. Complete the following table (assuming $k = 0.8$ and $j = 0.4$).

Year	Y	$Y - Y^P_{-1}$	Y^P	C
0	$20,000	$0	$20,000	$16,000
1	26,000		22,400	
2	30,000	7,600		
3	18,000			

By how much did consumption change from Year 0 to Year 1? _____

By how much did permanent income change from Year 0 to Year 1? _____

What was the marginal propensity to consume (MPC) from *permanent* income during this period?

_____

What was the marginal propensity to consume from *actual* income during this period?

_____

e. Explain why the two values for MPC differ. _____

_____

_____

What was the MPC from actual income during Year 2? _____

In light of these effects of the PIH on the marginal propensity to consume, what initial conclusions can be reached regarding the implications of PIH for the stability of the economy, for example, in response to changes in A_p?

_____

_____

_____

_____

f. In Milton Friedman's version of the PIH, the part of current income that is not expected to be permanent is called

_____

income, and the MPC out of that part of income is assumed to be equal to _____

That will make the difference between the long-run and the short-run MPC *greater/less*.

Question 3

Let us examine how the PIH can reconcile the conflict between cross-section data and time-series data.

a. To see how PIH can explain cross-section results, we note that not everyone will be in a situation where actual income for the year equals permanent income. In Year 1, some people will have actual income above permanent income (a good year) and some people will have a bad year with actual income below permanent income. Assume there are sixty persons in the economy grouped in the following way for the initial year:

Group	Number of Persons	Y^P
A	20	$10,000
B	20	20,000
C	20	30,000

When income data are published, they are actual income figures; thus, in these reports people are grouped not according to permanent income, but according to actual income. Assume that $j = 0.2$ and $k = 0.9$. Complete the following table.

Number	Original Group	This Year Actual Income	Last Year Permanent Income	This Year Permanent Income	Actual Consumption
		Low-Income Group			
16	A	$10,000	$10,000	$18,000	$16,200
3	B	10,000	20,000		
1	C	10,000	30,000		
		Middle-Income Group			
3	A	20,000	10,000		
14	B	20,000			
3	C	20,000			
		High-Income Group			
1	A	30,000	10,000		
3	B	30,000			
16	C	30,000			

Using the data from the above table, complete the following table. (*Hint*: You are using actual income and actual consumption. To find average consumption for each group, calculate the total consumption within the group and divide by 20.)

Income Group	Average Income	Average Consumption	APC
Low income	$10,000	$10,800	
Middle income			
High income			

Use this information to plot a consumption function in Figure 15A. Label it C_1.

b. What would be the APC for each group if everyone's actual income in Year 1 equaled his or her permanent income?

In Figure 15A, plot the consumption function associated with this situation ($Y = Y^P$). Label it C_2.

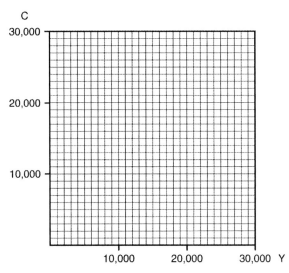

Figure 15A   *Figure 15B*

c. Now assume that we are considering an entire economy and that when $Y = \$300$ billion, the same
    number of people are having good years as are having bad years so that the total Y for the economy is
    $300 billion. What would be the level of consumption in the economy if $k = 0.9$?

    _____

    If suddenly the economic situation improves so that actual Y increases to $360 billion, the number
    of people having good years will be *greater/less* than the number having bad years, and permanent
    income will *increase/decrease*. What will be the relationship between Y and Y^P for the entire
    economy? Explain.

    _____

    _____

    If $j = 0.4$ and $k = 0.9$, what will be the level of Y^P? _____

    What will be the level of C? _____

    What is the observed APC for the economy? _____

    What is the APS? _____

    Alternatively, if originally $Y^P = \$300$ billion and the economy headed into a recession so that Y fell to
    $270 billion, what would be the level of Y^P?

    _____

    What would be the level of C? _____

    APC? _____

    APS? _____

Using your answers from Part c, plot the points for $Y = \$300$ billion, $\$360$ billion, and $\$270$ billion in Figure 15B, and draw the cyclical consumption function. Label this curve C_3.

Describe the behavior of APS as the economy heads into a recession. _____

_____

Describe the behavior of APS as the economy heads into a boom period. _____

_____

d. Assume that the three levels of output ($Y = \$270$ billion, $\$300$ billion, and $\$360$ billion) were points along a long-run growth path for the economy so that at each point $Y = Y^P$. Plot the three points associated with this situation in Figure 15B and draw the long-run consumption function. Label this curve C_4.

What is the level of APC along this curve? _____

APS? _____

e. For each type of consumption function listed below, describe the behavior of the APS as income changes and explain the behavior of APS according to the PIH.

1. Cross-section consumption function:

    Behavior: _____

    Explanation: _____

    _____

    _____

    _____

2. Cyclical time-series consumption function:

    Behavior: _____

    Explanation: _____

    _____

3. Long-run time-series consumption function:

    Behavior: _____

    Explanation: _____

Question 4

A second approach to explaining consumption behavior is the life-cycle hypothesis (LCH). This question analyzes the foundations of this approach and some of the implications of the hypothesis.

a. Assume the consumer attempts to stabilize his consumption over his entire lifetime. For our consumer, life begins at 20, when he begins earning income, and ends at 80, when he dies. The consumer earns income each year from age 20 to 60, when he retires. The consumer begins his earning lifetime with zero initial assets.

If we consider the beginning of earning power (age 20) to be Year 0, the length of life (L) equals

_____

and the years until retirement (R) equal _____

Assume that the consumer earns \$22,500 per year (Y_0). How much income will he earn over his lifetime?

_____

If he wishes to consume an equal amount every year, how much will he consume per year?

_____

Given these assumptions about income and consumer behavior, what are his APC and APS out of actual income?

APC = _____

APS = _____

Fill in the following table.

End of Year	Total Assets
1	\$7,500
10	
40	
50	
60	

b. Assume that the consumer receives an increase in income of \$6,000 in the thirtieth year. How many years are left in his life?

_____

If he considered this increase to be temporary (a one-time increase), how much should he spend during the thirtieth year?

_____

What would he do with the rest of his increased income? _____

_____

_____

What is the MPC related to this temporary increase in income? _____

c. If the consumer considers the income increase to be permanent (that is, expects to receive an extra $6,000 per year from the thirtieth year until retirement), by how much will his lifetime income increase?

_____

If he spreads this increase over his remaining life, by how much will his annual consumption increase?

_____

What is the MPC in the thirtieth year related to this permanent increase in income?

_____

According to the LCH, what conclusion can be reached about the response of the consumer to temporary and permanent changes in income?

_____

_____

d. In an economic boom, part of the consumer's increase in income might be considered temporary. If this is so, the MPS from this temporary increase will be *greater/less* than the MPS from a permanent increase. Therefore, the total percentage of income saved, the APS, will be *greater/less* in a boom that in a normal growth year. Explain why, according to the LCH, the APS will decrease when the economy heads into a recession.

_____

_____

_____

e. Now assume that the consumer does not begin his earning life with zero assets, but instead has an initial endowment of assets (A_1) equal to $90,000.

What is the total amount that the consumer can now consume over his lifetime? _____

What is his consumption each year? _____

If his income remains at $22,500, what is his APC? _____

APS? _____

What is the effect on the APS of having an increase in the initial level of assets? (Compare your answers in Parts e and a.)

_____

_____

f.   How does the LCH help support the view of rules advocates that without erratic government intervention, spending would be stable?

_____

_____

_____

_____

g.   What do the LCH and PIH suggest about a consumer's behavior in response to a tax cut perceived to be a temporary change versus a tax cut perceived to be a permanent change?

_____

_____

Question 5

While the PIH and LCH have effectively explained much of the difference between the short-run and long-run values of the marginal propensity to consume, there are other real-world phenomena they do not explain so well. Consequently, in recent years several economists have begun to qualify the simple versions of these theories. This question examines some of these qualifications.

a.   A qualification of the PIH comes from the rational expectations hypothesis, one of the key assumptions of the new classical economics.

In the rational expectations version of PIH, how is the estimate of permanent income formed?

_____

_____

_____

Under the rational expectations version of the PIH, changes in consumption depend only on

_____

changes in income.

b.   The LCH theory assumes that consumption is constant over the lifetime. In our example of the LCH, labor income was also assumed to be constant over the working years, but in fact labor income tends to rise during the first part of the working years, peaking in later middle age. To maintain a constant consumption, young people would have to borrow during the early part of their working years. A recent and important qualification of the LCH has come from the consideration of liquidity constraints.

What is mean by liquidity constraints? _____

_____

What is the effect of liquidity constraints on the MPC out of temporary changes in income?

_____

_____

What percentage of households is estimated to be subject to these constraints? _____

_____

c. Under the simple LCH, people are supposed to consume all of their earnings and all of their assets during their lifetimes. This means that all of their lifetime savings would be consumed during retirement. In fact, however, a large part of accumulated wealth is passed on to heirs, an apparent contradiction of the assumption that the proper time horizon is the lifetime.

In Chapter 12 of the text, we examined the Barro-Ricardo equivalence theorem, which assumes that people leave bequests because they care about their children. Under this theory, what would be the effect on consumption and saving of a deficit-financed tax cut?

_____

_____

The critics of the Barro-Ricardo theorem explain the existence of bequests in other ways. What are they?

_____

_____

d. Both the PIH and the LCH assume that families try to maintain a constant level of consumption services. For consumer services and nondurables, consumption and expenditure occur at roughly the same time. However, consumer durables (automobiles, washing machines, and so forth) provide a flow of consumer services over a long period of time, well after the expenditure to purchase them takes place. It is not the expenditures for durables that are assumed to be fixed fraction of permanent income, but the flow of services from durable goods. If permanent income rises, people will want to increase their enjoyment of the flow of services from consumer durable goods. As a result, total consumption expenditures (including durable goods) may *rise/fall/remain the same* as a fraction of income as actual income rises if that increase raises permanent income.

e. For the six most recent quarters for which data are available, find the ratio of personal saving to personal income and the ratio of personal saving plus consumer durable expenditures to personal income.*

Period	Personal Saving/ Personal Income	Personal Saving + Consumer Durable Goods Expenditure/ Personal Income
20: Q		
20: Q		
20: Q		
20: Q		
20: Q		
20: Q		

What ratio supports the PIH and LCH better? Explain.* _____

_____

_____

_____

When we include the behavior of consumer durables, do the PIH and LCH support the contention that non-government spending is stable? Explain.*

_____

_____

_____

Chapter 16
The Economics of Investment Behavior

This chapter continues the examination of the instability of private spending, begun in the previous chapter with consumption spending. Now, we turn our attention to private investment. It is the inherent instability in private investment spending that is, along with the behavior of consumer durable goods expenditures, the primary support for an activist stabilization policy.

Chapter 15 showed that when the desired stock of consumer durable goods is a constant ratio of permanent income, a revision of households' permanent income could lead to sharp variations in spending for consumer durables. In this chapter a similar approach, known as the accelerator hypothesis, is applied to private investment spending. Tobin's q theory, an alternative approach to explaining private investment spending, is also noted.

Question 1

We begin by examining some recent data for various components of GDP.

a. In the table below, give the percentages of real GDP represented by each of the following types of real expenditure for the periods indicated.*

	Percentage of Real GDP	
Expenditure Type	**Most Recent Quarter (20:Q)**	**Four Quarters Earlier (20:Q)**
Personal consumption expenditures		
Gross private domestic investment		
Government expenditures		
Net exports		
Total	100.0	100.0

b. A long tradition in economics—including such notable economists as J.M. Keynes, K. Wicksell, J.A. Schumpeter, and A. Hansen—associates cyclical movements in the economy with the inherent instability of private investment spending. In the table below, enter the changes (both absolute and percentage) that took place in the major categories of private domestic investment for recent trough-peak, peak-trough, and trough-peak periods.*

Cyclical Changes in Real Gross Private Domestic Investment (2000 Dollars)

Investment Type	Type of Change	Trough-Peak 1982:Q4–1990:Q3	Peak-Trough 1990:Q3–1991:Q1	Trough-Peak 1991:Q1–2001:Q1
Nonresidential fixed investment	Absolute percentage			
Residential investment	Absolute percentage			
Change in business inventories	Absolute percentage			

Question 2

In this question, we examine the simple accelerator theory and show why it predicts instability in private investment spending. We assume that firms attempt to keep a constant ratio of capital stock to expected output; as estimates of the expected sales level (output) are revised, there is a change in the desired level of capital stock, and sharp variations in the level of investment spending can result.

The first step in developing a simple accelerator model is to determine how the estimate of the amount of expected sales (Y^e) is formed. For this purpose we use the same error-learning adaptive expectations hypothesis as we did in the inflation and permanent income cases. We assume that this period's estimate of expected sales, Y^e, is related to the difference between last period's expected sales, Y^e_{-1}, and last period's actual sales, Y_{-1}, as follows:

$$Y^e = Y^e_{-1} + j(Y_{-1} - Y^e_{-1}),$$

where j is the weight given to the error term when the previous period's expectation is revised. We can rewrite the equation in the following way:

$$Y^e = jY_{-1} + (1-j) Y^e_{-1}.$$

a. Assume that last period's expected sales, Y^e_{-1}, were equal to 100 and that last period's actual sales, Y_{-1}, were equal to 110. Complete the following table (round figures to one decimal place.)

j	jY_{-1}	$(1-j) Y^e_{-1}$	Y^e
1.00	110.0	0	110.0
0.75			
0.50			
0.25			

b. The second step in the accelerator theory is the assumption that a firm's desired stock of capital (K^*) is a constant ratio (v^*) of the current period's expected sales, that is, $K^* = v \times Y^e$.

If $v^* = 4$, what is K^* for each of the four values of Y^e found in Part a above?

j	K^*
1.00	
0.75	
0.50	
0.25	

c. The third step in the accelerator model is determination of net investment (I_n). Net investment in the current period equals the change in the capital stock from the previous period to the current period. Thus,

$$I_n = \Delta K = K - K_{-1}.$$

If the previous period's capital stock (K_{-1}) were 460 and the current capital stock were 490, then

$I_n =$ _____

If the previous period's capital stock were 500 and the current capital stock were 485, then

$I_n =$ _____

Explain how this last value of I_n is possible. _____

_____

_____

d. The next step in the accelerator theory is the assumption that a firm can always put enough plant and equipment in place to make the current capital stock equal the desired capital stock, that is, $K = K^*$. Thus,

$$I_n = K - K_{-1} = K^* - K^*_{-1}.$$

We are now ready to show how net investment will vary with revisions in expected sales. Since $K^* = v \times Y^e$, then $K^*_{-1} = v \times Y^e_{-1}$. Combining these equations with the above equation for I_n, we get

$$I_n = v \times Y^e - v \times Y^e_{-1} = v \times (Y^e - Y^e_{-1}) = v \times \Delta Y^e.$$

We conclude that net investment in the current period depends on the change in expected sales (ΔY^e).

If we assume the values of Y^e_{-1} and Y_{-1} from Part a and v^* from Part b, what is I_n when:

$j = 0.25$? _____

$j = 0.75$? _____

For any given values of Y^e and Y^e_{-1}, the higher the value of the desired capital-output ratio (v^*), the

_____

will be net investment (I_n).

e. Total business spending on plant and equipment depends not only on spending for new capital goods to increase the stock of capital, but also on spending for the replacement of worn-out capital goods that have been used up in the process of producing goods and services. Gross investment spending (I) is equal to net investment (I_n) plus replacement investment (D). As a final step in our model of investment spending, we have to consider replacement investment spending.

Let us assume that a given fraction of a firm's old plant and equipment wears out each period and that replacement investment is a constant fraction of the previous period's capital stock, that is, $D = dK_{-1}$.

If one-fifth of the initial capital stock wears out each period ($d = 0.2$), what are the levels of gross investment related to the two values of net investment calculated in Part d above? (*Note:* $K_{-1} = 400$.)

j	I_n	D	I
0.25			
0.75			

The longer-lived the plant and equipment a firm has, the *greater/smaller* the fraction of its capital that must be replaced each period, and the *more/less* sensitive the firm's gross investment will be to changes in output.

f.   Assume that for the Magic Macro Textbook Company, $j = 0.75$, $v^* = 5$, $d = 0.1$, and actual sales for Periods 0 through 6 are as given below. Fill in the rest of the table (round answers to two decimal places). In the figure 16A, graph variables Y, Y^e, I_n, D, and I.

Variables	Periods						
	0	1	2	3	4	5	6
Actual sales (Y)	100	120	120	120.00	110.00	110.00	110.00
Expected sales (Y^e)	100	100	115				
Desired capital (K^*)	500						
Net investment (I_n)	0						
Replacement investment (D)	50						
Gross investment (I)	50						

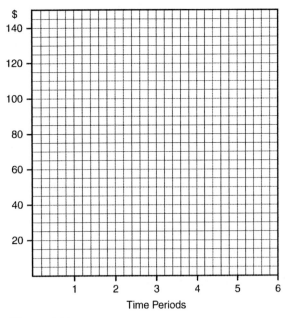

Figure 16A

g. Answer the following questions based on the results in the above table (round your answers to the nearest whole number).

The increase in actual sales between Periods 0 and 1 leads to an increase in expected sales and a change in net investment in Period 2. What is the percentage increase in sales in Period 1?

_____

What is the percentage increase in I (gross investment) in the following period (Period 2)?

_____

There is no change in actual sales in Periods 2 and 3. What is the percentage change in I:

in Period 3? _____

in Period 4? _____

What is the percentage change in actual sales from Period 3 to Period 4? _____

What is the percentage change in I in Period 5? _____

What happens to net investment (I_n) in Period 5 as a result of the fall in actual sales in Period 4 and the resulting revision of expected sales in Period 5?

_____

Could this same situation happen to replacement investment? Explain. _____

_____

_____

Question 3

The example of the accelerator theory of investment presented in Question 2 was in terms of an individual firm. Let us now assume that a similar theory holds for the economy as a whole and that there is a stable value of v^* for the economy. Also, we assume that $j = 1$ so that current expected sales equal last period's actual sales, $Y^e = Y_{-1}$.

Thus, $\Delta Y^e = \Delta Y_{-1} = Y_{-1} - Y_{-2}$, and since $I_n = v \times \Delta Y$, then $I_n = v \times (Y_{-1} - Y_{-2})$. Using this formulation allows us to see how previous levels of income (sales for the economy as a whole) can influence current investment and lead to an inherent instability in private investment spending.

a. The higher is the immediate past period's income (other things equal), the *higher/lower* is current net investment. The higher is income in the period before last (other things equal), the *higher/lower* is current net investment.

b. Because $I_n = K^* - K_{-1}^*$, the statement in Part a can be reinterpreted in the following way: The higher is current desired capital stock (other things equal), the *higher/lower* is current net investment. The higher is desired capital stock in the past (other things equal), the *higher/lower* is current net investment.

c. In general, investment varies *directly/inversely* with the recent past levels of output and current desired stock of capital, and *directly/inversely* with the size of the capital stock inherited from the past.

d. The simple accelerator model in this question employs three assumptions. Complete the following sentences, noting what those assumptions are and providing a more realistic version of each.

1. With respect to expected output (Y^e), it was assumed that _____

    _____

    More realistically, _____

    _____

2. With respect to the relationship between K^* and Y^e, it was assumed that _____

    _____

    More realistically, _____

    _____

3. With respect to the relationship between K^* and K, it was assumed that _____

    _____

    More realistically, _____

    _____

Question 4

In the previous questions on the accelerator theory, we assumed that the desired capital-output ratio (v^*) was constant. In this question, we examine some of the factors that determine v^* and conclude that v^* is not a constant. We will see how an erosion of business confidence can change v^* and add to the instability of private investment spending. We will also see what policy actions might be taken to offset the changes in v^*.

a. Define the user cost of capital. _____

    _____

    _____

    _____

    The two main elements of user cost are: _____

    and _____

b. Define the marginal product of capital (MPK). _____

    _____

    To maximize its profits, a firm will add to its capital stock until the expected MPK is *greater than/ equal to/less than* the user of cost of capital (u).

As more and more units of capital are added to the firm's capital stock (other inputs remaining constant), the MPK will *increase/remain constant/decline*. Consequently, if there is a fall in the user cost of capital, the firm's desired stock of capital (K^*) will *rise/remain the same/fall* and the desired capital-output ratio (v^*) will *rise/remain the same/fall*. On the other hand, if the user cost of capital increases, the firm's K^* will *rise/remain the same/fall* and its v^* will *rise/remain the same/fall*.

If the expected MPK falls and the user cost of capital remains the same, v^* will _____

and if increased business confidence raises the expected MPK, v^* will _____

c. Suppose the economy has the following expected MPK schedule, where MPK is expressed as a function of the desired capital-output ratio (v^*).

v^*	Expected MPK (%)
3.00	25
3.25	20
3.50	15
3.75	10
4.00	5

If the user cost of capital consists of a real interest rate of 8 percent and a depreciation rate of 7 percent, the desired capital-output ratio (v^*) would be

_____

If monetary policy and fiscal policy are used to reduce the real interest rate to 3 percent, the desired capital-output ratio would change to

_____

This would cause net investment to _____

Would this be a permanent or a temporary change in private net investment? Explain. _____

_____

_____

_____

d. Suppose that current domestic and international political and economic events cause a serious deterioration in business confidence so that the expected MPK is reduced by five percentage points for each value of v^*.

If once again the real interest cost is 8 percent and the depreciation rate is 7 percent, the desired capital-output ratio would be

_____

To what level must the real rate of interest be moved to make $v^* = 3.75$? _____

Is this possible? _____

_____

e. There are three elements of the user cost of a capital good: (1) the interest cost on the funds used to purchase the capital good, (2) the economic depreciation (physical deterioration and obsolescence) of the capital good, and (3) the change in the resale price of the capital good.

The first two elements have already been discussed. Explain why the third element will have an effect on user cost.

_____

_____

_____

If interest costs rise, u will _____

If the depreciation rate rises, u will _____

If the resale price of capital goods rises over time, u will _____

f. Because it is the *net* costs that are important in determining user costs, fiscal policy can have a major effect on user cost. Explain how each of the following can be used to *reduce* user cost.

1. Corporate income tax _____

_____

_____

_____

2. Depreciation allowances _____

_____

_____

_____

3. Investment tax credits _____

_____

_____

_____

g. Inflation can also have an effect on the desired capital-output ratio. One aspect of the effect of inflation on investment is its impact on business confidence, and therefore the expected MPK. Inflation may also affect user cost, however.

If the nominal rate of interest (i) and the expected inflation rate (p^e) increase by the same amount, u will _____

If i increases by less than p^e, then u will _____

Explain your answer. _____

_____

_____

Inflation can have an important effect on business profits. If profits increase, internal sources of funds will _____

and *u* will _____

Explain your answer. _____

_____

_____

Question 5

Tobin's *q* theory offers an alternative explanation of investment.

a. While the accelerator theory defines a desired level of capital stock (K^*) and assumes a gradual adjustment of the capital stock toward the desired level, Tobin's *q* theory explains the attractiveness of new spending on capital equipment by comparing _____

_____

b. In Tobin's theory, *q* is the ratio of _____

_____

and investment is *an increasing/a decreasing* function of the *q* ratio.

c. Tobin's *q* suggests that higher stock prices will *have no influence on/increase/decrease* aggregate demand.

Chapter 17
New Classical Macro Confronts
New Keynesian Macro

In Chapter 7, we derived and studied the properties of aggregate demand (*AD*), short-run aggregate supply (*SAS*), and long-run aggregate supply (*LAS*). Having developed these concepts, we studied two very different kinds of adjustments to changes in exogenous variables. In the first case, we assumed that the nominal wage rate and the price level were not completely flexible, i.e., that they took some time to adjust. This led to a model of the business cycle in which an increase (a decrease) in aggregate demand led, at first, to higher (lower) real GDP and the price level, and later, to lower (higher) real GDP and an even higher (lower) price level. The second case assumed flexible wages and prices. Here we saw that real GDP would not diverge from its natural level but that the price level was directly related to the level of aggregate demand.

Neither of these models is entirely satisfactory. The former, Keynesian model doesn't explain why wages and prices should be inflexible, or why workers are willing to supply labor off their supply curve. Furthermore, the real wage is countercyclical, falling when real GDP rises and vice versa. The latter, classical model fails to explain why there are business cycles, i.e., fluctuations in real GDP, that last for one or more years.

This chapter deals with some recent theories designed to provide a better explanation of reality. The theories presented first are in the classical tradition of market-clearing models and are called *new classical macroeconomics*. We specifically treat the following models: Friedman-Phelps "fooling model," the Lucas model, and the real business cycle model.

Next, those recent theories that are in the Keynesian tradition of non market-clearing are presented. These are called *new Keynesian macroeconomics*. The original Keynesian model relied on the somewhat arbitrary assumption of a fixed nominal wage, which led to the "sticky" behavior of wages and prices during economic downturns. The new Keynesian approach also relies on wage and price stickiness, but it emphasizes the microeconomic foundations of this stickiness.

Question 1

The Keynesian model of the business cycle depended on an arbitrary assumption: rigid nominal wages. A number of economists have attempted to develop alternative theories that relax this assumption yet also explain how the economy can produce a business cycle. In this question, we study the theory proposed by Milton Friedman.

In Figure 17A, an aggregate demand curve, AD_0, is drawn. Assume that the short-run aggregate supply curve for the economy has the equation $Y = 600 + 2{,}000(P - P^e)$, where P is the actual price level and P^e is the expected price level.

a. Assume that in the original situation, the expected price level equals 1.00. Draw the aggregate supply curve in Figure 17A under this assumption, and label it $SAS_0(P^e = 1.00)$. What is the equilibrium level of output?

$Y =$ _____

What is the equilibrium price level?

$P =$ _____

Label this Point E_0 in Figure 17A.

b. During Period 1, the Fed increases the money supply, and the aggregate demand curve shifts to AD_1. Assuming that the expected price level remains at 1.00, what is the equilibrium level of output after the expansionary monetary policy?

$Y =$ _____

What is the new price level?

$P =$ _____

Label this new equilibrium Point C.

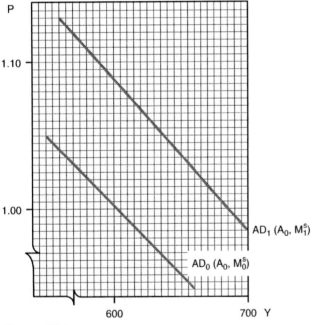

Figure 17A

c. Since output has increased, there must have been an *increase/decrease* in the number of people employed. If firms are moving along the labor demand curve, the actual real wage has to *rise/decline* in order to encourage firms to hire more workers. But in order to get workers to want to work more, workers must receive a *higher/lower* real wage.

    The previous statement seems to suggest a paradox: Firms will increase labor only if the real wage declines, yet workers will not be willing to increase the amount of labor supplied if they receive a decreased real wage. Milton Friedman has suggested a way of resolving the paradox.

d. According to Friedman, the supply curve for labor does not depend on the actual real wage. It depends on

_____

How is this variable defined? _____

_____

If, in response to an increase in aggregate demand, nominal wages rose but expected prices remained the same, the expected real wage would

_____

With this movement in the expected real wage, what would happen to the amount of labor supplied?

_____

e. Is Point C in Figure 17A a long-run equilibrium? _____

Explain your answer. _____

_____

If workers realize that their price expectations are too low, they will adjust their expectations. As the workers make their adjustment, they will demand higher wages. As a result, the aggregate supply curve will shift upward. Assume that workers set their expectations according to the following formula: $P^e = P_{-1}$.

f. What was the actual price level in Period 1 (i.e., the first period after the demand shift)?

$P =$ _____

Is the short-run aggregate supply the same or different from SAS_0? _____

Label it accordingly.

What is the expected price level in Period 2?

$P^e =$ _____

Draw the short-run aggregate supply curve for Period 2 and label it SAS_2. If the aggregate demand curve remains at AD_1, what is the equilibrium level of output in Period 2?

$Y =$ _____

What is the new price level?

$P =$ _____

Label this Point D in Figure 17A.

g. In long-run equilibrium, the actual price level must equal the _____

When this condition is met, output will equal the _____

Identify this point of long-run equilibrium in Figure 17A, and label it *F*.

What is the expected price level at this point?

$P^e =$ _____

Draw the short-run aggregate supply curve associated with this expected price level, and label it $SAS_n(P^e = 1.09)$.

Question 2

In the previous question, we examined Friedman's theory of the business cycle. Now we will study how Robert E. Lucas extended Friedman's model and developed what has come to be known as the Lucas model.

a. Friedman's model is often called the "fooling" model. Why is that? _____

_____

_____

b. To improve Friedman's model, Lucas assumed that workers form their expectations using rational expectations.

What is meant by this term? _____

_____

_____

_____

c. The aggregate supply curves in the Friedman model and the Lucas model are very similar in that changes in output supplied come about due to a disparity between

_____

and _____

In Friedman's case, this "price surprise" is due to workers being fooled; in Lucas' case, the explanation for the difference between actual prices and expected prices is

_____

If firms are profit maximizers, they will increase output in response to an increase in demand that raises the price of their own product only if that price increases relative to

_____

A distinction is made by Lucas between local and aggregate behavior in prices.

Give an example of a local price increase. _____

_____

Give an example of an aggregate price increase. _____

_____

Explain how the distinction between local and aggregate price increases is used by Lucas to explain how output can increase beyond Y^N when there is an increase in aggregate demand.

_____

_____

_____

In a country where firms interpreted the price increases they observed to be part of a general increase in prices, the aggregate supply curve would be *flatter/steeper* than in a country in which price increases were considered to be more localized.

Explain the importance of this difference in the slope of the aggregate supply curve in explaining how business cycles develop.

_____

_____

_____

Question 3

One important conclusion from the new classical models relates to the efficiency of monetary policy. In this question, we examine this conclusion.

Assume that the original demand curve in the economy is AD_0 as shown in Figure 17A. The supply curve for the economy is the same as in Question 1: $Y = 600 + 2,000(P - P^e)$. As in Question 1, the original equilibrium output is 600 and the equilibrium price is 1.00.

a.   Assume that the Fed increases the money supply so that the new aggregate demand curve is AD_1 in Figure 17A. If the public knows that in the past, expansionary monetary policy of that magnitude has led to an increase in the price level of 9 percent, what will be the new expected price level according to the new classical macroeconomists?

$P^e =$ _____

Describe the short-run aggregate supply curve corresponding to this situation.

_____

What is the new equilibrium output?

$Y =$ _____

What is the new price level?

$P =$ _____

b. If expectations are set as described in Part a, what will be the effect of expansionary monetary policy?

_____

_____

What is the name given to this belief regarding the effectiveness of monetary policy? _____

_____

Question 4

In this question we examine one additional theory proposed as an alternative to the Keynesian theory of the business cycle: the real business cycle (RBC) model.

a. What is real about the RBC theory? _____

_____

_____

b. According to the RBC, how can a business cycle develop even if markets are in continuous equilibrium?

_____

_____

c. The slope of the labor supply curve is very important in RBC theory. Why?

_____

_____

d. How do RBC theorists justify an upward sloping labor supply curve? _____

_____

_____

_____

_____

_____

_____

_____

e. What role do interest rates play in the intertemporal substitution of work and leisure?

_____

_____

_____

_____

f. Gordon identifies three major problems with the RBC theory. Identify these three problems and briefly describe them.

1. _____

_____

2. _____

_____

3. _____

_____

g. One distinction between the Keynesian model and the new classical models is that the latter theories are examples of *market-clearing/non market-clearing* models.

What market or markets are referred to in this case? _____

Based on this assumption of market clearing, what would be the new classical theorist's explanation for people not working in a recession?

_____

_____

Question 5

One effect of an adverse supply shock is the reduction of natural real GDP. In this question we see how this decline comes about, and we examine the economic conditions that affect the size of the decline. (*Note*: the aggregate supply curve incorporated here is not exposited in Gordon. It is, however, only a minor extension of the analysis presented in the text.)

The table below summarizes the relationship between employment and output both before and after a supply shock.

	Output	
Employment	**Before Supply Shock**	**After Supply Shock**
N_0	1,000	960
N_1	970	940
N_2	920	900

a. The relationship between an input and the corresponding maximum output is called a

_____

b. The labor supply curve is drawn in Figure 17B below. Assume that the nominal wage is 210. Using the data for the original production function (i.e., before the supply shock), complete Table 17A.

Table 17A

	Demand for Labor	Before-Shock Supply	Conditions
P	**W/P**	**N**	**Y**
0.954		N_2	
0.976		N_1	
1.000		N_0	

Plot the real wage and employment in Figure 17B. Draw a line connecting the points and label that line N_0^d.

Plot the price and quantity values in Figure 17C. Draw a line connecting the points, and label that line SAS_0.

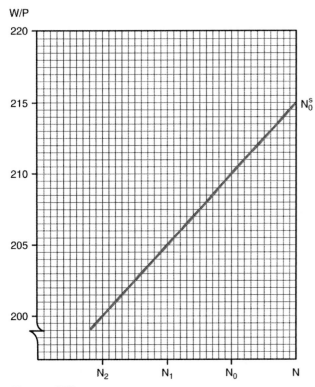

Figure 17B

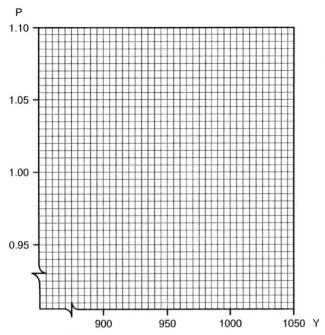

Figure 17C

What are the two parameters of an aggregate supply curve? _____

and _____

Write the values for these parameters next to SAS_0.

What is the equilibrium real wage?

$W/P = $ _____

Label the labor market equilibrium Point B in Figure 17B.

In equilibrium, real output is:

$Y = $ _____

and the equilibrium price level is:

$P = $ _____

Find the equilibrium point in Figure 17C, and label it B.

c.   Assume that the nominal wage remains at 210. Using the data for the new production function (after the supply shock), complete the following table.

Table 17B

	Demand for Labor	After-Shock Supply	Conditions
P	W/P	N	Y
	210	N_2	
	205	N_1	
	200	N_0	

Plot the real wage and employment in Figure 17B. Draw a line connecting the points, and label that line N_1^d.

Plot the prices and quantities in Figure 17C. Draw a line connecting the points, and label that line SAS_1. Write the values for the two parameters next to SAS_1.

d.   What effect does this shift in the production function have on the demand-for-labor curve?

_____

Explain your answer. _____

_____

Because of the supply shock, there is a new short-run and long-run aggregate supply curve for the economy. Where the economy operates in this new situation depends on what happens to the real wage. Assume that the economy is operating on the new labor demand curve N_1^d in Figure 17B and that the nominal wage remains at 210.

e. If the price level remains at the initial level, $P = 1.00$, the real wage equals

$W/P =$ _____

Find this point on the new labor demand curve in Figure 17B, and label it X. What must be the shape of the labor supply curve for this case to be an equilibrium situation?

_____

Find the corresponding point on the new aggregate supply curve in Figure 17C, and label it X. At Point X, output equals

$Y =$ _____

f. If the labor supply curve were N_0^s, what would be the equilibrium real wage?

$W/P =$ _____

Label this Point Y in Figure 17B.

Find the corresponding point on the new short-run aggregate supply curve in Figure 17C, and label it Y. At Point Y, output equals

$Y =$ _____

g. If the labor supply curve were vertical at N_0 in Figure 17B, the real wage would _____

The new equilibrium real wage would be $W/P =$ _____

Label this Point Z in Figure 17B.

Find the corresponding point on the new short-run aggregate supply curve in Figure 17C, and label it Z. At Point Z, output is:

$Y =$ _____

h. Review:

In each of the alterative cases, Parts e–g above, the economy would be in equilibrium, given different assumptions regarding the shape of the labor supply curve. Since Points X, Y, and Z are equilibriums in the labor market, the corresponding levels of output are alternative levels of

_____

After a supply shock, the more flexible the real wage, the *larger/smaller* the decline in the natural level of real output that will result.

In each of the cases, Parts e–g above, natural real GDP was below the original level, $Y = 1,000$. Now we will examine why natural real GDP must fall.

i. There will be a decline in natural real output that will exist regardless of the labor supply response.

The cause of this decline is _____

_____

In Figure 17C, this change in natural real GDP is shown as a movement from Point _____

to Point _____

This represents a decline in output from _____

to _____

j. If the labor supply curve is positively sloped (for example, N_0^s in Figure 17B) relative to the original position, the real wage will

_____

and employment will _____

In Figure 17B, this new situation is shown as Point _____

Because of this response, natural real GDP would decline from _____

to _____

Since labor was responding to a change in real wages, this reason is called the _____

labor supply response.

k. To reach the case described in Part j, the real wage must be _____

If the real wage is rigid, then the economy will operate at Point _____

Because of real wage rigidity, natural GDP would decline from _____

to _____

Question 6

In Question 5, we saw how one effect of an adverse supply shock is to cause natural real GDP to fall. In Question 6, we will study the options that are available to policymakers facing such a shock. In Figure 17D, the aggregate supply curves that were derived in Question 5 are drawn. The labor market conditions derived in Tables 17A and 17B, and shown in Figure 17B, should be used for this question. Assume that the original aggregate demand curve is AD_0 and that the economy is in equilibrium, with $P = 1.00$ and $Y = 1,000$. The initial equilibrium is shown as Point B. The long-run aggregate supply curve is shown as LAS. (*Note*: The aggregate demand-aggregate supply analysis incorporated here is not exposited in Gordon. It is a substantial expansion of the analysis, so you or your instructor may wish to consider this an optional exercise.)

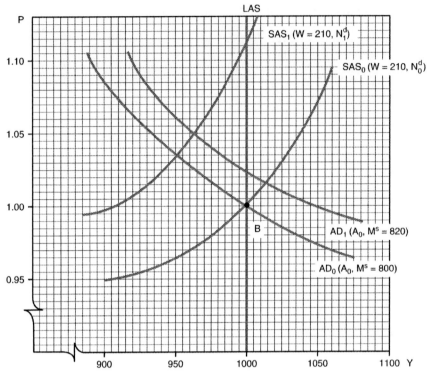

Figure 17D

a. Assume the economy is hit by the adverse supply shock described in Question 5. If the labor supply curve is vertical, the number of people employed after the shock is

_____

The new equilibrium real wage is

$W/P =$ _____

The output that can be produced by this amount of labor is

$Y =$ _____

This level of output is the new _____

In Figure 17D, draw the new long-run aggregate supply curve based on the assumptions given here, and label it LAS′.

b. If the nominal wage remains at 210, the short-run aggregate supply curve will shift due to the supply shock. The new short-run aggregate supply curve is shown in Figure 17D as SAS_1.

What would happen to the aggregate demand curve? _____

_____

At the price level $P = 1.00$, how much output would be demanded in the economy?

$Y =$ _____

How much output would firms be willing to produce at $P = 1.00$?

$Y =$ _____

Given this condition of *excess supply/excess demand*, there will be a tendency for the price level to *increase/decrease*.

c. Find the new short-run equilibrium point, and label it H. At Point H,

$Y =$ _____

$P =$ _____

$M^s/P =$ _____

$W/P =$ _____

At Point H, what is the relationship between the actual real wage and the equilibrium real wage?

_____

_____

d. There is involuntary unemployment at Point H. To bring employment back to the natural level, employment must increase to

$N =$ _____

This level of employment is associated with an output level of

$Y =$ _____

The Fed could bring the economy to this level of output by increasing the money supply to 820, causing a shift in the aggregate demand curve to AD_1. Find the new short-run equilibrium point that would result from this policy action, and label it Z. Would this point also be a long-run equilibrium? Explain your answer.

_____

e. In fact, the Fed could increase the money supply by a sufficient amount to bring output back to 1,000, the original level. Draw the demand curve that would lead to this result. Label that curve AD_2. Find the short-run equilibrium point that would result, and label it E.

What is the real wage rate at Point E?

$W/P =$ _____

How is employment related to N_0? _____

At Point E, real output is *greater than/less than/equal to* the natural level of output that exists after the supply shock. As a result of this situation, there would be a tendency for the nominal wage to *increase/decrease/stay the same*, and the short-run supply curve would

_____

If the Federal Reserve attempted to maintain output at 1,000, what would happen to the price level?

_____

f. Review:

If the Fed chose to increase the nominal money supply so that the aggregate demand curve shifted to AD_1, the level of real output would

_____

relative to the initial (pre-shock) level. However, the actual level of output would be

_____

the new (post-shock) natural level of output. If the Fed follows this policy, it is said to have

_____

the supply shock.

The above results assumed that the real wage was flexible. In Parts g–i below, we examine the results when the real wage is *not* flexible.

g. Assume that all employees have COLAs (cost-of-living adjustments) in their labor contracts. If these COLAs give full protection to the workers, then when the price level increases to 1.05 at Point Z, the new nominal wage rate will be

$W =$ _____

If the real wage is rigid, employment will be

$N =$ _____

Is the labor market in equilibrium at this real wage and level of employment? _____

h. Based on your answers above, what would be the natural level of real GDP when the real wage is perfectly rigid?

$Y^N =$ _____

Identify the $P - Y$ point in the rigid-real-wage case, and label that Point X in Figure 17D.

What would the Fed have to do to reach this output level? _____

i. Describe the situation in the economy if the Fed did not decrease the money supply when the real wage was perfectly rigid but instead kept the nominal money supply equal to 800 (keeping the aggregate demand curve at AD_0).

_____

_____

_____

_____

Find the point that indicates where the economy would end up if the situation described above took place. Label that Point X'.

Review:

When real wages are rigid, the Fed must accept a level of natural real GDP that is *higher/lower* than the level in the flexible-real-wage case (Part d above). This level of real GDP could exist with the same price level as before the supply shock if the Fed *increased/decreased/maintained* the money supply, or with a

_____

price level if the Fed maintained the nominal money supply at the initial level.

All of the above (short-run) cases assumed that the nominal wage rate was constant; that is, changes in the real wage came through price changes. In the following part of the question, we examine what would happen if the nominal wage were flexible.

j.   Assuming a vertical labor supply curve, natural GDP will fall to 960. Find the point in Figure 17D at which $P = 1.00$ and $Y = 960$. Label that Point Z''.

What is the equilibrium real wage at Point Z''?

$W/P =$ _____

What is the nominal wage?

$W =$ _____

What would happen to the short-run aggregate supply curve relative to SAS_1 in the circumstances described above?

_____

What would the Fed have to do to maintain the price level at 1.00? _____

Question 7

In this question, we show how a profit-maximizing monopoly responds to a reduction in demand when there is no cost to changing price.

a.   The demand curve of the monopoly firm, Consolidated Zoomby, is given by the equation, $Y = 15 - 2P$, and its total cost curve is given by the equation, $TC = 3Y$ (there are no fixed costs).

What is the equation of the firm's inverse demand function? _____
Graph this function in Figure 17E, and label it D_0.

What is the equation of the firm's marginal cost function? _____

What is the relation among the firm's marginal cost function, average variable cost function, and average total cost function?

_____

Graph the firm's marginal cost function in Figure 17E, and label it MC_0.

What is the equation of the firm's marginal revenue function? _____

(For linear demand, marginal revenue has the same vertical intercept as inverse demand and twice the absolute value of the slope.) Graph this function in Figure 17E, and label it MR_0.

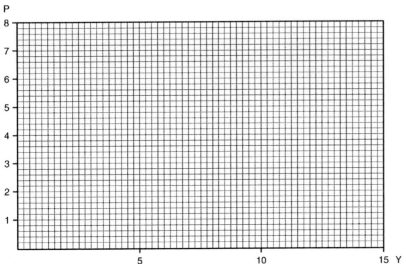

Figure 17E

b. What is the profit-maximizing output for this firm?

    $Y =$ _____

    What is the profit-maximizing price for this firm?

    $P =$ _____

    Find these quantities in Figure 17E, and label them P_0 and Y_0. Identify this profit-maximizing point along D_0 in Figure 17E, and label it E_0.

    What is the total profit of the firm? _____

c. In this part of the question, we assume that there has been a drop in the demand for zoombies. Suppose the equation of the demand function is now given by $Y = 13 - 2P$.

    What is the equation of the firm's inverse demand function? _____

    Graph this function in Figure 17E, and label it D_1.

    What is the equation of the firm's marginal revenue function? _____

    Graph this function in Figure 17E, and label it MR_1.

d. What is the profit-maximizing output for this firm?

    $Y =$ _____

    What is the profit-maximizing price for this firm?

    $P =$ _____

    Find these quantities in Figure 17E, and label them P_1 and Y_1. Label the corresponding point on the demand curve E_1.

    What is the total profit of the firm? _____

Question 8

As can be seen from your answers to the above question, a decline in the demand for zoombies, with no decline in the firm's marginal cost, will lead to a decrease in price and output for Consolidated Zoomby. In this question, we examine the conditions that must exist for Consolidated Zoomby when faced with a fall in demand: (1) to keep production constant and (2) to keep price constant.

In Figure 17F, we have drawn D_1 and MR_1.

a.   For the marginal revenue curve, MR_1, what is the value of marginal revenue for an output of 4.5?

_____

Thus, output would remain at 4.5 zoombies only if MC *rose/fell* to

_____

Draw this new *MC* curve in Figure 17F, and label it MC_1.

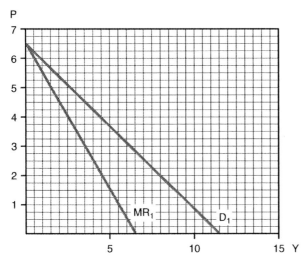

Figure 17F

If $MC_1 = 2.00$, how many zoombies will the firm produce and what price will it charge to maximize profit?

$Y = $ _____

$P = $ _____

What is the firm's profit under these circumstances? _____

In Figure 17F, label these profit-maximizing price and output quantities P_2 and Y_0, respectively. Identify that profit-maximizing point along D_1, and label it E_2.

Summary: If the vertical shifts in demand and marginal revenue are *greater than/equal to/less than* the vertical shift in marginal cost, the firm will continue to produce the same output as before these shifts, but price will *rise/remain the same/fall* and profit will *rise/remain the same/fall*.

For the rest of this question we'll assume that costs have fallen in conjunction with the fall in demand and that the marginal cost curve is MC_1.

b. If, despite the fall in demand from D_0 to D_1 and the fall in marginal cost from MC_0 to MC_1, Consolidated Zoomby keeps its price constant at $5.25 (the initial level, P_0), how many zoombies will it sell?

$Y =$ _____

What is its profit in this case? _____

In Figure 17F, label these price and output quantities P_0 and Y_1, respectively. Find the associated point on D_1, and label it E_3.

c. After the demand decrease from D_0 to D_1, if Consolidated Zoomby lowered its price from $5.25 to $4.25, its sales would increase from 2.5 to 4.5; however, it would lose revenue of $1 on each of the 2.5 units it would have sold at the higher price. Shade the area representing this loss, and label it *A* in Figure 17F. As a result of lowering its price, Consolidated Zoomby increased its sales from 2.5 to 4.5 and thus gained revenues of $4.25 on each of its additional sales. Shade the area representing this gain, and label it *B* in Figure 17F.

Which area is larger: A or B? _____

What is the change in profit if the firm lowers its price to $4.25 rather than keeping the price at $5.25?

_____

How are these answers related? _____

_____

_____

d. From the answers to Parts a–c above, it appears that Consolidated Zoomby would increase its profits if, after the demand fall, it lowered its price from $5.25 to $4.25 as opposed to keeping price at the initial level of $5.25. However, this analysis ignores the fact that there might be transactions costs involved with changing prices.

Economists refer to these transactions costs as _____

If these menu costs are *greater/less* than _____

Consolidated Zoomby would not lower its price and would keep its output constant in response to the fall in demand.

e. Review: In Questions 7 and 8, we examined the response of a firm to a fall in the demand for its product. In Question 7, we presented the "standard" microeconomic theory. In Question 8, we assumed that marginal cost fell in conjunction with the decline in demand. Although it would appear that holding output constant and lowering prices would maximize profits, if the menu costs associated with this change are greater than the expected profit increase, the firm would want to *increase price/leave price unchanged/decrease price* and *increase output/leave output unchanged/decrease output*.

Question 9

The new Keynesian approach relies heavily on the existence of rigidities that prevent wages and other costs from responding completely to changes in aggregate demand. Gordon explains that menu costs and long-term contracts cause *nominal rigidities*. In this question, we compare these *nominal rigidities* with several theories developed to explain *real rigidities* in the behavior of wages.

a. Menu costs and long-term contracts for wages and prices are referred to as nominal rigidities. What is the distinction between nominal rigidities and real rigidities?

_____

_____

_____

b. The efficiency wage theory is based on a key assumption regarding worker behavior. What is that assumption?

_____

_____

According to the efficiency wage theory, why would firms be unwilling to cut wages in response to a decrease in demand?

_____

_____

c. Would a firm be more willing to cut wages if it believed that all firms were willing to cut their wages at the same time? Explain.

_____

_____

As indicated in your answer to Part c, a key part of the rigidity argument is the lack of coordination among firms. One form of coordination would be if all firms indexed their nominal wages to the growth rate of nominal GDP, called nominal indexation.

d. Give an example of how nominal indexation would work. _____

_____

_____

One explanation why this type of indexation might not work is called the *input-output approach*. Explain how this approach lends some doubt to the viability of nominal indexation.

_____

_____

_____

Chapter 18
Conclusion: Where We Stand

This chapter represents a summing up of what has been learned throughout the course. We begin with a review of the evolution of macroeconomic events and ideas since 1930 including recent events in the world economy. We then revisit the macroeconomic puzzles and try to present short summary answers to them. Finally, we look at some unsettled issues in macroeconomics.

Question 1

This question deals with the evolution of events and ideas.

a. How does the Great Depression illustrate Gordon's contention that events affect ideas?

b. What economist do we most associate with development of an alternative theory to explain events like the Great Depression?

c. Did the behavior of the economy during World War II support or reject Keynesian economics? Explain.

d. What happened during the recessions of 1953–54 and 1957–58 that was different from the experience since the 1930s?

_____

_____

e. What happened to inflation after 1965 when unemployment fell to its lowest levels since the Korean War?

_____

f. Did these events support the Phillips curve? Explain. _____

_____

g. Why did President Kennedy's and President Johnson's economic advisors urge a tax cut in the early 1960s and a tax increase in the late 1960s?

_____

_____

_____

h. Why did this kind of fiscal activism fall out of favor? _____

_____

_____

i. What were the most notable economic features of the period from 1970 to 1982?

_____

_____

_____

_____

j. What was the generally accepted view regarding the efficacy of monetary and fiscal policy during this period?

_____

_____

k. What major economic ideas were developed during this period? _____

_____

_____

l. What event or events most likely led to the development of the supply-shock theory of inflation?

    _____

m. How was the Phillips curve modified during this period? _____

    _____

    _____

    _____

n. During the 1980s, what event further weakened fiscal policy? _____

    _____

    _____

o. During the period from 1979 to 1982, what was the Fed targeting? _____

    _____

p. What event led the Fed to abandon this policy? _____

    _____

q. During the 1980s and early 1990s, how did economists come to view fiscal and monetary policy?

    _____

    _____

r. In what respect was the behavior of inflation and unemployment in the 1990s a surprise to the Fed?

    _____

    _____

s. What were the so-called "preemptive strikes" conducted by the Fed in the 1990s?

    _____

    _____

t. What new economic idea emerged regarding the NAIRU in the 1990s?

    _____

    _____

Question 2

This question deals more specifically with the influence of events in the world economy.

a. What happened to the value of imports and exports relative to GDP in the United States between 1965 and 1999?

b. What was the benefit from the movement away from fixed exchange rates and toward the flexible exchange system after 1973?

c. How did exchange rates behave under the flexible exchange rate system?

d. What happened to the consensus among economists and politicians regarding the benefits of a flexible exchange rate system?

Question 3

This question explores some unsettled issues in macroeconomics.

a. How can poor countries achieve growth?

b. Why does productivity growth ebb and flow?

c. Should zero inflation be a policy goal of the United States? _____

_____

_____

d. Why did the natural rate of unemployment decline? _____

_____

_____

e. Which is the better policy framework: rules or discretion? _____

_____

_____

_____

_____

_____

f. Why are there differences in growth, saving, and stability among nations?

_____

_____

_____

Answers

■ Chapter 1

Question 1

a. Large.

Macroeconomics is the study of major economic totals or aggregates, e.g., total production, total employment and unemployment, the average price level of all goods and services.

Small.

Microeconomics is the study of economic relationships among individual firms and households. It is concerned primarily with the determination of the price of one product relative to other products.

b. Macroeconomic.

Microeconomic.

Microeconomic.

Macroeconomic.

Macroeconomic.

c. Gross domestic product. GDP is the value of all currently produced goods and services sold on the market during a particular time period. (A more detailed definition is given in Chapter 2.)

Question 2

The answer to Parts a and b depends on the time period used.

Question 3

a. Actual real GDP is the amount of goods and services actually produced and sold at any given time.

Too much real GDP is undesirable because it strains the nation's ability to produce and leads to increases in nominal wages and other costs which, in turn, can lead to inflation.

Too little real GDP is undesirable because it leads to unnecessary unemployment of people and equipment, and wastes resources.

b. The natural level of real GDP is the level at which inflation is constant, i.e., has no tendency to accelerate or decelerate.

The natural rate of unemployment is the minimum attainable level of unemployment compatible with avoiding an acceleration of inflation.

c. From 1960 through 1963, $U > U^N$. From 1964 through 1970, $U < U^N$. In 1971, $U > U^N$. From 1972 through 1974, $U < U^N$. From 1975 through 1978, $U > U^N$. In 1979, $U < U^N$. From 1980 through 1987, $U > U^N$. From 1988 through 1990, $U < U^N$. From 1991 through 1994, $U > U^N$. From 1995 to 2001 $U < U^N$. From 2001 to 2007 $U > U^N$.

d. Target; policy instruments.
    1. Monetary policies
    2. Fiscal policies
    3. A miscellaneous group of policies, such as policies to provide workers with the skills needed to qualify for jobs

e. 1. Positive economic theory is used to explain or predict the behavior of important economic variables. Positive economics is concerned with *what is* or *what would be under certain circumstances*.

2. In normative economics, economic theory is used as a basis for recommending changes in economic policy. Normative economics is concerned with *what ought to be* normative.

Question 4

Short-run macroeconomics is concerned with the business cycle, or the short-run stability, of the economy. The main short-run concern of macroeconomists is to close the gap between actual and natural real GDP. Long-run macroeconomics is concerned with the economy's long-run growth rate in real GDP and real GDP per capita. The main long-run concern of U.S. macroeconomists is to increase the rate of growth of these magnitudes.

Question 5

While the depression experienced in the United States and Germany in the 1930s, and the hyperinflation of the early 1920s in Germany were important, neither had a significant effect on standards of living a decade or two later. By contrast, the higher economic growth rates in South Korea relative to the Philippines from 1960 to 2005 caused the material standard of living in South Korea to increase more than six times that of the Philippines.

Question 6

a. A theoretical closed economy has no foreign trade. An actual economy can be approximated as a closed economy if it has only a "small" amount of foreign trade.

b. A theoretical open economy has foreign trade. An actual economy with a "large" amount of foreign trade would be modeled as an open economy.

c. In the 1940s and 1950s, foreign trade amounted to about 5 percent of the U.S. economy, exchange rates were fixed, and international financial flows were restricted. In 2004, exchange rates were flexible, international financial flows were virtually unrestricted, and U.S. exports were $1,097.3 billion, or 10.2 percent of U.S. GDP, while imports were $1,781.6 billion, or 15 percent of gross domestic purchases (purchases by U.S. residents of goods and services wherever produced). (The 2004 figures are from the *Bureau of Economic Analysis*.)

■ Chapter 2

Question 1

a. Equal to; zero

A flow magnitude is an economic magnitude that moves from one economic unit to another at a specified rate per unit of time (e.g., income earned per week).

A stock magnitude is an economic magnitude that is measured at a moment or point in time.

b. Examples of stock magnitudes: money supply, capital stock, government debt, stock of housing, labor force.

The National Income and Product Accounts (NIPA) is an income statement that measures flows, e.g., the amount of output produced during a specified period of time.

c. 1. A good must be currently produced.
2. A good must be sold in the market and valued at its market price.
3. A good must not be resold during the current period.

d. Merely adding up the total goods and services produced would result in double-counting because the value of output from one firm includes the value of intermediate goods purchased from other firms.

e. Value added is the value of a firm's output minus the value of the intermediate goods that the firm produces. It includes wages paid to the firm's employees, rental of buildings and equipment, and the firm's profit.

f. $100 + $1,500 + $5,000 = $6,600; no.

Step	Amount
Ned Dustman	$ 100
Solomon Deli	1,400
Leo Jelli	3,500
Total	$5,000

Yes.

g. Personal saving; private investment
1. Households buy stocks and bonds issued by the firms.
2. Households put the funds in banks, which lend them to firms.

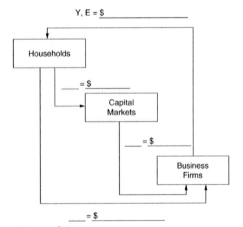

Figure 2A

Question 2

a.

Ajax	Beeline	Coastal
450	450	900
+50	−250	+600

$2,800

b. Honey, 900; Towels, 1,200; Tools, 300; Total 2,400

No. It does not include the value of goods produced during this period and not sold during the period, and it wrongly includes the value of goods sold this period but produced in previous periods.

c. $400; $700; $2,800.

It is a good measure because it includes only those goods actually produced during the period.

Question 3

Gross domestic product = 1,090.2 + 243.0 + 359.5 + 7.4 = 1,700.1.

Gross national product = 1,700.1 + 30.0 − 27.0 = 1,703.1.

Net domestic product = 1,700.1 − 177.8 = 1,522.3.

Domestic income = 1,522.3 − 163.1 = 1,359.2.

Undistributed corporate profits = corporate profits after tax − corporate dividends = 62.7 − 37.9 = 24.8.

Personal income = 1,359.2 − 64.3 − 125.1 − 24.8 + 209.9 + 26.0 = 1,380.9.

Personal disposable income = 1,380.9 − 196.5 = 1,184.4.

Question 4

The Magic Equation shows how the government spending and taxes, domestic investment, net exports, and private savings are related. When the government spending is greater than taxes, the government is running a deficit. The government deficit (1) could make investment smaller, (2) could require private saving to rise to avoid any downward pressure on the sum of domestic and foreign investment, (3) could require more borrowing from other nations (larger negative NX) or cause decline in lending to other nations.

Question 5

a. A nominal magnitude is an economic variable measured in current prices.

A real magnitude is an economic variable measured in the prices of an arbitrarily chosen base year.

1. Prices are constant, and there is an increase in the quantities of goods and services produced.
2. The quantities of goods and services are constant, but prices increase.

b. 2007—$8,800.

2008—$12,790.

c. At 2007 prices—$8,800 and $11,300.

At 2008 prices—$10,050 and $12,790.

d.   45.34 percent.

28.41 percent; 27.26 percent.

Prices for 2008 give a lower increase in real GDP because 2008 prices place lower values on quantities which have increased most rapidly.

e.   27.83 percent.

f. $11,249.04.

g. $2865.98 billion.

Question 6

The answers to both parts of this question depend on the time period chosen.

Question 7

(1) Employed; (2) Unemployed; (3) Not in labor force; (4) Unemployed; (5) Employed; (6) Employed; (7) Not in labor force; (8) Unemployed; (9) Not in labor force; (10) Employed; (11) Not in labor force.

Question 8

Individuals laid off by large firms may go into business for themselves as consultants (a large number of individuals did this during 2002–07). By moving to self-employment from establishments covered by the payroll survey, these individuals can be missed by the payroll survey yet included in the household survey.

■ Chapter 3

Question 1

a. $C = 200 + 0.8Y.$

b. See Figure 3A.

c. See Figure 3B.

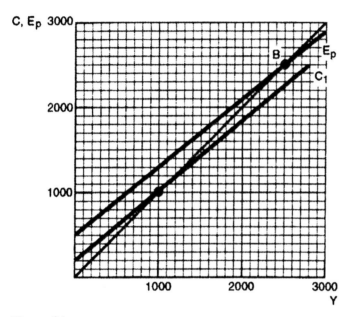

Figure 3A

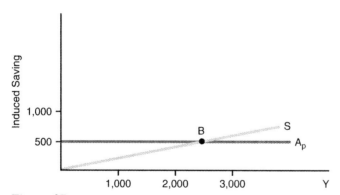

Figure 3B

Question 2

a. $A_p = a + I_p = 500.$

b. $E_p = 500 + 0.8Y$; Induced Consumption $= 0.8Y$

c. See Figure 3A and Figure 3B.

d. $Y = A_p/s = (a + I_p)/s.$

   $Y = 500/0.2 = 2,500.$

e.

E_p	I_u	A_p	sY
1,300	−300	500	200
1,700	−200	500	300
2,100	−100	500	400
2,500	0	500	500
2,900	+100	500	600

f. Unintended inventory accumulation is negative because total production is less than planned expenditure. Alternatively stated, autonomous expenditure is greater than induced saving. Business will increase production to meet this shortfall.

g. Unintended inventory accumulation is positive because total production is greater than planned expenditure. Alternatively stated, autonomous planned expenditure is less than induced saving. Business will decrease production because of this shortfall.

h. $Y = 2,500$.

At this level of output, production equals planned expenditure. There is no unplanned accumulation or decumulation of inventories, and as long as spending plans do not change, there is no reason to change the level of production.

Question 3

a. $A_{p1} = a + I_{p1} = 200 + 500 = 700$.

b. $k = \Delta Y/\Delta A_p = 1/s = 1/0.2 = 5$.

c.

$Y_1 = A_{p1}/s$	$Y_1 = 700/0.2 = 3,500$
$Y_0 = A_{p0}/s$	$Y_0 = 500/0.2 = 2,500$
$\Delta Y = (A_{p1} - A_{p0})s = \Delta A_p/s$	$\Delta Y = (700 - 500)/0.2 = 200/0.2 = 1,000$

Question 4

a. $A_{p0} = a + I_p = 200 + 400 = 600$.

$E_{p0} = 600 + 0.8Y$.

See Figure 3C and Figure 3D.

$Y = 600/0.2 = 3,000$.

See Figure 3C and Figure 3D.

b. $A_{p1} = a + I_p + G = 200 + 400 + 300 = 900$.

$E_{p1} = 900 + 0.8Y$.

See Figure 3C and Figure 3D.

$Y = 900/0.2 = 4,500$.

See Figure 3C and Figure 3D.

$\Delta Y = 1,500$.

$\Delta G = 300$.

$k = \Delta Y/\Delta G = 5$.

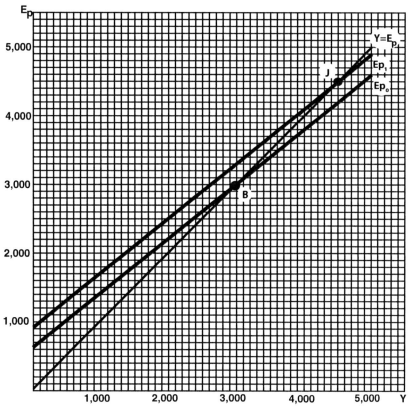

Figure 3C

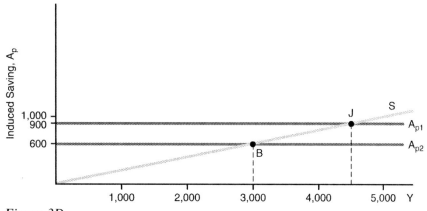

Figure 3D

c. See Figure 3E and Figure 3F.

$A_{p2} = a - cT_0 + I_p + G = 200 - 0.8(250) + 400 + 300 = 700.$

$E_{p2} = 700 + 0.8Y.$

See Figure 3E and Figure 3F.

$Y = 3,500.$

See Figure 3E and Figure 3F.

$\Delta Y = -1,000.$

$\Delta T_0 = +250.$

$\Delta Y / \Delta T_0 = -4.$

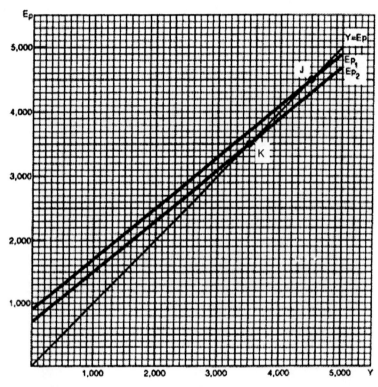

Figure 3E

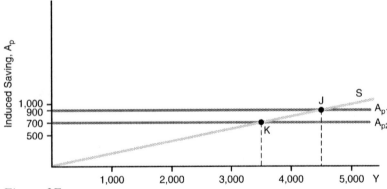

Figure 3F

d. Gap $= Y^N - Y = 3,500 - 3,000 = 500.$

Gap $= Y^N - Y = 3,500 - 3,500 = 0.$

The combination of the increase in government expenditure and the increase in taxes provided a net stimulus to the economy and increased real GDP by enough to erase the GDP gap.

Question 5

a. 1. A change in autonomous consumption (a).
    2. A change in autonomous taxes (T_0).
    3. A change in planned investment (I_p).
    4. A change in government spending (G).
    5. A change in autonomous net exports (NX_0).

b. 1. $A_p \uparrow I_p \uparrow$.
    2. $A_p \uparrow G \uparrow$.
    3. $A_p \uparrow T_0 \downarrow$.
    4. $A_p \downarrow a \downarrow$.
    5. $A_p \downarrow I_p \downarrow$.
    6. $A_p \downarrow T_0 \uparrow$.
    7. $A_p \uparrow NX_0 \uparrow$.

c. No, the multiplier for both (c) and (f) is smaller than the multipliers for the others. The difference is due to the fact that in (c) and (f), A_p changes only by the amount of the marginal propensity to consume (c) times the change in T_0; in the other cases, A_p changes by an amount equal to the change in the variable.

d. 1. Fewer or smaller "shocks" that cause changes in real GDP
    2. Improvement in monetary and fiscal policy

Question 6

a. $Y - T = Y - (T_0 + t_0 Y) = -T_0 + (1 - t_0)Y = -50 + 0.9Y$.

b. $A_p = a - cT_0 + I_p + G = 200 - 0.8(50) + 400 + 350 = 910$.

c. The marginal leakage rate is the fraction of a change in real GDP that does not go into induced consumption, i.e., the sum of the fraction going into induced saving and the fraction going into induced tax revenues.

d. $MLR = s(1 - t_0) + t_0 = (0.2)(0.9) + 0.1 = 0.28$.

e. $Y = 910/0.28 = 3{,}250$.

f. $T - G = T_0 + t_0 Y - G = 50 + 0.1(3{,}250) - 350 = 375 - 350 = 25$.

g. $k = \Delta Y / \Delta G = 1/0.28 = 3.57$.

    This multiplier is smaller than the one found in Question 3 because in this case there is an additional leakage into induced taxes.

Question 7

a. $A_p = a - cT_0 + I_p + G + NX_0 = 200 - 0.8(50) + 400 + 350 + 65 = 975$.

b. $MLR = s(1 - t_0) + t_0 + nx_0 = 0.2(1 - 0.1) + 0.1 + 0.02 = 0.18 + 0.10 + 0.02 = 0.3$.

c. $Y = 975/0.3 = 3{,}250$.

d. $k = 1/0.3 = 3.33$.

This multiplier is smaller than in the previous question because of the added leakage into imports.

e. $NX = 65 - 0.02(3{,}250) = 0$.

Question 8

a.   Sample answer provided in the question.

b. $70. Price $= \$70/(1.07) + \$70/(1.07)^2 + \$70/(1.07)^3 + \$1{,}000/(1.07)^3 = \$65.42 + \$61.14 + \$57.14 + \$816.30 = \$1{,}000$.

c.   Price $= \$100/(1.07) + \$100/(1.07)^2 + \$100/(1.07)^3 + \$1000/(1.07)^3 = \$93.46 + \$87.34 + \$81.63 + \$816.30 = \$1{,}078.73$.

d.   increases; fixed; variable

Question 9

a.   ($3,200 – $2,800)/$2,800 = $400/$2,800 = 0.1429, or 14.29 percent.

b.

$1 + r$	$(1 + r)^2$	$\$1{,}600/(1 + r)$	$\$1{,}600/(1 + r)^2$	Discounted Value
1.07	1.1449	$1,495	$1,398	$2,893
1.08	1.1664	1,481	1,372	2,853
1.09	1.1881	1,468	1,347	2,815
1.10	1.2100	1,455	1,322	2,777
1.11	1.2321	1,441	1,299	2,740
1.12	1.2544	1,429	1,276	2,705

$r = 9.4\%$ (by interpolation between $2,815 and $2,777; specifically, $14/38 = 0.39$; $0.39 \times 0.01 = 0.0039$; $0.094 + 0.0039 = 0.0939$).

r would fall to about 7 percent; r would rise to 11 percent.

c.   10 percent (present value of $1,998); 8.4 percent (present value of $553.5 + $1,446.7); 7.8 percent (present value of $1,493.5 + $1,505.9)

Project A has more of its return in the first year than does Project B so that more of B's gross return has to be discounted over two periods.

None. $0.

A; $2,000.

A, B, and C; $7,000.

d.   11.9 percent; 10.0 percent; 9.1 percent

e.

Before CEA Report		After CEA Report	
Projects Undertaken	**Total Value**	**Projects Undertaken**	**Total Value**
None	$ 0	A	$2,000
A	$2,000	A, B, C	$7,000
A, B, C	$7,000	A, B, C	$7,000

Question 10

a.

I_p	A	A_p
180	170	350
220	180	400
260	190	450
300	200	500
340	210	550
380	220	600

b. $A_p = 600 - 25r$.

c. $k = 5$.

d.

A_p	$Y = kA_p$	sY
350	1,750	350
400	2,000	400
450	2,250	450
500	2,500	500
550	2,750	550
600	3,000	600

e.

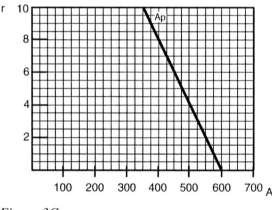 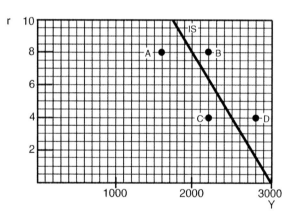

Figure 3G

f. Induced saving and autonomous planned spending are equal at each point on the *IS* curve.

g. $Y = 3000 - 125r$.

h.

sY	A_p	I_u
320	400	−80
440	400	40
440	500	−60
560	500	60

i.   left; greater than; decrease; increase

2,000; 2,500

■ Chapter 4

Question 1

a. $MPC = 0.75$.

$A_p = 550 - 40r$.

A_0 is the amount of autonomous planned spending that occurs when the interest rate is zero.

$A_0 = 550$.

$A_p = 150$.

$A_p = 350$.

$Y = 600$; $Y = 1,400$; $Y = 2,200$.

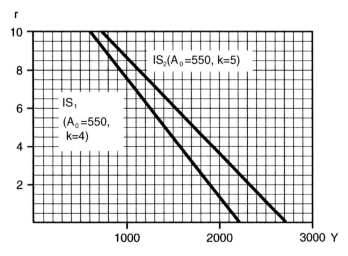

Figure 4A

$\Delta Y / \Delta r = -160$.

b. $A_0 = 580$.

$A_p = 580 - 40r$.

$A_p = 180$.

$A_p = 380$.

$A_p = 580$.

When government spending increases by 30, the A_p curve shifts to the right by a horizontal distance of 30.

$\Delta Y / \Delta r = -160$.

The answers would be the same because the increase in investment of 30 would have the same effect on IS and A_p as did the increase of 30 in government expenditure.

$\Delta T_0 = -40$. $(-0.75 \Delta T_0 = 30 \qquad \Delta T_0 = -40.)$

c. $k = 5$.

   $A_p = 142$.

   $A_p = 342$.

   $A_p = 542$.

   The value of A_p is slightly less because $-cT_0$ is part of A_p (i.e., when c increases, A_p shifts leftward).

   $Y = 710$.

   $Y = 1,710$.

   $Y = 2,710$.

   $\Delta Y / \Delta r = -200$.

   The multiplier of 5 in Part c is larger than in the multiplier of 4 in Part a, so the change in Y due to a one-percentage-point change in r is greater numerically. The A_p and IS curves are flatter.

d.

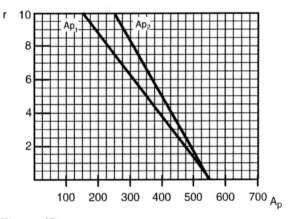 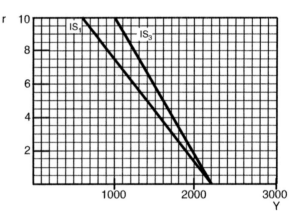

Figure 4B

   $A_p = 550 - 30r$.

   $A_p = 250; A_p = 400; A_p = 550$

   A_p responsiveness refers to the amount by which A_p changes as a result of a change in r. In this case, A_p has become less responsive to changes in r.

   $\Delta Y / \Delta r = -120$.

Question 2

a. $(M/P)^d = 350$.

   $(M/P)^d = 400$.

   $(M/P)^d = 500$.

b.

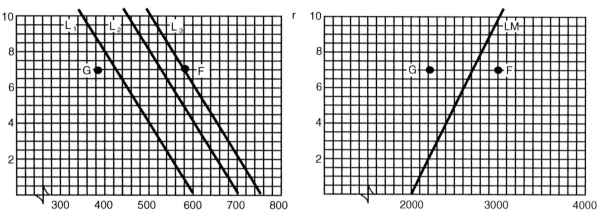

Figure 4C

demand curve for real money balances.

c. $(M/P)^d = 450$; excess supply; 50

People holding the excess money will try to exchange it for other assets. This action bids up the price of those assets and lowers their yield (the interest rate).

$r = 4$.

d. $(M/P)^d = 500$; $(M/P)^d = 600$; excess demand

People will attempt to increase their money balances by selling other assets. This action bids down the price of those assets and raises their yield, causing the interest rate to rise.

$r = 8$.

e. $(M/P)^d = 700 - 25r$

$r = 10$.

f. See Figure 4C.

g. $Y = 2,000 + 100r$.

For equilibrium, $(M/P)^d = M^s/P$. M^s/P is constant along the *LM* curve, so any increase in $(M/P)^d$ due to an increase in Y must be matched by a decrease in $(M/P)^d$ due to a rise in r (and vice versa), so Y and r are directly related.

h. $V = 4.8$; $V = 5.6$; $V = 6.0$

With a fixed money supply, the only way the economy can support a higher Y is to use the given money supply more intensively; r must rise to encourage people to reduce their desired money balances.

i. excess *demand*; r must rise to 10

To eliminate the excess demand, r must rise; this would cause some people to hold less money.

j.   excess supply; r must fall to 2

The fall in r will cause some people to want to hold more money. This increased in quantity demanded will absorb the excess supply.

k.   1.   on; remain unchanged;
2.   to the right of; increase;
3.   to the left of; decrease

Question 3

a. $(M/P)^d = 400 - 20r$.

$r = 4$.

b. $Y = 800 + 50r$.

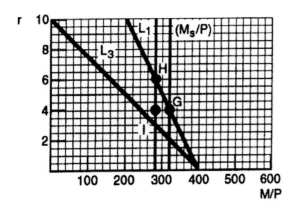 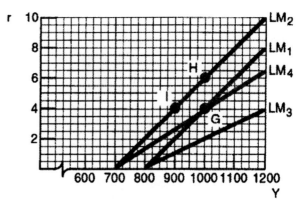

Figure 4D

c.   The decrease in the money supply will cause an excess demand for money, and people will sell some of their financial assets to increase their money balances, causing a fall in asset prices and an increase in the rate of interest.

$r = 6$; $Y = 900$; $Y = 700 + 50r$

d. L_3 is flatter than L_1

$Y = 800 + 100r$

LM_3 is flatter than LM_1. As the demand for money has become more sensitive to the interest rate, so has the LM curve. A smaller change in the money supply produces a greater change in the interest rate and hence in real output.

e. $Y = 680 + 80r$.

Both curves go through Point G ($Y = 1,000$ and $r = 4$), but LM_4 is flatter than LM_1. As income increases, the necessary rise in r is less along LM_4 than along LM_1.

Question 4

a. $A_0 = 960$; $A_p = 960 - 80r$; $k = 2.5$; $Y = 2,400 - 200r$

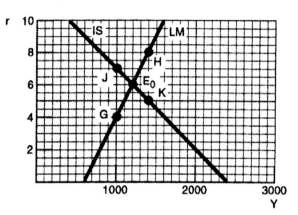

Figure 4E

b. $Y = 600 + 100r$.

c. $Y = 1,200$; $r = 6$.

$(M/P)^d = 150$; $M^s/P = 150$.

The money market is in equilibrium.

$A_p = 960 - 80r = 960 - 80(6) = 480$; Induced Saving $= 0.4Y = 480$.

The commodity market is in equilibrium.

d.

$(M/P)^d$	Condition in Money Market	I_p	auto C	sY	Condition in Goods Market
150	EQ	520	120	400	$-\Delta I_u$
150	EQ	200	120	560	$+\Delta I_u$
75	ES	280	120	400	EQ
225	ED	440	120	560	EQ

e. is not; decrease; increase; increase

E_0.

−1

increase.

25.

200.

increase; 50.

increase; 75.

supply; 75.

f. is not; increase

E_0.

200.

increase; 50.

increasing; 2.

decrease; 50.

Question 5

a. $Y = 2,400.$

   $r = 8.$

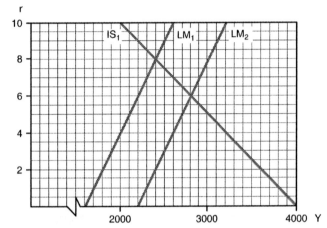

Figure 4F

b. $V = 6.0.$

c. $Y = 2,200 + 100r.$

   See Figure 4F.

   $Y = 2,800.$

   $r = 6.$

   $V = 2.67.$

d. $V = 2,800/550 = 5.09$

   The velocity of money is lower here because of the fall in the interest rate.

e.   A change in the rate of interest has no effect on the demand for money.

   LM: $Y = 2,400.$

   $Y = 2,400;\ r = 8;\ V = 4$

f.   *LM*: $Y = 3,000$

   $Y = 3,000;\ r = 5;\ V = 4$

   Velocity is the same as in Part e.

g. $\Delta Y/\Delta(M^s/P) = 4.$

   This ratio is much higher because in Part c the velocity of money declines as the rate of interest falls. Here, velocity is independent of the interest rate.

Question 6

a. $Ap = a - cT_0 + Ip + G = 200 - 0.8(200) + 300 + 260 + 0 = 600.$

In this question, planned autonomous spending is unrelated to the interest rate.
$k = 1/s = 1/0.2 = 5.$
IS: $Y = 3,000.$
LM: $Y = 2,200 + 100r.$

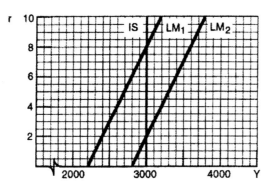

Figure 4G

$Y = 3,000; r = 8$

b. $Y = 3,000; r = 2$

c. $\Delta Y / \Delta (M^s/P) = 0.$

d. In Question 1, Part g, when the interest rate fell, A_p increased and real GDP increased. Here, the fall in the interest rate does not prompt any increase in autonomous spending; thus, the level of real GDP does not increase.

e. The *LM* curve is a horizontal line at $r = 2$.

Neither bond prices nor interest rates change as the real money supply increases. When the money supply increases, everyone is willing to hold the new money; thus, there is no need for bond prices to rise and interest rates to fall as a way of encouraging people to hold money.

f. $Y = 2,600; r = 2$

$Y^N - Y = 600.$

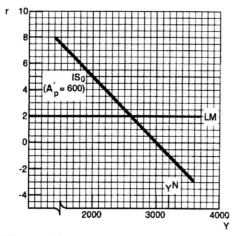

Figure 4H

g. The Fed cannot remove the GDP gap through the use of monetary policy. Regardless of the amount of money created, the interest rate would not fall below 2 percent and Y would remain at 2,600.

h. The size of the desired increase in real GDP is 600. The multiplier is 5, so government expenditure should increase by 120.

Since the tax multiplier is 4, tax revenue would have to fall by 150.

i. For monetary policy to be impotent, either the IS curve must be vertical or the LM curve must be horizontal.

It is unlikely that the curves would ever have these shapes. A vertical IS curve suggests that changes in the interest rate have no effect a desired spending. A horizontal LM curve suggests that people are willing to hold an unlimited amount of money at the current interest rate. There are economists who suggest that Japan may have experienced a very flat LM curve, the so-called "liquidity trap," in 1998–1999.

Question 7

a. $A_p = a - cT_0 + I_p + G = (300 - 10r) - 0.8(250) + (400 - 30r) + 180 + 0 = 680 - 40r.$

$IS: Y = 3,400 - 200r.$

$LM: Y = 2,200 + 100r.$

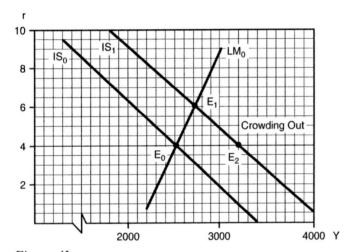

Figure 4I

$Y = 2,600; r = 4.$

b. $IS: Y = 4,000 - 200r.$

$Y = 2,800; r = 6.$

c. $Y = 3,200.$ $(\Delta Y = k\Delta G = 5(120) = 600.)$

To move to E_2, the interest rate must remain at 4 percent. When real GDP increases, people want to hold more money; i.e., the demand for money increases. Since the money supply does not increase, the interest rate must rise. The interest-rate rise causes A_p and Y to decline relative to their levels at E_2.

d.

E_0	E_1
540	460
180	300
250	250
520	560
2,600	2,800

Private *autonomous* expenditure falls by 80 (540 – 460, or 340 – 260, after taxes) because of the higher interest rate at E_1 compared to E_0. However, *total* private spending increases from 2,420 (2,600 – 180) to 2,500 (2,800 – 300).

e. *LM*: $Y = 2,600$.

$Y = 2,600$; $r = 4$

$Y = 2,600$; $r = 7$

Crowding out = 600

All of the potential increase in Y due to the change in G is crowded out by the rise in the interest rate.

f. $Y = 2,600$; $r = 4$

$Y = 3,200$; $r = 4$

Crowding out = 0

In Part a, a rise in r causes a reduction in a and I_p, and hence in Y relative to E_2. In Part b, there is no rise in the interest rate; hence there is no reduction in a or I_p.

g. Both are unlikely. Again, however, there is some evidence that Japan may have experienced a very flat *LM* curve in 1998–99.

Question 8

Low, liquidity trap, monetary policy, decrease, horizontal *LM* curve, fiscal policy, combined monetary and fiscal policy, decrease, monetizing

Question 9

a. Fed kept interest rates too low for too long

b. Fed did not regulate the sub-prime mortgage market

■ Chapter 5

Question 1

a. Tax revenues net of transfers minus government expenditures, or $T - G$.

Because the bases for the different types of taxes (income, sales, value of property) fluctuate as GDP fluctuates, the level of tax revenues is a function of the level of real GDP. (Autonomous net taxes, T_0, are omitted for simplification.)

b. 0; 8; 16.

Average tax rate; government expenditures

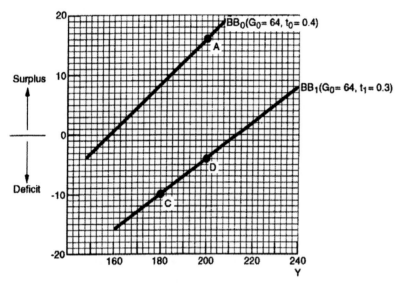

Figure 5A

c. We can't tell unless we know the actual level of real GDP in the economy: the level of the deficit depends on the level of output.

Using the actual budget deficit would not give a clear picture of the government's fiscal policy because it would ignore the two-way interaction between the budget and the economy.

d. 16.

The government would have to use expansionary fiscal and/or monetary policy.

The government would have to either decrease taxes or increase government spending; either of these choices would increase the deficit (lower the surplus) in the government budget.

–4, i.e., a deficit of 4.

Tax revenues are tied to the level of Y. Since the value of Y fell, so will tax revenues, and the budget will move toward a deficit.

Automatic stabilization policy.

e. The economy would have fallen further than $Y = 150$ if there were no built-in stabilization policy.

When there is no automatic stabilization, $t = 0$.

f. Discretionary fiscal policy.

–4; –10; 213.3; expansionary; lower; below.

g. Surplus of 16; deficit of 4.

h. Surplus of 16; deficit of 4.

   The answers are the same since the structural surplus or deficit and the natural employment surplus or deficit are two names for the same concept.

i. Deficit of 10; deficit of 6.

Question 2

See Gordon Figure 5-5

Question 3

See Gordon Figure 5-6

Question 4

a. Data presented in Figure 5-1 reveals that the size of government (measured by total government expenditures) spiked in war years with World War II have a much larger impact than World War I.

b. Data presented in Figure 5-1 reveal that tax revenues also spiked during war years. However, the spike in tax revenue was smaller than that of government expenditures. Consequently, budget deficits increased as well.

c. For the most part, for several decades prior to World War II the size of government remained below 10 percent of natural GDP. After the war, the size of government increased to between two and three times that amount.

d. During the 1980s and continuing into the 1990s, the budget ran a substantial deficit. None of it was due to a drop in tax revenues, because tax revenues were stable throughout the decade. Budget deficits arose from the fact that government expenditures were increasing at an even faster rate than tax revenues.

e. In the late 1990s and very briefly in the first moments of the 21st century there were budget surpluses, but these were quickly turned to deficits by a recession.

Question 5

a. $G - T \alpha - NX + (S - I)$

b. If $G > T$ (i.e., there is a budget deficit), then NX will have a negative value (i.e., there will also be a foreign trade deficit) if personal saving is insufficient to fund both domestic investment spending **and** the budget deficit. This is commonly the case.

c. S and I must be equal if the budget deficit and trade deficit are to be the same size. As your text notes, however, there is little reason to expect this.

d. During a part of the 1990s $G < T$ and $N > X$ or $-NX$. In this case personal saving *along with the budget surplus* was sufficient to fund both domestic investment spending **and** the budget deficit. Ordinarily we may think of budget deficits as causing increased interest rates, increased foreign investment, increased demand for dollars and increased value of the dollar in foreign exchange markets, a drop in exports, and ultimately a trade deficit. In this case, however, there is a budget surplus, which alone would tend to drive interest rates downward. However, domestic investment is so much greater than private saving that it overwhelms the dampening effect of the budget surplus on interest rates and leads to an increase in interest rates in the United States. This in turn leads to a trade deficit as explained above, but this time with federal budget that is still in a surplus.

■ Chapter 6

Question 1

a. The balance of payments is the record for a given period of a country's transactions in goods, securities, and money with the rest of the world.

A deficit occurs when the amount of goods and services that a nation purchases from other countries plus the amount of capital that it exports is greater than the amount of goods and services that it exports plus the amount of capital that it borrows from other countries.

The deficit is financed by borrowing from foreign firms, households, governments, and central banks.

Net exports are the excess of exports over imports (net exports are negative if imports exceed exports).

Current account; capital account.

The current account is that portion of the balance of payments that includes the flow of goods, services, and transfers between a nation and the rest of the world.

The capital account is that portion of the balance of payments that includes direct investment and trade in both long-term and short-term securities between a nation and the rest of the world.

b. 1. current account, –;

2. current account, +;

3. capital account, +;

4. current account, +;

5. current account, –;

6. capital account, +

c. Capital inflows that gave a surplus in the capital account were the main factor balancing the large deficit in the current account in the 1980s.

Negative; net debtor

The interest and dividend payments going to foreign owners of U.S. assets are a deduction from domestic output and income and will reduce real income in the United States.

d. After 1981; about 1984.

e. The reduction in U.S. net foreign investment from 1981 to 1998 cost the United States a flow of income equal to about 1.2 percent of GDP.

Question 2

a. The foreign exchange rate is the amount of another nation's money that residents of a country can obtain in exchange for a unit of their own currency.

b. The international demand for a country's currency, i.e., the demand for foreign exchange, depends on the country's exports and its capital inflows, both of which require that foreigners obtain the country's currency to pay for their purchases of its exports and its real and financial assets.

The supply of foreign exchange depends on a country's imports and capital outflows, both of which require that the country's citizens acquire foreign currency to pay for their purchases of foreign goods and services as well as foreign real and financial assets.

The demand curve for a country's currency depends on the foreign demand for that country's exports. If the foreign demand is negatively sloped, then the demand for the country's foreign exchange will also be negatively sloped.

The supply curve of a country's currency depends on the price elasticity of that country's demand for foreign goods and services. If the demand for foreign products is elastic, then the supply curve of foreign exchange will be positively sloped. If the demand is unit-elastic, the supply curve will be vertical, and if the demand curve is inelastic, the supply curve will be negatively sloped.

c. Excess demand: The foreign exchange rate would rise as those demanding the currency bid up its price, thereby inducing those supplying the currency to offer it in exchange.

Excess supply: The foreign exchange rate for Country A's currency would fall as those supplying Country A's currency would accept less of Country B's currency in exchange, thereby inducing those demanding Country A's currency to accept more.

The U.S. government would have to buy up the excess supply of dollars on the foreign exchange market.

d. The answers to the first part of this question depend on the date chosen.

If the spot rate is higher than the future rate, people expect the exchange rate to fall in the future; if the spot rate is lower than the future rate, they expect the exchange rate to rise in the future.

e. 1. flexible exchange-rate policy.
    2. fixed exchange-rate policy.

f. 1. With flexible exchange rates, the deficit will create an excess supply of a country's currency and an excess demand for foreign currencies; the exchange rate will fall. (The reverse is true for a surplus.)
    2. With fixed exchange rates, a country will adjust to a deficit by losing international reserves. (The reverse is true for a surplus.)

g. Fixed exchange rates. The central bank of a country with fixed exchange rates will have to raise interest rates to offset the inflationary effect of a substantial increase in capital imports.

Question 3

a. P = domestic price level; P^f = foreign price level; e' = nominal exchange rate (in units of foreign currency per unit of domestic currency)

b. e' = \$0.167/euro.; depreciate; e' = \$0.15/euro.

c. $\Delta e'/e' = P^f - p$ (the foreign inflation rate minus the domestic inflation rate); –3.8
    1. differences in technology and natural resources among countries;
    2. capital movements between countries;
    3. government policy to affect exchange rates.

d. The real exchange rate is the average nominal foreign exchange rate between a country and its trading partners, adjusted for the difference in inflation rates between that country and its trading partners; $e = e' (P/P^f)$

zero. Since $\Delta e/e = (\Delta e'/e') + p - p^f$ and $\Delta e'/e' = p^f - p$, then $\Delta e/e = p^f - p + p - p^f = 0$.

$\Delta e/e = 0.8$. ($\Delta e/e = (\Delta e'/e') + p - p^f = -3.0 + 7.4 - 3.6 = 0.8$.)

The rise in the real exchange rate will tend to reduce net exports in Spain.

Question 4

a. $39.4; 35.2, increase.

b. 1140 euros; 1275 euros; decrease.

c. Net exports will decrease because exports will decrease and imports will increase.

d. 30; fall to –30.

Question 5

a. Larger; selling; buying; increase; increase.

b. Increase; decrease.

Question 6

a. The marginal leakage rate (MLR) is the fraction of the change in income that does not go into induced consumption.

$MLR = 0.2; k = 5; A_p = 680 - 40r; Y = 3,400 - 200r; Y = 2200 + 100r$; closed

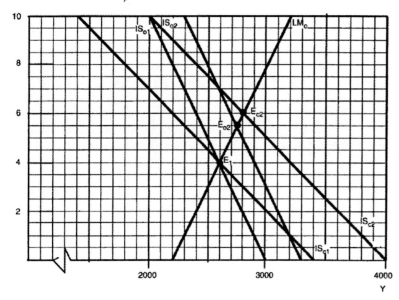

Figure 6A

$Y = 2,600; r = 4$

b. $MLR = 0.2; k = 5; A_p = 800 - 40r; Y = 4,000 - 200r$

$Y = 2,800; r = 6$

$\Delta Y/\Delta G = 200/120 = 1.67$

The value of k is the multiplier only if the interest rate remains constant; it would equal the government-spending multiplier if the *LM* curve were horizontal so that the interest rate would not change due to a shift of the *IS* curve. If the interest rate rises, however, there will be some amount of crowding out and the government-spending multiplier will be lower than the simple Keynesian multiplier.

c. The definition remains the same, but now there is an additional type of leakage (induced imports).

MLR $= 0.4$; $k = 2.5$; $A_p = 1,200 - 40r$; $Y = 3,000 - 100r$

IS_{c1} is flatter than IS_{o1}.

Since the general equation of the IS curve is $Y = k(A_0 - br)$, then the slope is $\Delta Y/\Delta r = -kb$. Under the assumptions of this question, the slope of the closed economy's IS curve is $-(5)(40) = -200$, and the slope of the open economy's IS curve is $-(2.5)(40) = -100$. Hence, the closed economy's IS curve is flatter than the open economy's because there is more change in Y for any given change in r.

$Y = 2,600$; $r = 4$

The equilibrium values are the same as in Part a.

d. MLR $= 0.4$; $k = 2.5$; $A_p = 1,320 - 40r$; $Y = 3,300 - 100r$

$Y = 2,750$; $r = 5.5$

$\Delta Y/\Delta G = 150/120 = 1.25$; No

The same answer given in Part c applies here as well. There is some crowding out because of the rise in the interest rate.

e. $\Delta Y = 200$; $\Delta Y = 150$

In the open economy, there is leakage of spending into induced imports; hence, less of the increased income resulting from the increased government spending is spent on *domestic* consumption.

Question 7

a. If real GDP increases (decreases), consumers want to buy more (fewer) consumer goods. Since some of these goods are imported, there is an increase (a decrease) in induced imports.

If the foreign exchange rate increases (decreases), the domestic economy's consumers and businesses want to buy more (less) imports and foreign economies' consumers and businesses want to buy less (more) of the domestic economy's exports, so the domestic economy's net exports decrease (increase).

b. $NX = 520 - 0.2Y$; $A_p = 1,200 - 40r$; $k = 2.5$; $Y = 3,000 - 100r$

c. increase; increase; decrease; decrease

$NX = 840 - 0.2Y - 80r$; $A_0 = 1,520$; $A_p = 1,520 - 120r$; $k = 2.5$; $Y = 3,800 - 300r$

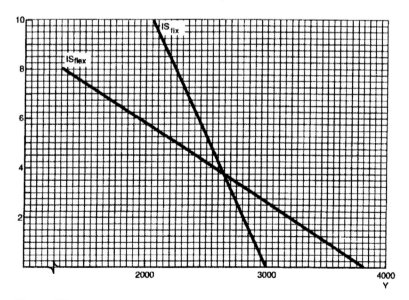

Figure 6B

d. $A_p = 960$; $Y = 2,400$

To get A_p, use the equation for A_p from Part b of this question and substitute 6 for r. To get Y, multiply A_p ($= 960$) by k ($= 2.5$), or substitute $r = 6$ into the equation of IS_{fix} in Part b, or simply read Y from the graph of the IS_{fix} curve at $r = 6$.

e. $A_p = 800$; $Y = 2,000$

To get A_p, use the equation for A_p from Part c of this question and substitute $r = 6$. To get Y, multiply A_p ($= 800$) by k ($= 2.5$), or substitute $r = 6$ into the equation of IS_{flex} in Part c, or simply read Y from the graph of the IS_{flex} curve at $r = 6$.

f.   Since a rising interest rate leads to an increase in the exchange rate in the flexible exchange-rate model, there is an additional crowding-out effect in the flexible exchange-rate model, which makes the total effect larger in the flexible exchange-rate model.

Question 8

a. $Y = 3,000 - 100r$; $Y = 2,200 + 100r$; $Y = 2,600$; $r = 4$

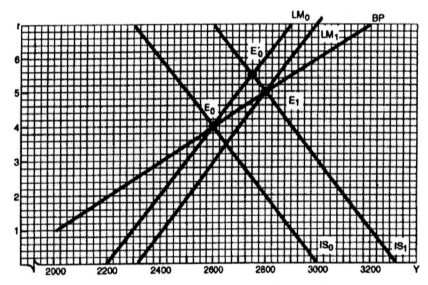

Figure 6C

b. $NX = 0$; 0; 0

c. $Y = 3,300 - 100r$; $Y = 2,750$; $r = 5.5$

d.   Equilibrium; surplus

$NX = -30$.

Into; increase; increase; fell; equilibrium

e. $Y = 2,800$; $r = 5$

f. $\Delta(M^s/P) = +25$; $M^s/P = 575$; $Y = 2,300 + 100r$

g. $NX = -40$; inflow; 40

h.   The fiscal policy stimulus has been more effective than in Question 6 because real GDP of 2,800 is greater than Question 6's real GDP of 2,750. The additional real GDP is due to the fact that money supply growth caused the interest rate to fall from 5.5 percent to 5 percent; hence, there is less crowding out of private spending.

Question 9

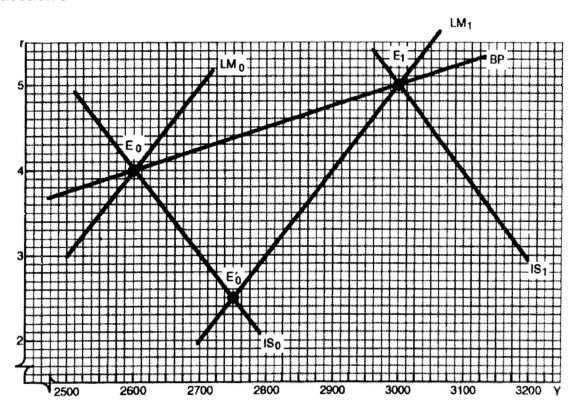

Figure 6D

a. $Y = 2,500 + 100r$; $Y = 2,750$; $r = 2.5$

b. Out of; increase; fall

c. $Y = 3,000$; $r = 5$

As the exchange rate depreciated, spending on U.S. exports would increase and U.S. spending on imports would decrease, thereby increasing net exports. The increase in net exports would increase real GDP. The exchange rate would continue to fall until the balance of payments was again in equilibrium. Graphically, increased *NX* shifts *IS* to the right until it intersects LM_1 and *BP* at their joint intersection at Point E_1.

d. $A_0 = 1,400$; $A_p = 1,400 - 40r$; $Y = 3,500 - 100r$

e. $NX_0 - 4e = 840 - (4)(80) = 520$; $\Delta A_0 = 1,400 - 1,200 = 200$; $NX_0 - 4e = 520 + 200 = 720$;

$e = 30(840 - 4e = 720 \quad e = 30)$

Depreciated; 120; outflows; 120; effective.

■ Chapter 7

Question 1

a. The nominal money supply is the actual amount of money in existence at a given time.

   The real money supply is the nominal money supply divided by a relevant price index (e.g., the GDP deflator).

b. Real money supply: 200; 400; 600; 800.

c. $Y = 1,600 + 200r$; $Y = 2,800$; $r = 6$

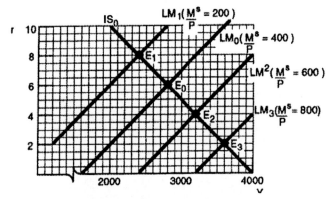

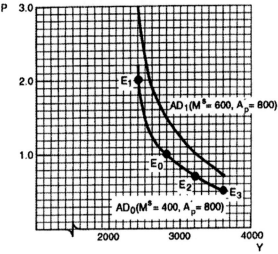

Figure 7A

d. The *LM* curve will shift to the right because the fall in prices makes each nominal dollar worth more; it is equivalent to an increase in the nominal money supply with constant prices.

   The *LM* curve will shift to the left because the increase in prices makes each nominal dollar worth less.

e.

M^s/P	*LM* Curve	Y	r
200	$Y = 800 + 200r$	2400	8
400	$Y = 1,600 + 200r$	2800	6
600	$Y = 2,400 + 200r$	3200	4
800	$Y = 3,200 + 200r$	3600	2

f. The two exogenous variables of the aggregate demand curve are M^s and A_0.

g. 1. The aggregate demand curve shows all the possible intersection points of a single *IS* curve with *LM* curves drawn for each possible price level.

2. Each point along the curve is an equilibrium in *both* the commodity and the money markets.

3. The aggregate demand curve slopes down because a lower price index (P) raises the real money supply and stimulates planned expenditures, requiring an increase in actual real output (Y) to keep the commodity market in equilibrium.

4. The position of the aggregate demand curve depends on all the factors that can shift the *IS* and *LM* curves, except the price level.

Question 2

a.

Ms/P	LM	Y	r
200	$Y = 800 + 200r$	2,400	8
300	$Y = 1,200 + 200r$	2,600	7
400	$Y = 1,600 + 200r$	2,800	6
600	$Y = 2,400 + 200r$	3,200	4
800	$Y = 3,200 + 200r$	3,600	2

b. Right; increased; higher

Question 3

a.

M^s/P	Y	r
200	2,800	10
400	3,200	8
600	3,600	6
800	4,000	4

b.

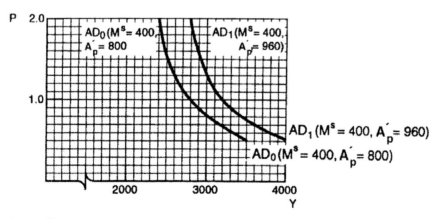

Figure 7B

c. Increase; increase; higher

Question 4

a.   the law of diminishing marginal product.

b.   marginal product of labor (MPL); demand-for-labor

c.   the demand curve for labor

technology and the quality and quantity of other resources used

d.   amount of labor to be employed

total output or real GDP

e.   decrease; increase; opposite

short-run aggregate supply curve

Question 5

a.   Marginal product of labor.

b.   A higher price level reduces the real wage and firms can increase profits by hiring more labor and producing more output.

c.   To produce more output, a higher price must exist; thus, the *SAS* curve will shift up.

d.   The *SAS* curve will shift up and to the left.

Question 6

a.   The nominal wage rate is the wage rate in current dollars. In our theory, the nominal wage (W) represents an average of nominal wage rates for the entire economy.

The real wage rate is the nominal wage rate divided by an index of the price level. In our theory, the real wage is W/P, where P is the GDP deflator.

Real wages have increased by 15 percent.

There will be no change in the real wage.

b.   Real wages stayed the same from Period 0 to Period 1 ($W_1/W_0 = P_1/P_0 \quad W_1/P_1 = W_0/P_0$). Real wages rose from Period 1 to Period 2 ($W_2/W_1 > P_2/P_1 \quad W_2/P_2 > W_1/P_1$).

c.   Upward; A higher real wage is required to bring more people into the labor force or to persuade those in the labor force to work longer hours.

d.   The equilibrium real wage is the real wage that equates the supply of and the demand for labor, i.e., brings about a long-run equilibrium in the labor market.

Rise; At the current real wage, there will be an excess demand for labor, and firms will bid up the real wage in an attempt to obtain more workers or worker-hours.

Rise; The supply of labor has fallen (i.e., shifted to the left), leading to an excess demand at the current real wage.

Question 7

a.

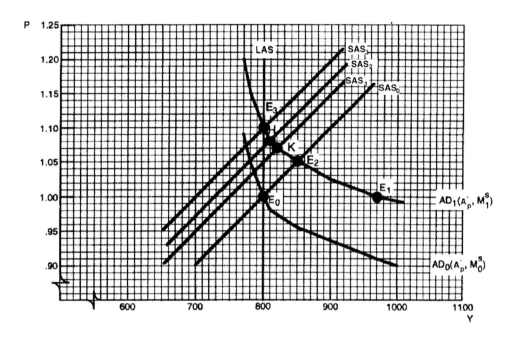

Figure 7C

b. The natural level of real GDP

c. *AD* represents the output people want to buy at various price levels. *SAS* represents the output firms want to produce at various price levels. *LAS* represents the output that would be produced if the actual real wage equaled the equilibrium real wage.

d. Since the *IS* curve will not change, the economy will stay at the same Y only if M^s/P remains unchanged. Since M^s increased by 10 percent, a 10-percent increase in P will bring M^s/P back to its original level (i.e., the *LM* curve will be the original one) and therefore bring output back to its original level (i.e., at the intersection of the original *IS* and *LM* curves).

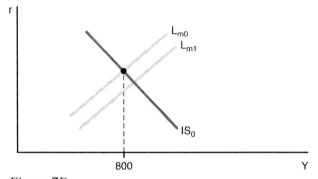

Figure 7D

e. Point E_1 represents the output that would be demanded after the increase in the money supply if the price level did not change.

The economy would reach E_1 if the short-run aggregate supply curve were horizontal, i.e., if firms were willing to produce an unlimited amount of output at a price level of P_1. It is unlikely this point would be reached because producers' costs increase as output increases, resulting in the need for higher prices.

f. $P = 1.05$; $W = 100$; $Y = 850$; $X = 892.50$

The actual real wage is lower at E_2 than at E_0 ($W/P = 100/1.05 = 95.2$).

E_2 is an equilibrium point because at that Point $AD = SAS$; thus, the amount of output desired is equal to the amount firms are willing to produce at $P = 1.05$ when $W = 100$.

E_2 is not a long-run equilibrium because at that point the actual real wage is less than the equilibrium real wage; thus, workers are not satisfied and will demand a higher real wage.

g. $P = 1.05$; If $P = 1.05$, no discrepancy would exist between the actual real wage and the equilibrium real wage; therefore, output would be at the natural level.

$P = 1.07$; $W/P = 98.13$; $Y = 820$; $X = 877.4$

Since workers realize at E_2 that the actual real wage is less than the equilibrium real wage, they will revise their wage demanded upwards (i.e., they will be willing to supply enough labor to produce 850 only at a higher real wage). Producers will be willing to pay this higher real wage only if they can sell the output produced at a higher price. The rising price level causes the real money supply to decline (since the nominal money supply is unchanged), and therefore the quantity demanded to decrease (shown by the movement along AD_1 from E_2 to K).

h. $W = 107$; $P = 1.08$; $W/P = 99.07$; $Y = 810$; $X = 874.8$

i. $P = 1.10$; $Y = 800$; natural real GDP

Question 8

a.   Rise; remain the same.

Fall; remain the same.

The rise in prices (in the first case) will cause the real money supply to decline, interest rates to rise, and the desired level of spending to fall. This process will continue until the level of desired spending equals the natural level of real GDP. In the second case, the real money supply increases because of falling prices, and the level of desired spending increases until it reaches the level of natural real GDP.

b.

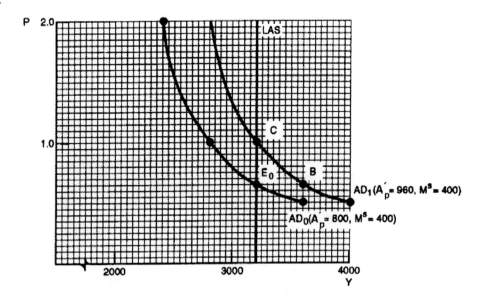

Figure 7E

Output is independent of the price level.

c. $Y = 3,200$; $P = 0.67$; $X = 2,134.4$

d. $Y = 2,400 + (800/P)$; $Y = 3,600$

e. $Y = 3,200$; $P = 1.00$; $X = 3,200$

f. No. The increase in the money supply can temporarily increase real GDP, but prices will begin to rise and this will drive the real money supply back to its original level and the level of real GDP back to the natural level.

Question 9

a. $r = 8 - (4/P)$; $Y = 1,600 + (800/P)$

b.

M^s/P	Y	r
200	2,000	6
400	2,400	4
600	2,800	2
800	3,200	0
1,000	3,600	-2

c. No. The demand curve will become vertical at $Y = 3,200$. Lower prices will not drive the interest rate any lower.

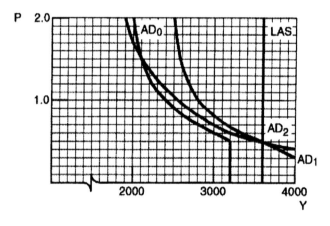

Figure 7F

d. Vertical

There is no equilibrium real GDP.

There is no equilibrium price level.

The price level will fall indefinitely.

e. The aggregate demand curve will shift to the right. This new aggregate demand curve is AD_0 for Figure 7E.

$Y = 3,600$; $P = 0.5$; $r = 2$

Question 10

a. $r = 7 - (2.5/P)$.

  $Y = 1,400 + (1,100/P)$.

  the aggregate demand curve

b.

M^s/P	A_0	IS Curve	Y	r
200	620	$Y = 3,100 - 200r$	1,950	5.75
400	680	$Y = 3,400 - 200r$	2,500	4.50
600	740	$Y = 3,700 - 200r$	3,050	3.25
800	800	$Y = 4,000 - 200r$	3,600	2.00
1,000	860	$Y = 4,300 - 200r$	4,150	0.75

c. $Y = 3,600; P = 0.5$

d.   More

■ Chapter 8

Question 1

a.

Policy	Y	P	p	W/P
A	100	1.00	0	100.0
B	104	1.05	5	95.2

It is a short-run equilibrium because the AD_1 and SAS_0 curves cross at that point; however, it is not a long-run equilibrium because the actual real wage is below the equilibrium real wage.

Workers will demand higher wages, and the actual real wage will rise.

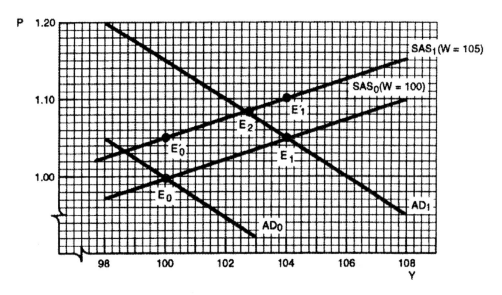

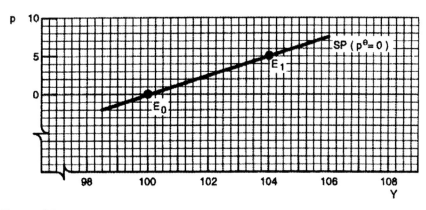

Figure 8A

b. They are not expecting any inflation because the current price level is 1.05 and the expected price level is also 1.05.

The government would have to use restrictive monetary or fiscal policy so that AD passes through that point.

102.7; 1.08; 105/1.08 = 97.2.

Increase AD_1 by expansionary monetary or fiscal policy so it would intersect SAS_1 at $P = 1.10$ and $Y = 104$.

$P = 1.10$.

c.

Policy	Y	P	p	W/P
C	100.0	1.05	0	100.0
D	102.7	1.08	3	97.2
E	104.0	1.10	5	95.5

d. In each case, the expected inflation rate is zero. In Part a, the initial P is 1.00 and people expected $P = 1.00$. In Part b, the initial P is 1.05 and people expected $P = 1.05$.

Question 2

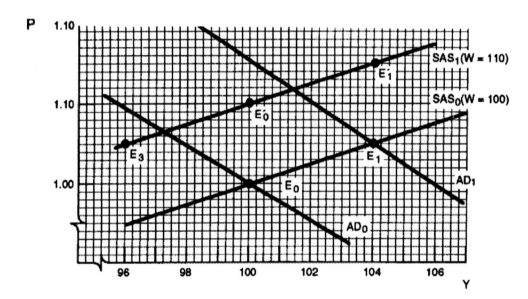

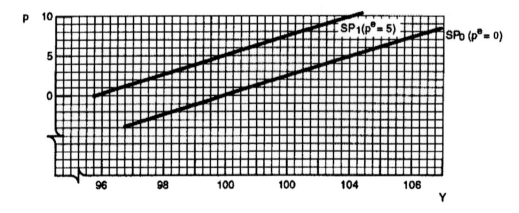

Figure 8B

a. p^e; 0

b. $P = 1.05$; $p = 5$; $p^e = 5$; $p^e = 1.10$; $W = 110$

c. The government would have to use restrictive monetary or fiscal policy to shift the AD curve to the left so that it passed through $P = 1.10$ and $Y = 100$.

It would have to shift the AD curve to the right through $P = 1.15$ and $Y = 104$.

$P = 1.05$; $Y = 96$

d.

Y	P	p	W/P
100	1.10	5	100.0
104	1.15	10	95.7
96	1.05	0	104.8

The expected inflation rate for this Phillips curve is higher than the expected rate for the original Phillips curve; thus, at every level of real GDP there will be a higher level of inflation along the new Phillips curve compared with the original curve.

e. The rate of inflation would continually accelerate. Note that in the first period the inflation rate at $Y = 104$ was 5 percent, and in the second period the inflation rate was 10 percent.

f. Since expected inflation of 5 percent actually occurred, workers would expect 5-percent inflation again and demand $W = 115$, which would shift SAS upward parallel to SAS_1 but through the Point $P = 1.15$ and $Y = 100$.

The SP curve would be the same as SP_1 since each would have $p^e = 5$.

g. At this Point $p = 10$ and $P = 1.15$, so workers would expect $p = 10$ and $P = 1.25$. They would therefore ask for $W = 125$. Hence, SAS would shift up through the Point $P = 1.25$ and $Y = 100$.

The SP curve would shift up parallel to SP_0 and SP_1 through the Point $p = 10$ and $Y = 100$.

h. A decrease; off; disequilibrium; pressure; rise.

Increase

Labor productivity increases over time.

The natural level of real GDP will grow over time.

i. The SP curve slopes upward because the SAS curve slopes upward. (If the SAS were horizontal, there would be no price increase as AD increased, and hence no inflation.) In classical or new-classical theory, the SAS curve slopes upward because firms' marginal cost curves slope upward. In new Keynesian theory, SAS slopes upward because some prices are set by fixed or variable price markups and some are set on auction markets.

The slope of the SP curve depends on the slope of the SAS curve. In classical and new-classical theory, the slope of SAS depends on the slope of firms' marginal cost curves, i.e., how fast marginal cost rises with output. In new Keynesian theory, the slope of SAS depends on the how much firms raise their markups as output expands, and on the proportion of prices that is determined in auction markets.

The position of the SP curve is fixed by the rate of inflation expected at the time wages and other input prices are negotiated.

Question 3

a. $X = 2,000$; $X = 2,080$; $X = 2,080$; $\%\Delta X = 4$; $X = 2,080.8$; $\%\Delta X = 4.04$

b.   Alternative A: $Y = 2,080$; $P = 1.00$; $x = 4$; $y = 4$

Alternative B: $Y = 2,039$; $P = 1.02$; $x = 4$; $y = 2$

Alternative C: $Y = 1,962$; $P = 1.06$; $x = 4$; $y = -2$

c.

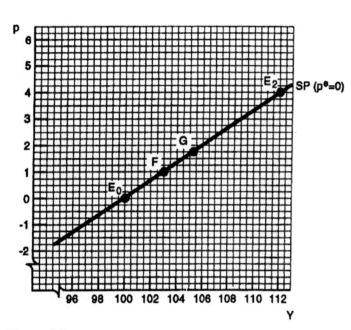

Figure 8C

(1) The economy is on the *SP* curve. (2) $x = p$, so that $y = 0$. (3) $p = p^e$.

d.   No. To get to $Y = 104$ will require $y = 4$, but since $x = 4$, this would also require $p = 0$. However, as we can see from the *SP* curve, the economy cannot get to $Y = 104$ unless $p = 1.33$.

$Y = 103$; $p = 1.00$

No. Two of the three conditions are not met: (1) $x \neq p$ ($x = 4$, while $p = 1$); (2) $p \neq p^e$ ($p^e = 0$, while $p = 1$).

e.   No. For $y = 3$, p must be 1; but to increase Y above 103, p must increase as the economy moves up the *SP* curve.

$Y = 105.3$; $p = 1.75$

f.   No. E_2 lies on the *SP* curve, and $x = p$; however, price expectations are incorrect, i.e., $p \neq p^e$ ($p^e = 0$, while $p = 4$).

Question 4

a.   Forward-looking expectations

b.   Backward-looking expectations

First, people may have no reason to believe that the change in nominal GDP growth is permanent; second, long-term wage and price contracts keep the inflation rate from responding immediately to changes in nominal GDP growth.

c.   adaptive expectations

	$j = 1$		$j = 0.6$	
Period	p^e	$p - p^e$	p^e	$p - p^e$
0	1.0	0	1.0	0
1	1.0	0.5	1.0	0.5
2	1.5	0	1.3	0.2
3	1.5	0	1.42	0.08
4	1.5	0.5	1.47	0.53
5	2.0	0.5	1.79	0.71
6	2.5	0	2.22	0.28

When $j = 1$, expected inflation catches up with actual inflation after one period.

d.   When $j < 1$, expected inflation does not catch up after one period but does get steadily closer to actual inflation if the inflation rate remains at the new level.

e.   The speeds of adjustment differ. When $j = 1$, adjustment to a new p occurs after one period; when $j < 1$, adjustment occurs over several periods.

Question 5

a. $j = 0$.

This would not be a realistic assumption if inflation has persisted for some time. In that case, it is likely that people would begin to expect inflation.

$p^e = p_{-1}$.

b.   The SP curve for Period 1 depends on p^e in Period 1. We are assuming that $p^e = p_{-1}$ and that $p_{-1} = 0$ in this case. Thus, the SP curve with $p^e = 0$ is the correct curve for the first two periods.

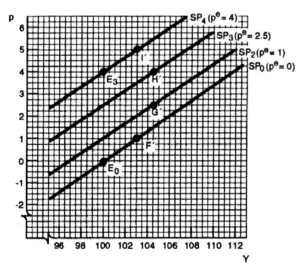

Figure 8D

$Y = 103; p = 1$

c.   In the last period, the inflation rate was 1 percent, so $p^e = 1$. We have to draw the SP curve (SP_2) with the parameter $p^e = 1$. The earlier SP curves assumed that $p^e = 0$.

$Y = 104.6; p = 2.5$

d. $p^e = 2.5$; $Y = 104.5$ (actually, 104.3); $p = 4.0$ (actually, 3.9)

e. SP_4 lies above SP_3 because expected inflation has increased from 2.5 to 4.
    $Y = 103.3$; $p = 5.1$

f   In Figure 8C, the SP curve was stable because people's expectations regarding the inflation rate remained constant. In this case, expectations change when $p \neq p^e$. As a result, the SP curve is constantly shifting.

g. The economy will head toward the Point $Y = 100$ and $p = 4$. This point would be a long-run equilibrium since when $x = 4$ and $p = 4$, $y = 0$ and Y will remain at 100.

h. If x remains equal to 4, the actual inflation rate would be greater than the expected inflation rate, and the SP curve would shift upward. There would be a rising inflation rate and a falling level of real GDP for a time. The path of the economy would eventually circle around Point E_3 and head toward that point.

Question 6

a. $x = 8$; Since the economy is in a long-run equilibrium, $x = p$ and $p = p^e$, so that $x = p^e$.

b. $y = -5$; -4; -3; -2; -1; 0; 1; 2.

c. The point is on the SP curve, but if $p = 6$, then y must equal -4 and Y would have to be 96, not 98. It is the equilibrium point because $p + y = x$, and it is on the SP curve.

d. SP_1 is not the appropriate curve for the second period because p^e has changed from 8 to 5, so SP must shift.

    If $p = 5$, p would equal p^e and the economy would be at Y^N.

e.

p	y	Y
3	−1	96
2	0	97
1	1	98

$p = 2$; $Y = 97$

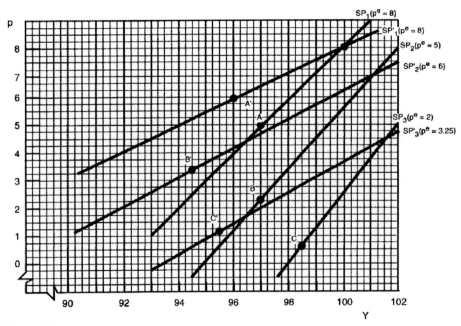

Figure 8E

f. $p^e = 2$; $p = 0.5$; $Y = 98.5$

Question 7

a. See Figure 8E.

b. $p = 6$; $Y = 96$

c. $p^e = 6$

p	y	Y
4	−2	94
3	−1	95
2	0	96

$Y = 94.8$; $p = 3.25$ (actually, 3.4)

d. $p^e = 3.25$

p	y	Y
2	0	94.8
1	1	95.8
0	2	96.8

$Y = 95.8$; $p = 1$

e. $Y = 100$; $p = 2$; cold-turkey

f. Question 7. The slope of SP is smaller in Question 7; a change in p of 1 percentage point causes a change in Y of 2, whereas the slope is one in Question 6.

Question 7; deeper; longer; more

g. Gradualism

x would be slowly (gradually) decreased.

Inflation decelerates more slowly, but real GDP does not fall as far; over time, the total output loss is about the same with both approaches.

The cold-turkey approach will lead to shorter and sharper recessions than will the gradualist approach; however, the cold-turkey approach might cause more disruption to businesses and workers.

Question 8

a.   endogenous; exogenous; exogenous

b.   adverse; sharp increase in oil or farm prices

c.   beneficial; sharp decrease in oil prices or large farm harvests

d.   The direct effect is the decrease in natural GDP.

It is called the direct effect because it is unavoidable and cannot be escaped through the use of monetary and fiscal policies.

The indirect effect is the aggravation of inflation and unemployment due to policy responses to the supply shock.

Question 9

a.   In a temporary supply shock, such as a crop failure, there is a temporary increase in prices followed by a return to the original level of prices. Consequently, a temporary supply shock is unlikely to cause any adjustment in the expected rate of inflation.

In a permanent supply shock, such as the OPEC oil price increases, the increase in prices is considered to be permanent, and there is a permanent change in relative prices. If the shock is considered to be a one-time increase in relative prices, there may not be any effect on the expected rate of inflation.

b.

Variable	Period 1	Period 2	Period 3
Price level	107	110	115
Inflation rate	7	3	5

c.

Variable	Period 1	Period 2	Period 3
Price level	107	112	117
Inflation rate	7	5	5

d.   will not; fall back to their original position; may not be

Question 10

a. long-run equilibrium.

Actual output is at the natural level, and the expected rate of inflation is equal to the actual rate of inflation.

SP: $p = 9 + 100[(Y/Y^N) - 1]$.

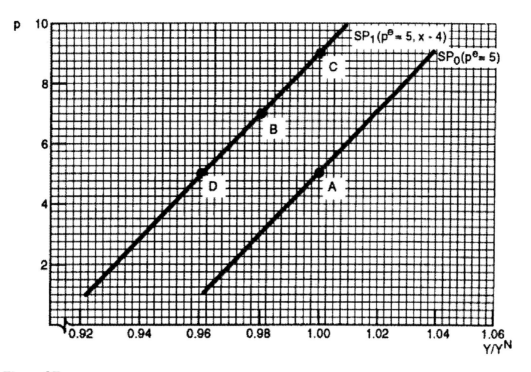

Figure 8F

$Y/Y^N = 0.98$; $p = 7$; short-run

$p + y$ must equal x. If $Y/Y^N = 0.98$, then $y = -2$. Therefore, when $x = 5$, $p = x - y = 5 + 2 = 7$.

b. neutral; accommodating; extinguishing; neutral; fell; rose

c. $x = 5 + 4 = 9$.

$Y/Y^N = 1.00$; $p = 9$; short-run

Although Y is at the natural level, the actual rate of inflation is greater than the expected rate. The movement of the economy will depend on how price expectations respond to the supply shock.

d. $x = 5 - 4 = 1$

$Y/Y^N = 0.96$; $p = 5$; long run

There would be no tendency for the economy to leave that point as long as the supply shock existed, since at Point D the actual and expected rates of inflation are the same.

e. $p = p^e + 100[(Y/Y^N) - 1]$.

SP would return to SP_0 if the expected inflation rate remained at 5 percent.

With COLAs, the one-period increase in inflation will be incorporated automatically into a faster growth of nominal wage rates next period.

The Fed could use an extinguishing policy in response to the initial impact of the supply shock; this policy would prevent any increase in inflation.

Although it would stop any increase in inflation, the extinguishing policy would decrease output and increase unemployment.

Question 11

a.   a drop in the relative price of energy or of imports; technological developments that lead to a sudden increase in productivity; price and wage controls

b. $x = 10$; $p^e = 10$; $Y/Y^N = 1.00$; $p = 10$; long-run

$p^e = p$, $x = p$, and $y = 0$

c.   downward.

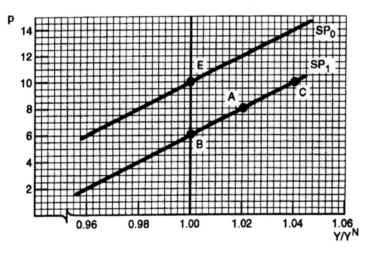

Figure 8G

d.   It would not change x; $Y/Y^N = 1.02$; $p = 8$

e.   It would lower x to 6; $Y/Y^N = 1.00$; $p = 6$

f.   It would raise x to 14 $(10 + 4)$; $Y/Y^N = 1.04$; $p = 10$

g.   An extinguishing policy best describes the policy because x increased from 8.0 in 1971:Q_2 to 11.6 in 1973:Q_1, in effect increasing GDP growth at the same time the SP curve was shifting downward.

h.   downward; below; accommodating

i.   will not; shift upward; E

j.   If the government were successful in reducing inflationary expectations, the policy might permanently decrease inflation.

Question 12

a.

Labor Force (000s)	Number of		Unemployment Rate (%)	Average Hours/ Employee	Productivity (Y/hr.)	Output (000s)	Y/Y^N
	Unemployed (000s)	Employed (000s)					
100	8	92	8	8	20	14,720	0.968
100	7	93	7	8	20	14,880	0.979
100	6	94	6	8	20	15,040	0.989
100	5	95	5	8	20	15,200	1.000
100	4	96	4	8	20	15,360	1.011

Y/Y^N changes by approximately one percentage point (0.01) in the opposite direction when the unemployment rate changes by one percentage point.

b.

Year	Y/Y^N	$U(U^N = 5)$	$U(U^N = 6)$	$U(U^N = 7)$
1	1.060	2.0	3	4
2	1.025	3.75	4.75	5.75
3	0.920	9	10	11.0
4	0.960	7	8	9

c. The answers to this question depend on the period chosen.

■ Chapter 9

Question 1

a.   The misery index is the inflation rate plus the unemployment rate.

They are the same because a one-percentage-point change in either changes the misery index by the same amount.

b.   decrease; inversely

c.   unemployment

Question 2

a.   Gordon defines hyperinflation as an inflation rate equal to or greater than 1,000 percent per year, or 22 percent per month.

b.   Argentina, Brazil, Nicaragua, Peru, Poland

c.   Most of these countries are now successfully managing their inflation rates.

Question 3

a. $M^sV = PY$ or $M^sV = X$. M^s is the nominal money supply; V is the velocity of money; P is the price level; Y is real GDP, and X is nominal GDP.

b. $m^s + v = p + y$, or $m^s + v = x$.

c. $X = PY; p = x - y$

d. $p = (x - y^N) - (y - y^N)$.

e. $y = y^N$.

f. $p = x - y^N$.

Yes. The equation says that the inflation rate is the amount by which nominal GDP growth exceeds natural real GDP growth.

g. $p = m^s + v - y^N$; $v = 0$; $p = m^s - y^N$

Yes. The equation says that the inflation rate is the amount by which the growth in the nominal money supply exceeds the growth in natural real GDP.

Question 4

a.   The nominal rate of interest is the rate actually observed in financial markets.

The expected real rate of interest is what people expect to pay on their borrowing or earn on their savings after deducting expected inflation.

$r^e = i - p^e$; 3%; 8%; 2%

b. $r = i - p$; 5%; 7%

Question 5

a.

Tom	Steve
$300	$300
—	300
312	312
—	312
300	—
$ 12	$ 0

b.   11 percent.

Tom	Steve
$300	$300
—	300
333	333
—	333
321	—
$ 12	$ 0

c.   Neither Tom nor Steve is better off (or worse off). Because the inflation was expected and all markets adapted perfectly to the expectation, the inflation had no effect on economic well-being.

d.   1. Inflation is universally and accurately anticipated.

    2. All savings are held in assets that earn the nominal interest rate.

    3. Only real (not nominal) interest income is taxable, and only the real cost of borrowing is tax deductible.

    4. An inflation of p^e percent raises the nominal interest rate for both saving and borrowing by exactly p^e percent above the no-inflation interest rate.

    5. Inflation raises the prices of all goods by the same percentage, i.e., relative prices are unaffected by inflation.

    All of the assumptions are invalid in the real world.

e.   –3 percent.

Tom	Steve
$300	$300
—	300
312	312
—	312
321	—
–$ 9	$ 0

f.   Tom is worse off; his savings are eroded by an unanticipated inflation.

g.   Steve's situation is the same as in Cases 1 and 2; both his assets and his debts are eroded by unanticipated inflation.

Question 6

a.

January 1	December 31
$250,000	$267,500
225,000	225,000
25,000	42,500
25,000	39,720

gain; $17,500; gain; $14,720

b.

January 1	December 31
$80,000	$76,000
72,000	72,000
8,000	4,000
8,000	4,211

loss; $4,000; loss; $3,789

c.   liabilities; assets; assets; liabilities

Question 7

a.   basic deficit; interest payments on outstanding bonds; iB; increases; bonds held by the public; B; high-powered money; H; the government budget constraint

b.   right; IS; in the money supply; right; LM

c.   remain unchanged; higher; crowding-out; supply of; decrease; increase; increase.

d.   The deficit will have a bigger impact on aggregate demand if the bonds are sold to the Fed. If bonds were sold to the public, there would be a crowding-out effect.

Selling bonds to the Fed would be the preferred alternative.

inflation to accelerate.

e.   Inflation aggravates government debt financing because inflation tends to raise interest rates, including government bond rates.

Inflation eases government debt financing because the government receives revenue from the inflating value of its high-powered money.

This revenue source is called *seignorage*.

Since the government pays only real interest on its debt, it gains by paying a lower real interest rate if the nominal interest rate rises by less than the rate of inflation.

Question 8

a. 1. Currency pays no interest.

2. The Fed does not pay interest on reserves.

3. There are costs for banks to service checking accounts; hence, checking accounts pay less than the market rate of interest one could receive by investment in an alternative security without check-writing privileges.

b. $r = i = 6$.

c. $i = 10$; shrink; $M^s/P = 200$; $i = 10$

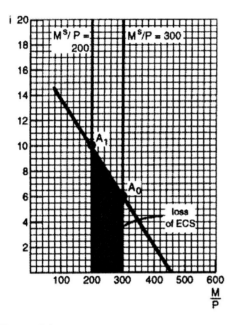

Figure 9A

d. extra convenience services; ECS = 6 percent; ECS = 10 percent; loss

e. ($100 billion)(0.06) + (0.5)($100 billion)(0.04) = $8 billion.

f. The loss comes about because businesses and households try harder to synchronize cash inflow and cash outflow; this requires the inconvenience of more frequent trips to make deposits and withdrawals. These trips use up shoe leather.

g. If financial assets had zero returns, then there would be no incentive to own assets alternative to money and there would be no shoe-leather costs. Alternatively, if interest (equal to the return on financial assets) were paid on money, there would be no incentive to own assets alternative to money.

Question 9

a. 7.5 percent; 7.5 percent for each type of worker; 5 percent for each type of worker

b.

Overall $U = 7.5\%$		Overall $U = 5\%$	
Required	U Rate (%)	Required	U Rate (%)
462.5	9.3	475	6.9
277.5	4.3	285	1.7
185.0	7.5	190	5.0
925.0	7.5	950	5.0

The market for engineers is very tight, especially at an overall unemployment rate of 5 percent.

There would probably be higher rates of wage changes in Part b than in Part a because one key industry would have very tight conditions, even at the fairly high overall unemployment rate in Part a.

c.

Overall $U = 7.5\%$		Overall $U = 5\%$	
Required	U Rate (%)	Required	U Rate (%)
462.50	7.5	475.0	5.0
286.75	4.4	294.5	1.8
175.75	12.1	180.5	9.8
925.00	7.5	950.0	5.0

The market for engineers is very tight; the market for teachers is quite loose, with a large surplus of workers.

There would probably be higher rates of wage changes in Part c than in Part a because of the tightness in the engineering market and in Part c because of both the looseness in the market for teachers and the tightness in the market for engineers.

d. mismatch or structural unemployment

Question 10

a. See the answer to the last question. The problem is that those who are mismatched don't get into other occupations. Among the reasons for this are inflexibility of relative wages, lack of incentives for firms to train workers, and discrimination.

b. The solutions to the problem fall into two general categories: First, alleviate the problem of lack of skills among workers. Second, improve the match between the location of workers and the location of jobs. Possible policies to solve the problem are training subsidies, modified minimum-wage legislation, better schooling, reduced discrimination, improved services of employment offices, and moving subsidies.

c. Turnover unemployment emphasizes that it takes time for a worker to find the job that is best for him or her; during this search period, the worker is classified as unemployed.

d. Both views agree that job openings and workers are diverse and must be matched up. Both views agree that there could be problems in making those matches.

e. The mismatch approach suggests that it is possible that no opening will be found for certain types of workers. The turnover approach emphasizes that although it might be difficult to make the match and that the process will take time, the match can eventually be made.

f. 1. Decrease in teenage population.
   2. Increase in prison population.
   3. Increase in the temporary help agencies.
   4. Invention of the World Wide Web.

■ Chapter 10

Question 1

a. Economic growth is measured by the annual growth rate of real GDP per person.

b.

Y	Y^N	Y/Y^N	$\%\Delta Y$
100	100.0	1.00	—
106	103.0	1.03	6.0
108	106.1	1.02	1.9
105	109.3	0.96	−2.8
112	112.6	0.99	6.7
116	115.9	1.00	3.6

For each year, Y would have been equal to Y^N.

less; less; greater, greater; economic growth; economic stabilization

c.

2%	5%	8%
1.0404	1.1025	1.1664
1.0612	1.1576	1.2597
1.0824	1.2155	1.3605
1.1041	1.2763	1.4693

d. Y for 1995: 440.8; 382.9; 331.2.

Ratio: 1.33; 1.16; 1.00.

33

e. 16.7 percent; 3 years

f. 2 percent: 35; 3 percent: 23; 5 percent: 14; 7 percent: 10

Question 2

a. $Y = 28$; $Y = 32$; $Y = 56$; a production function

b. $Y = 480$; $Y = 528$; $\%\Delta Y = 9.5$; $\%\Delta K = 19$; the elasticity of real GDP with respect to capital; 0.5; $Y = 540$; $\%\Delta Y = 11.8$; $\%\Delta L = 23.4$; 0.5

c. $Y = 640$; $\%\Delta Y = 28.6$; equal to

d. $K = 120$; $N = 307.2$; $Y = 588$; $\%\Delta Y = 20$; constant returns to scale

e.

Y	K/N	Y/N
480	2.56	4.80
600	4.00	6.00
300	1.00	3.00
576	0.56	2.25
768	1.00	3.00

f. $Y/N = 3(K/N)^{0.5}$

The values for Y/N are the same in both cases.

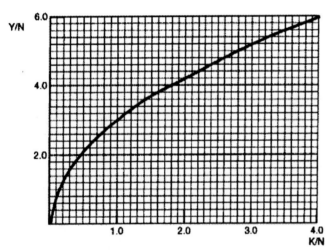

Figure 10A

g. Y increased from 300 to 768; Y/N remained the same (3.0); K; N; K/N; remain unchanged

Question 3

a. ΔK is the change in the capital stock from one period to the next, i.e., net investment.

dK is the amount of capital that is being replaced to keep the capital stock at its original level, i.e., replacement investment or depreciation.

Gross investment is net investment plus depreciation.

b.   The steady state is a situation in which Y and K grow at the same rate so that Y/K is fixed.

constant; K/N is constant; same rate as; equal to

c. $S = (n + d)K$ $sY = (n + d)K$ $sY/N = (n + d)K/N$.

total national saving per person; amount of steady-state investment per person

Capital per person (K/N) will grow until the steady-state level of output is reached.

decreases; diminishing returns to capital along the production function

d.

Table 10E

Period	*K*	*N*	*K/N*	*Y*	*Y/N*	*Y/K*	*k*	*n*
0	100.00	100.00	1.00	25.00	0.2500	0.2500	—	—
1	103.00	103.00	1.00	25.75	0.2500	0.2500	0.03	0.03
2	108.15	106.09	1.02	26.78	0.2524	0.2476	0.05	0.03
Steady State	—	—	1.96	—	0.3500	0.1786	0.03	0.03

Yes. *K/N* and *Y/N* are growing at the same rate (zero), and *Y/K* is constant.

e. $S = \Delta K + dK$ $\Delta K = S - dK$ $\Delta K/K = (sY/K) - d$ $k = (sY/K) - d$ $k - n = (sY/K) - (d + n)$.

equal to; $k - n = 0.20(0.2500) - (0.03 + 0.02) = 0$

f. $sY = \Delta K + dK$ $\Delta K = sY - dK$. Hence, $\Delta K = (0.28)(25.75) - (0.02)(103) = 5.15$. Hence, $K = 103 + 5.15 = 108.15$.

The level of *K/N* will continue to rise. Output will increase but at a diminishing rate as the economy moves along the production function.

g. growth rate of population; will not; will

It will be greater than the rate of population increase during the period of adjustment from one steady state to the next steady state.

Question 4

a. *Y/N* has risen significantly in those countries; technological change

b. 3%

Table 10F

Period	*K*	Population	*N*	*K/N*	*Y*	*Y/N*	*Y/K*	*Y/Pop*
0	100	100	100	1.0	25.00	0.25	0.25	0.2500
1	103	101	103	1.0	25.75	0.25	0.25	0.2549
2	106	102	106	1.0	26.50	0.25	0.25	0.2598

c. remains unchanged; rises; slower; labor-augmenting

d. capital; neutral technological change; increase

The change in output could be included in the production function by allowing *A* to increase.

e.

Table 10G

Period	*K*	*N*	*A*	*K/N*	*Y*	*Y/N*	*Y/K*
0	100.0	100.0	0.2500	1.00	25.00	0.2500	0.25
1	106.0	103.0	0.2536	1.03	26.50	0.2573	0.25
2	112.4	106.1	0.2576	1.06	28.10	0.2651	0.25
3	119.1	109.3	0.2610	1.09	29.78	0.2730	0.25

f. Both remained constant; both are increasing

In both cases, *Y/N* and *K/N* are increasing at the same rate, which allows *Y/K* to remain fixed.

Question 5

a. A; *K*; *N*

b. Gordon calls *a* multifactor productivity growth.

Conditions, other than changes in capital and labor, that change productivity. Examples are urbanization, economies of scale, environmental degradation, government regulations, crime, and technological change.

It explained 7/8 of the growth of output per hour of work

Question 6

a. Technological change is exogenous to Solow's model, yet it is usually the greatest contributor to economic growth. There is no consideration of market incentives for inventors or research workers to generate technological change. Also, since technological knowledge should be available to all countries, we should observe that countries' per capita incomes converge over time. Empirically, this is not the case, however.

b. The determinants of per-capita growth are *A*, multifactor productivity, the capital-labor ratio, *K/N*, and *b*, the output elasticity of the capital input. (The output elasticity of the labor input, $1 - b$, is implicitly a determinant of growth, also.)

Capital-labor ratios. (The output elasticity, *b*, is also the share of output going to capital, and *A* is the parameter representing technology. By assumption, *b* and *A* are the same for both countries, so any difference in the countries' growth rates must be attributable to differences in their capital-labor ratios.)

The capital-labor ratios must differ by a factor of 10,000. To see this, solve the per-capita production function for $K/N = (Y/NA)^{1/b}$. If $A = 1$ and $b = 0.25$, then $K/N = (Y/N)^4$. Let $Y/N = 10$ for the rich country, then $K/N = 10^4 = 10,000$.

c. Poor-country $MP_K = 0.25$. ($MP_K = 1(0.25)(1)^{-0.75} = 0.25$.); Rich-country $MP_K = 0.00025$. ($MP_K = 1(0.25)(10,000)^{-0.75} = 0.25.(0.001) = 0.00025$.)

Investment in the poor country would yield more output per unit of new capital.

Capital would flow from the rich country to the poor country.

No

d. Human capital is the existing stock of a nation's human knowledge. Gordon also defines it as the value, for a person or a society as a whole, of the extra future earnings made possible by education. Physical capital is the existing stock of a nation's structures and business equipment.

An economy accumulates physical capital by positive net investment (either by foreigners or domestically).

An economy accumulates human capital by acquiring educated and well-trained residents through immigration and by adding to the stock of human knowledge residing in the country, e.g., by education, training, and research.

Physical capital is likely to accumulate faster. Financial flows to support the acquisition of physical capital can occur overnight, and flows of physical capital, depending on the nature of the capital, can also occur quickly. Human capital, aside from migration, requires years to accumulate as citizens become better educated and trained and while research activity grows.

Rich countries have greater stocks of human capital than poor countries. Consequently, even if the capital stocks were the same, which they are not, the poor countries' economies would still not grow as fast as the rich countries' economies, and their standards of living would remain lower for some time.

e. $Y/N = (K/N)^b (H/N)^c$

contribution of uneducated labor $= 1 - b - c = 1 - 0.25 - 0.60 = 0.15$

$K/N = (Y/N)^{1/0.85} \cong 15$

Question 7

No. Immigrant incomes increase rapidly when they move from poor countries to rich countries. Many immigrants rapidly achieve the same average living standard as native residents of rich countries. If human capital alone was the key to faster growth, the incomes of immigrants would not increase as rapidly. Some other factors at work in the rich country cause this to happen.

Endogenous growth theory focuses on how rich countries use ideas and techniques to produce more and better goods per person. These ideas work within a context of appropriate physical and human capital and cannot simply be transplanted to any location. For this reason people from poor countries can migrate to such an economy and experience significant increases in income.

■ Chapter 11

Question 1

a. Labor productivity = (Y/N) where N = hours of work

Standard of living = (Y/Q) where Q = population

$y - n, y - q$

If $n < q$, then the number of hours of work is growing more slowly than population. When $n < q$ the standard of living grows more slowly than labor productivity.

In Europe over the past few decades, people have taken longer vacations, and experienced higher unemployment and lower participation rates.

b. $y = a + bk + (1 - b)n$

$a = y - bk - (1 - b)n = (y - n) - b(k - n)$

multifactor productivity growth.

Conditions, other than changes in capital and labor, that change productivity. Examples are urbanization, economies of scale, environmental degradation, government regulations, crime, and technological change.

If $k = n$ then there is no change in K/L. However, if $k > n$ the ratio of capital to labor increases and a is smaller than $y - n$, i.e. MFP growth will be lower than the growth of labor productivity.

c. $1 - b = WN/PY = (W/P) \times (N/Y) = (W/P)/(Y/N)$ where W/P is the real wage and Y/N is output per unit of labor. The growth rate of $1 - b = (w - p) - (y - n)$. If the growth rate of labor's share is zero, then $(w - p) = (y - n)$.

at the same rate as

Question 2

does not, has not, is not

a. Copy modern products made in rich countries, purchase imported machinery that embodies the latest technology, obtain investment by foreign firms.

b. Political/Legal environment (political capital), infrastructure, geographical location.

c. $Y = A(G, P, T) F(K, R, H, N)$

Three new exogenous factors have been introduced: political capital (P), infrastructure capital (R), and geography (G). Because political capital and geography affect the entire production process they are specified as determinants of A along with technology (T). Infrastructure capital (R) is like physical capital and is specified in the same way.

Question 3

lower growth rate for capital per labor hour, higher relative prices of energy and raw materials, a reduction in the quality of the labor force, inadequate public investment in infrastructure, specific productivity problems particular to each of a number of different industries, and the depletion hypothesis.

Question 4

a. Productivity shocks which decrease demand for labor given the supply of labor will lead to a lower real wage rate.

b. Productivity shocks can also include changes which increase the supply of labor. Given the existing demand for labor, an increase in supply will lower the real wage rate and lead employers to hire more workers until the productivity of labor has fallen to the same level as the real wage.

c.

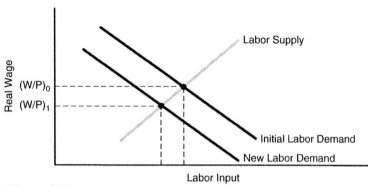

Figure 11A

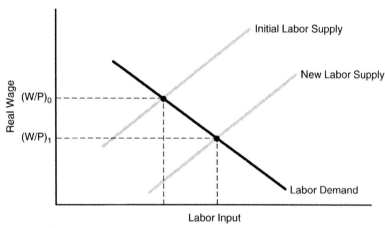

Figure 11B

d. Since 1973 the growth of the capital stock has slowed and the growth of labor hours has increased. The combined effect reduced capital per labor hour and possibly labor productivity.

Question 5

a. 3 percent per year, 1 percent, 1.5 percent, 2 percent, 1.8 percent

b. Solow's Paradox refers to Robert Solow's comment that "we can see the computer age everywhere except in the productivity statistics." The resurgent labor productivity growth proved the missing statistical evidence.

c. inflation, the budget deficit, the productivity slowdown, and the business cycle

d. Skeptics argued that 40 percent growth in computer investment could not be sustained, and that actual real GDP could not continue to grow faster than natural real GDP growth. By early 2000 investment in computer equipment had turned to negative growth. In 2001 productivity growth fell from 4 percent in the previous year to little more than 1 percent.

■ Chapter 12

Question 1

a.

Table 12A

Variable	1	2	3
Consumption	800	800	880
Investment	140	300	300
Government expenditure	560	400	320
Planned expenditure	1,500	1,500	1,500
Private saving	200	200	220
Government budget surplus	−60	100	80
National saving	140	300	300

Yes

b. A decrease in the interest rate to 5 percent.

No. If policymakers used monetary policy alone to lower the interest rate to 5 percent, output would rise to 2,300 (above Y^N); if only fiscal policy were used, output would fall to 500 (below Y^N).

interest rate; fiscal

c. national saving

Yes

1. private saving;
2. government saving

d.

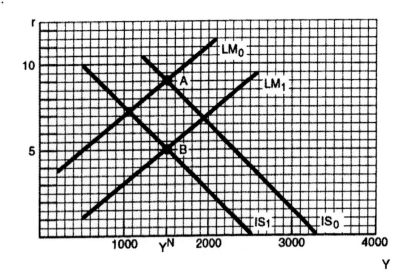

Figure 12A

160; government; 160

e. IS_1 is the same as IS_0 because A_p is the same in each case.

160; 20; 140

f. tight; easy

g. Probably Case 2. In Cases 2 and 3, investment is 300, but government spending is greater in Case 2. If some of the government spending cut in moving from Case 2 to Case 3 is investment, then the rate of growth in Case 2 would be greater than that of Case 3. Since in Case 2 the level of investment is greater than that in Case 1, Case 2 would probably lead to a higher rate of growth than would Case 1. The size of the difference between Cases 1 and 2 depends on the type of government spending that is cut from Case 1.

Question 2

a. lending to

Positive net exports by a country generate a flow of foreign income which upon being invested in foreign countries become an equal amount of net foreign investment.

b. Investment would have been even lower. Negative net exports imply negative net foreign investment, i.e., foreign borrowing. Foreign capital inflows into the United States helped fund U.S. investment.

c. Again, investment would have been lower since national saving was not sufficient to fund U.S. investment in that year.

Question 3

a. The consumption ratio decreases.

Year	Alternative 1 Y	C	Alternative 2 Y	C
0	100.0	95.0	100.0	95.0
1	104.0	98.8	104.0	93.6
2	108.2	102.8	108.2	97.4
3	112.5	106.9	115.8	104.2
4	117.0	111.2	123.9	111.5
5	121.7	115.6	132.5	119.3
6	126.5	120.2	141.8	127.6
7	131.6	125.0	151.8	136.6

780.5; 790.2

We can't tell for sure. Under Alternative 2, total consumption is greater over the seven-year period, but the increases all come in the fourth year and later. We must learn whether or not consumers are willing to cut back in the first three years to receive the later benefits.

b. We would know that members of that society would be willing to pay $1.06 to obtain a good today that they could have had for $1.00 one year from now; or alternatively, they would be willing to give up $1.00 today if they received $1.06 a year from now.

A rough approximation would be the real return earned on relatively risk-free investments, such as government bonds and savings accounts.

c. The rate of return on capital measures the extra output produced from a new capital good expressed as a fraction of the cost of that capital good.

The rate of investment would be too small. If society gave up a dollar's worth of consumption today, it could produce enough additional output next year to compensate savers at their rate of time preference and still have some output left over.

d. The United States now saves too little. The real rate of return on private investment has been around 12 percent, while the real interest rate paid to savers has been around 5 percent.

e. Private saving; larger; tighter

It must choose a looser monetary policy to keep output at $Y = Y^N$. If it did not follow the correct monetary policy, $Y \neq Y^N$. Inflation would accelerate if $Y > Y^N$, or a recession might occur if $Y < Y^N$.

Consumption; A tax policy that increased taxes on consumption goods or reduced transfer payments would best induce private investment.

f. Elimination of the corporate income tax, or indexation of the corporate income tax system.

If there were some inflation during the year, the real return would be less than the nominal return; however, taxpayers have to pay tax on the nominal return in an unindexed system. Thus, there is less incentive to save.

g. The saving rates depend on the dates used.

Question 4

a. Stabilization: The correct deficit or surplus ensures that $Y = Y^N$.

Economic Growth: Since private saving tends to be too small, a government surplus might be necessary to encourage more investment.

b. The government will make annual payments to cover the interest and a final payment on the principal at the bond's maturity.

If the government has spent its funds on productive public investments, future output and income will be higher. This would make servicing the government debt easier.

In the private case, the revenues earned from the additional output are paid voluntarily by those receiving the output. In the public case, higher future taxes might not be paid by those receiving the benefits of the government spending; therefore, there may be some redistribution of income.

c. 0.225; $6.75 billion; $231.75 billion; $1,040 billion; 0.223; fallen

d. $9 billion; $234 billion; $1,025 billion; 0.228; risen

The economy's growth rate of output and real income equals or exceeds its real interest rate.

Question 5

a. 1. The ratio increases during wars.
    2. The ratio increases during recessions because of automatic stabilization.

b. The debt/GDP ratio increased even though there was neither a war nor a recession.

c. It stabilized from 1994 to 1995, fell slightly from 1996 to 1997, and fell sharply during 1998–2001. The return of deficit in 2002–05 ended the decline in the ratio and began a new period in which the ratio increased each year.

■ Chapter 13

Question 1

a. 1. Money is a medium of exchange;

    2. Money is a store of value.

b. Checking deposits (transaction deposits): medium of exchange; money market deposit accounts: store of value; Traveler's checks: medium of exchange

c.

Item	M_1	M_2
Transactions (checking) accounts	yes	yes
Savings certificates (under $100,000)	no	yes
Gold	no	no
Money-market mutual funds	no	yes
Currency	yes	yes
Treasury bills	no	no
Traveler's checks	yes	yes
Savings deposits	no	yes
Commercial paper	no	no
Money-market deposit accounts	no	yes

Medium of exchange; Store of value, although much of M_2 can be used as a medium of exchange. M_2 is more inclusive and less subject to close substitution.

d. The development of interest-bearing transaction accounts increased the demand for M_1 as people shifted funds to savings accounts, but also made demand for M_1 more unstable because M_1 excludes some assets that are very similar to interest-bearing transaction accounts. The development of money market mutual funds reduced the demand for M_1.

e. The answers depend on the period covered.

Question 2

a.

Assets		Liabilities	
Required reserves	500	Deposits owed to settlers	5,000
Excess reserves	4,500		
Total assets	5,000	Total liabilities	5,000

b. 4,500 star credits; 4,500 star credits

Assets		Liabilities	
Required reserves	950	Deposits – settlers	5,000
Excess reserves	4,050	Deposits – cooper	4,500
Loan – vintner	4,500		
Total assets	9,500	Total liabilities	9,500

The proceeds of the loan were redeposited in the First World Bank. Most of this amount (90 percent) once again becomes excess reserves, for only 10 percent of the amount is needed as required reserves.

c.   40,500

Assets		Liabilities	
Required reserves	5,000	Deposits – settlers	5,000
Excess reserves	0	Deposits – cooper	4,500
Loan – vintner	4,500	Deposits – Galactic	40,500
Loan – logician	40,500		
Total assets	50,000	Total liabilities	50,000

d.   No. All of the reserves are being used as required reserves. There are no excess reserves.

10 percent

e.   1.   Bank money (deposits transferable by check) must be accepted as a means of payment *equivalent* to coin and currency.

2.   Any seller who receives the proceeds of a loan in coin or currency must redeposit it in his or her account at the same bank.

3.   Any seller who receives payment in the form of a check must redeposit it in his or her account at the same bank.

4.   The bank must hold cash reserves equal to some fraction of deposits.

5.   Someone must be willing to borrow from the bank at interest rates that will cover the bank's costs of operation.

Question 3

a.   The reserve requirement might be set by law, e.g., by the Fed in the United States. Even if there were not a *legal* reserve requirement, prudent banking practice would lead banks to hold some fraction of deposits in the form of a reserve to protect against sudden withdrawals by depositors.

High-powered money is the total amount of currency held by the non-bank public and other forms of money that qualify as legal bank reserves.

$$H = 5,000; \quad e = 10\%; \quad D = H/e; \quad 50,000 = 5,000/0.1$$

b.   33,333; 6.67; decreases; increases

c.   No. The second bank will gain the reserves that the first bank lost and will continue the money-creation process. The total reserves in the banking system do not change.

d.   Demand $= eD + cD$; Supply $= H$; $D = H/(e + c)$; $D = 5,000/0.2 = 25,000$

e. cD; $H/(e + c)$; $(1 + c)H/(e + c)$

f. $M = 5,250/0.2 = 26,250$; 25,000; 1,250

g. $(1 + c)/(e + c)$; $5.25 = 1.05/0.2$

Question 4

a. 1. *H* is controlled by the Fed and perhaps by banks through borrowing from the Fed.

 2. *e* is controlled by the Fed and perhaps by commercial banks if they hold excess reserves.

 3. *c* is controlled by the public.

b. 1. open-market operations influence *H*

 2. discount rate influences *H*

 3. reserve requirements influence *e*

c. open-market operations; government securities; *H* increases; *H* decreases; the Federal Open Market Committee

d.

Federal Reserve Banks		Commercial Banks	
Assets	**Liabilities**	**Assets**	**Liabilities**
Government securities 25	Commercial bank deposits 25	Reserve deposits at Fed 25	Deposits owed to security dealers 25

e.

Assets		Liabilities	
Required reserves	25	Original deposit	25
Excess reserves	0	New deposits	225
New loans	225		
Total assets	250	Total liabilities	250

f. *H* would decline by $8 million as a result of the sale (which is also a purchase by banks and/or the public). There would be a drop in deposits (and the money supply) of $80 million.

g. discount rate; discourage; encourage; increase *H*.

h. The answers to this question depend on the period chosen.

i. The Fed has been criticized because in periods of high interest rates it has tended to keep its discount rate low enough to induce substantial borrowing by banks; this tends to reduce the precision of the Fed's day-to-day control over *H*.

j. reserve requirements; *e*; reduce; increase

k. It will tend to increase the Fed's control over the money supply because it now allows the Fed to control all transactions deposits, which are very close substitutes for demand deposits at member commercial banks. Previously, the Fed did not have any authority over these deposits.

Question 5

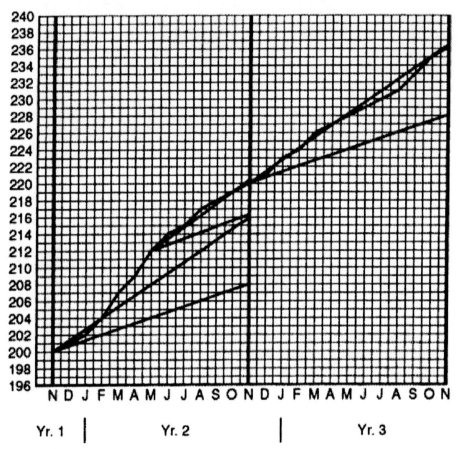

Figure 13A

a.   208; 216

b.   216.24; 220.48; Yes

c.   228.8; 236.7

d.   233.28; 236; Yes; Because the base from which the percentage increases were calculated was raised.

Question 6

a.   The *LM* curve will be a vertical line; remain constant

b.   identity;
    1. *M*: money supply;
    2. *V*: velocity of money;
    3. *P*: price level (GDP deflator);
    4. *Y*: real output

Economic units hold money because receipts and expenditures are not perfectly synchronized.

c. constant

The increase in the money supply will cause a temporary excess supply of money; this situation will lead to an increase in spending (PY) until the new higher amount of money is the desired fraction $(1/V^{*})$ of the new higher level of spending.

d. P; Y

1. Weak version: A change in the money supply causes a proportional change in nominal income in the same direction.

2. Strong version: Same as the weak version regarding nominal income, but it adds that almost all of the adjustment in nominal income takes the form of changing prices, and none or almost none, takes the form of changing output.

e. 1. decrease;

2. increase;

3. increase;

4. no change

Question 7

a. People hold money to bridge the interval between the receipt of income and its disbursement.

directly; the economy's total nominal income (PY); $L_1(PY)$

b. fall; rise; higher; rose; gain; rise; fall; loss; bonds; money

c. $1/0.3 = 33.33$; $1/0.5 = 20$; $1/0.01 = 100$; gain; $13.33; loss; $-$66.67

d. $L_2(r)$.

e. $M = L_1(PY) + L_2(r)$

f. The main problem is the idea that speculative money holding occurs only because some investors think that the interest rate is below normal (so bond prices are above nominal). This cannot explain why the demand for money remains high over a long period that would allow investors to revise their idea of the normal rate of interest.

Question 8

a. Savings deposits at commercial banks, savings and loan associations, mutual savings banks, and similar thrift institutions would also satisfy the speculative motive.

b. Broker's fees would include the time and transportation expense required to make an extra trip to the savings bank to obtain cash from a savings deposit; they would also include any charge that would have to be paid to a broker to make the transfer.

$Y = \$2,000$; $T = 2$; $C = \$1000$; 8

c. 1. $r = 0.00416667$, or 0.416667%; $C = \$979.80$; 2.04

2. $r = 0.00666667$, or 0.666667%; $C = \$774.60$; 2.58

3. $C = \$692.82$; 2.89

4. $C = \$547.72$; 3.65

d.   reduce; reduce

These developments reduce the cost of transferring funds from savings accounts into checking accounts. They therefore reduce the optimal amount of cash to be obtained in each transaction (C), thereby reducing the demand for money.

Question 9

a.   The change in real output due to a change in the interest rate; steeper; less

1.   Introduction of money market certificates. When treasury-bill interest rates increase, money market certificate rates increase by about as much, reducing disintermediation.

2.   Removal of the ceiling interest rate that banks and thrift institutions could pay on deposits. Banks and thrift institutions are now able to pay market interest rates, eliminating disintermediation.

3.   Growth of secondary markets for financial instruments backed by mortgages. Thrift institutions now have a steady supply of mortgage funds and do not have to restrict mortgages when interest rates rise.

4.   Adjustable rate mortgage. Potential home buyers are less likely to postpone buying when interest rates are high; with an adjustable rate mortgage initially at the high rate, home buyers know that the mortgage rate will fall with a fall in overall interest rates.

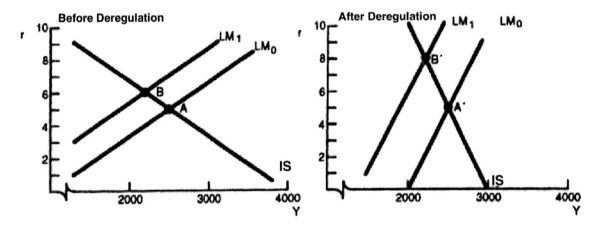

Figure 13B

b. $Y = 1,000 + 300r$; steeper

Before deregulation, when interest rates rose, the gap between interest on nonmonetary assets and money rose and individuals would reduce their holdings of money. Now, since some forms of money pay interest, a rise in the interest rate leads to a smaller gap between nonmonetary assets and money, leading to a smaller reduction in money holdings.

$Y = 2,000 + 100r$

c. $Y = 2,500$; $r = 5$; $Y = 2,500$; $r = 5$

d.   200; $Y = 400 + 300r$; $Y = 2,200$; $r = 6$

e.   700; $Y = 1,400 + 100r$; $Y = 2,200$; $r = 8$

f.   steeper, steeper; larger; deregulation of the financial markets

Question 10

a.

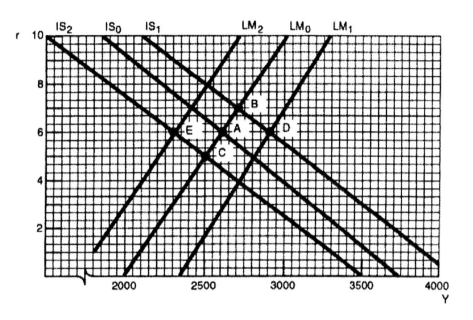

Figure 13C

$Y = 2,600$; $r = 6$

b.   The *LM* curve remains unchanged.

c. $Y = 2,700$; $r = 7$; $\Delta Y = 100$; $\Delta r = 1$

d. $Y = 2,500$; $r = 5$; $\Delta Y = -100$; $\Delta r = -1$

e. $Y = 2,900$; $r = 6$; $\Delta Y = 300$; $\Delta r = 0$

f. $Y = 2,300$; $r = 6$; $\Delta Y = -300$; $\Delta r = 0$

g.   money supply; interest rate.

h. $Y = 2,600$; $r = 7.5$; $\Delta Y = 0$; $\Delta r = 1.5$

i. $Y = 2,600$; $r = 4.5$; $\Delta Y = 0$; $\Delta r = -1.5$

j.   better; better

The major disadvantage is that a policy of countercyclical changes in the money supply causes a wider variation in interest rates than either of the other two policies.

k.   *LM* shifts left; *LM* shifts right

l.   2,400 and 2,800, 7 and 5; LM_2; increase; LM_1; decrease; Real GDP will remain at 2,600.

m.   better than; They are the same.

n.   In this case, neither a fixed money supply nor a fixed interest rate will work as well as countercyclical changes in the money supply.

■ Chapter 14

Question 1

a. Both groups have the same basic model of aggregate supply.

   They disagree on the sources of instability in the economy and on the effect of policy on aggregate demand.

b. One; real GDP; interest rate; monetary; fiscal; real GDP; interest rate; the natural rate of unemployment; a rising inflation rate; the natural rate of unemployment; manpower policy

c. (1) *S*; (2) *T*; (3) *I*; (4) *E*; (5) *T*; (6) *R*; (7) *I*; (8) *S*; (9) *E*; (10) *T*; (11) *I*; (12) *R*; (13) *E*; (14) *T*; (15) *E*; (16) *I*; (17) *S*; (18) *T*; (19) *I*; (20) *T*; (21) *E*; (22) *I*; (23) *S*; (24) *T*; (25) *S*; (26) *I*

d. Rules advocates propose a constant growth-rate rule (CGRR) for the money supply.
   1. Ability to make perfect forecasts of future changes in the private demand for and supply of goods and services.
   2. Ability to make perfect forecasts of the future effect of current changes in monetary and fiscal policy.
   3. Possession by policymakers of policy instruments that powerfully affect aggregate demand.
   4. No costs of changing policy instruments.
   5. No political constraints on use of policy instruments for the desired purposes.

Question 2

a. 1. demand shocks; erratic government policy; stable.
   2. stable; demand for money.
   3. planned private; demand for money; completely stable; monetary and fiscal policy; more harm than good.
   4. not completely flexible; wander away; the natural level of real GDP; short run; increased flexibility; longer

b. (1) 3; (2) 1; (3) *None*; (4) 4; (5) *None*; (6) 2; (7) *None*; (8) 1; (9) 2; (10) *None*; (11) 3; (12) 3;

c. (1) 3; (2) 4; (3) 2; (4) 1

Question 3

a. The answers to this question depend on the period chosen.

b. The answers to these questions depend on the answers to Part a above.

c. This is difficult to answer because the current behavior of these variables is not independent of the fiscal and monetary policies chosen in the past. However, to the extent that government spending is more volatile than the others, the rules advocates position is strengthened, and vice versa.

Question 4

a. 1. Lags prevent monetary changes from influencing the economy until it is too late.
   2. The extra fluctuations in the interest rate caused by an activist policy are undesirable.

   Yes

   The issue of lags is relevant for a nominal GDP target, but the issue of interest-rate volatility would not always be relevant if the source of instability were the demand for money.

b. 1. Data lag: Policymakers do not know what is going on in the economy the moment something happens.

2. Recognition lag: The usual rule of thumb is to wait and see if a trend continues for three months before acting.

3. Legislative lag: The period of time that passes until the next meeting of the FOMC at which policy can be determined.

4. Transmission lag: The time interval between the policy decision and the subsequent change in policy instruments.

5. Effectiveness lag: The length of time required for a change in the money supply to influence real output.

19 months.

Question 5

a.

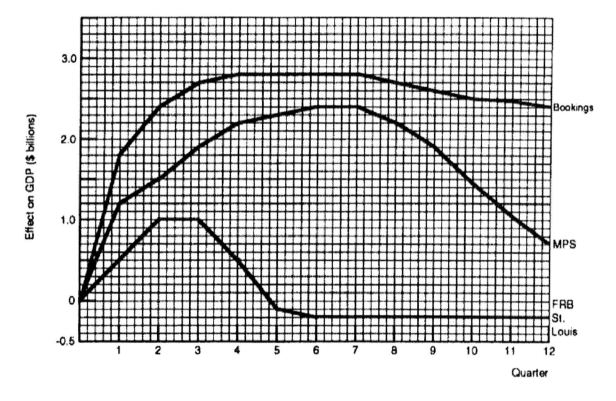

Figure 14B

b. After four quarters: Brookings, 56; MPS, 44; St. Louis FRB, 10

After eight quarters: Brookings, 54; MPS, 44; St. Louis FRB, –4

After twelve quarters: Brookings, 48; MPS, 14; St. Louis FRB, –4

c. The St. Louis FRB model most supports the rules advocates' position. It has a very small multiplier for fiscal policy, which becomes negative in the fifth quarter because of the high rate of crowding out.

The Brookings model best supports the activist case. It has the largest multiplier for fiscal policy, and the multiplier remains high throughout the entire twelve-quarter period.

Question 6

a. Feedback policy rules set stabilization policy to respond in a regular way to macroeconomic events, such as unemployment or inflation.

b. Zero.

    CGRR is a rigid-rule policy and allows the public to form accurate expectations about the future price level.

c. Zero.

    No, not if the public is able to see that the policymakers systematically act according to the feedback rule.

d. The rigid rule and the feedback policy are equivalent.

e. Time inconsistency describes the temptations of policymakers to deviate from a credible policy once it is announced.

    A rigid rule would be best since it would prevent any deviation from the announced policy due to time inconsistency.

f. A central invests in its reputation if it consistently succeeds in avoiding the temptation to boost monetary growth to reduce unemployment.

    This will convince private decisionmakers that a future upsurge in inflation is unlikely. Private decisionmakers will adjust their inflationary expectations downward, and the central bank can achieve lower, or even zero inflation, without recession.

Question 7

a. A fixed exchange rate target precludes the central bank from stimulating money supply growth because such a policy will lead to a drop in the exchange rate.

b. lower, lower, lower

c. It suggests that fixed exchange rates tend to reduce the average inflation rate in the future.

■ Chapter 15

Question 1

a. A consumption function shows a systematic relationship between disposable income and consumption.

The marginal propensity to consume is the ratio of *changes* in consumption to *changes* in disposable income (i.e., $\Delta C/\Delta(Y-T)$).

The average propensity to consume is the ratio of *total* consumption to *total disposable* income (i.e., $C/(Y-T)$).

APC + APS = 1.

b.

	Alternative 1			Alternative 2	
C	APC	APS	*C*	APC	APS
90	0.9	0.1	90	0.90	0.10
108	0.9	0.1	104	0.87	0.13
126	0.9	0.1	118	0.84	0.16
117	0.9	0.1	111	0.85	0.15
99	0.9	0.1	97	0.88	0.12
81	0.9	0.1	83	0.92	0.08
90	0.9	0.1	90	0.90	0.10

Expansion: Q_1 through Q_3; Recession: Q_3 through Q_6

The APC = 0.9 and the APS = 0.1 during all periods under Alternative A.

APC and APS fluctuate over the cycle under Alternative B. In the expansion, APC is decreasing and APS is increasing; in the recession, APC is increasing and APS is decreasing.

Alternative A is called a proportionate consumption function because consumption is always the same proportion of income, i.e., APC is constant. Alternative B is nonproportionate because consumption is not always the same proportion of income, i.e., APC fluctuates.

c. A cross-section consumption function relates the level of consumption to income for individuals in different income groups at a given time.

nonproportionate

d. A time-series consumption function measures the relationship between total consumption and total income for an entire economy over a period of time.

remained relatively constant

proportionate

Question 2

a. This year's permanent income is equal to last year's permanent income, modified by the amount by which this year's current income differs from last year's permanent income.

When $j = 0$, this year's permanent income equals last year's permanent income; any difference between permanent income and current income is ignored.

When $j = 1$, permanent income is always revised to equal the actual income of the current year.

Neither $j = 0$ nor $j = 1$ is likely. It is more likely that *some* (but not all) weight will be given to differences between previous permanent income and current income, i.e., a value of j between 0 and 1.

Permanent income in the current period is a weighted average of this year's actual income and last year's permanent income.

b. $23,200; $25,120; $26,272; $26,963

Actual income for each year is constant at $28,000; the individual will begin to expect this level of income and will gradually revise permanent income toward this amount.

c. $C = kY_{-1}^P + kj(Y - Y_{-1}^P)$

$C = 0.8\,Y_{-1}^P + 0.32(Y - Y_{-1}^P)$

$C = 0.8Y$

d.

$Y - Y_{-1}^P$	Y^P	C
$6,000	$22,400	$17,920
7,600	25,440	20,352
−7,440	22,464	17,971

$1,920; $2,400; 0.8; 1,920/6,000 = 0.32$

e.   Since the change in permanent income is smaller than the change in actual income, the MPC out of permanent income has to be larger than the MPC out of actual income.

$2,432/4,000 = 0.61$.

With the PIH, there is a smaller marginal propensity to consume out of actual income than there would be in the simple consumption-function case; therefore, with the PIH, there is a smaller multiplier than in the simple case, and the economy would be more stable.

f.   transitory; zero; greater

Question 3

a.

Y_{-1}^P	Y^P	C
$10,000	$10,000	$9,000
20,000	18,000	16,200
30,000	26,000	23,400
10,000	12,000	10,800
20,000	20,000	18,000
30,000	28,000	25,200
10,000	14,000	12,600
20,000	22,000	19,800
30,000	30,000	27,000

Group	Average Income	Average Consumption	APC
Low income	$10,000	$10,800	1.08
Middle income	20,000	18,000	0.90
High income	30,000	25,200	0.84

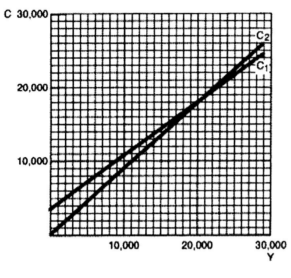

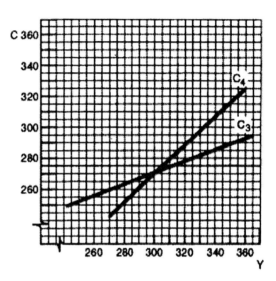

Figure 15A   Figure 15B

b.   APC = 0.9.

c. $270 billion; greater; increase

Actual income will be greater than permanent income because not all of the increased income is considered to be permanent.

$324 billion; $291.6 billion; 291.6/360 = 0.81; 0.19; $288 billion; $259.2 billion; 259.2/270 = 0.96; 0.04.

APS declines as the economy heads into a recession; APS increases as the economy heads into a boom period.

d.   APC = 0.9; APS = 0.1

e.   1. Behavior: APS increases as Y increases; APS decreases as Y decreases. Explanation: In high-income groups, a greater percentage of people are having good times than are having bad times; for people having good times, actual income is greater than permanent income so that APS out of actual income is greater than it would be. (The reverse holds for low-income groups.)

2. Behavior: Same as for cross-section. Explanation: Similar explanation as above except that *high income* and *low income* refer to the entire economy.

3. Behavior: APS constant. Explanation: In the long run, actual income equals permanent income.

Question 4

a.   60; 40; $900,000; $15,000; 0.67; 0.33; Total assets: $7500; $7500; $300,000; $150,000; 0.

b.   50; $200

He would put the rest of the income into an asset so that he could increase spending by $5,200 each year for the next 29 years.

MPC = 200/6000 = 0.033

c. $60,000; $2000; MPC = 2000/6000 = 0.33

The marginal propensity to consume out of a permanent increase in income is greater than the marginal propensity to consume out of a temporary increase in income.

d. greater; greater

When the economy heads into a recession, part of the fall in income will be considered temporary. The amount of that fall that comes out of consumption will be less than if the fall were permanent. Hence, the APC will increase and the APS will decrease.

e. $990,000; $16,500; 16,500/22,500 = 0.73; 0.27; APS decreases when the level of assets increases and income remains the same.

f. According to the rules advocates, without erratic government intervention, private spending would be stable. LCH helps to support this view by suggesting that private spending is stabilized because transitory increases in income have only a modest influence on current consumption and because the real-asset effect stabilizes the economy as higher prices cut the value of real assets and dampen spending.

g. They suggest that consumers will be more likely to increase consumption spending if they perceive the tax cut to be permanent rather than temporary.

Question 5

a. Expectations of future events are formed using the best available information, so that any information contained in past levels of income is already taken into account in estimating permanent income; unanticipated

b. The capital markets are not perfect, and young people may not be able to borrow against their future incomes.

Those subject to liquidity constraints will have a much higher MPC out of temporary changes in income than would be predicted by the PIH or LCH.

15 percent

c. A deficit-financed tax cut that raised the taxes to be paid by future generations would not stimulate consumption since people would save all of the increase to raise their bequests.

People are uncertain of their age of death and may tend to overestimate it; they also want to be sure of being able to cover the possibility of high medical expenses that may not be covered by insurance.

d. rise

e. Answers will depend on the data for the period selected, but normally the ratio of personal saving plus consumer durable expenditures to personal income will provide better support for the PIH and LCH theories. Since it is only the flow of services from durable goods that is treated as consumption expenditures, consumer durable goods should be treated as saving.

When consumer durable goods expenditures are included in consumer expenditures, it makes consumption expenditures much more cyclically sensitive and therefore less stable.

■ Chapter 16

Question 1

(a) & (b) The answers to these questions depend on the periods used.

Question 2

a.

jY_{-1}	$(1-j)Y_{-1}^e$	Y^e
110.0	0	110.0
82.5	25	107.5
55.0	50	105.0
27.5	75	102.5

b. $K^* = 440, 430, 420, 410.$

c. $I_n = 30.$

   $I_n = -15.$

   Net disinvestment is required since the desired capital stock is less than the actual capital stock. Disinvestment comes about when replacement investment is less than the amount of capital stock that wore our (depreciated) during the period.

d. $I_n = 10; I_n = 30;$ higher

e.

I_n	D	I
10	80	90
30	80	110

   smaller; more

f.

Variables	1	2	3	4	5	6
Y	120	120	120.00	110.00	110.00	110.00
Y^e	100	115	118.75	119.69	112.42	110.61
K^*	500	575	593.75	598.45	562.10	553.05
I_n	0	75	18.75	4.70	−36.35	−9.05
D	50	50	57.50	59.38	59.85	56.21
I	50	125	76.25	64.08	23.50	47.16

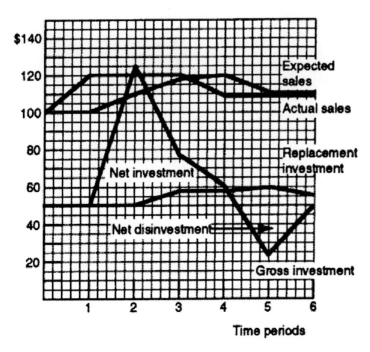

Figure 16A

g. 20; 150; –39; –16; –8; –63

Net investment becomes negative.

No. Since the capital stock cannot be negative, replacement investment cannot be negative.

Question 3

a. higher; lower

b. higher; lower

c. directly; inversely

d. 1. It was assumed that this period's expected output was always equal to last period's actual output. More realistically, only a fraction of expected output would be based on last period's actual output, and the rest would carry over whatever was expected last period.

2. It was assumed that v^* (the desired capital-output ratio) was a constant. More realistically, v^* may vary substantially depending on the cost of borrowing, the taxation of capital, and other factors.

3. It was assumed that K is equal to K^*, i.e., firms can instantly put in place any desired amount of capital stock. More realistically, some kinds of capital take a substantial period to construct, and we would not expect K to equal K^*.

Question 4

a. The user cost of capital is the cost to the firm of renting a capital good from itself (since most capital goods, unlike other factors of production, are owned by the firm and not rented from others). This cost must cover both the cost of financing the purchase of the capital good and the cost of maintaining its value intact.

the real interest rate; the depreciation rate.

b. The marginal product of capital is the additional output produced by an additional unit of capital.

equal to; decline; rise; rise; fall; fall; fall; rise

c. $v^* = 3.5$; $v^* = 3.75$; increase

It would be a temporary change. The increase in the firm's capital stock would reduce the gap between the desired higher level of capital stock, and the rate of investment would slow down.

d. $v^* = 3.25$; $r = -2$

Yes, but only if the rate of inflation of the prices of the capital goods were two percentage points greater than the nominal interest rate. (Recall that $r = i - p$.)

e.   Although used capital goods may depreciate, they may simultaneously have a market value that increases. In this case, the rising value of the capital goods can partially offset the interest and depreciation costs.

rise; rise; fall

f.   1.   To provide savers with a given market return, an investment project must pay a higher before-tax rate (and hence incur a higher user cost) when the corporation income tax rate is high than when it is low.

2.   For income-tax purposes, firms are allowed to deduct depreciation expenses from their income. If the guidelines determining how much can be deducted are changed so that an increased depreciation expense can be deducted, more corporate profits would be protected from taxation, and the user cost of capital would fall.

3.   With an investment tax credit, a firm could take a percentage of the value of investment made during the year and deduct that amount from its corporate tax. If the size of the credit increased, the deduction would increase, and the user cost of capital would fall.

g.   remain the same; fall

User cost depends on the real rate of interest. In the first case, the real rate of interest remains the same. In the second case, the real rate of interest falls.

increase; fall

Internally generated funds, e.g., profits, are cheaper than externally obtained funds since the firm's borrowing rate will generally be higher than the rate the firm could earn with its own funds

Question 5

a.   the market value of capital in the stock market with the cost of purchasing the capital.

b.   the firm's market value on stock and bond markets to the replacement cost of its capital stock, increasing

c.   increase

■ Chapter 17

Question 1

a. $Y = 600$; $P = 1.00$

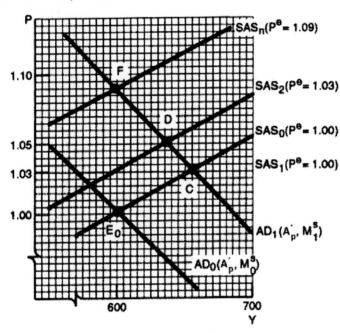

Figure 17A

b. $Y = 660$; $P = 1.03$

c.   increase; decline; higher

d.   the expected real wage; W/P^e; increase

The amount of labor supplied would increase.

e.   No. At Point C, the actual real wage is below the equilibrium real wage.

f. $P = 1.03$;

It is the same.

$P^e = 1.03$.

$Y = 640$; $P = 1.05$

g.   the expected price level.

the natural level of real GDP.

$P^e = 1.09$.

Question 2

a.   Business cycles can occur if workers inaccurately perceive the current price level.

b.   Expectations are rational when people make the best forecast they can with the available data. Errors can result, but people do not consistently make the same forecasting errors.

c. the actual price level; the expected price level; an information barrier shared by workers and firms alike; marginal cost

Local price increase: An increase in the price of a product not experienced equally by other firms.

Aggregate price increase: An increase in the price of a product accompanied by increases in the prices of other products.

If a firm perceives the price increase to be local, the firm will expect its price to rise relative to its marginal cost. Under these circumstances, the firm would increase its profits by increasing output; steeper

Countries with more localized price movements (flatter SAS curve) would have larger supply responses, i.e., more movement in real output around Y^N.

Question 3

a. $P^e = 1.09$.

It is identical to SAS_n.

$Y = 600$; $P = 1.09$

b. It will have no effect on real GDP but will raise the price level.

the policy ineffectiveness proposition

Question 4

a. The RBC theory assumes that business cycles are caused by real (or supply) shocks, rather than by monetary or fiscal policy (or demand) shocks. (As the text notes, however, more recent developments in RBC theory permit a role for demand shocks.)

b. Supply shocks cause changes in the level of natural real GDP. Thus, even if Y remains equal to Y^N, there would be fluctuations in Y.

c. If the labor supply curve is upward sloping, then supply shocks will affect *both* employment and output. If the labor supply curve is vertical, however, then supply shocks will affect output only.

d. RBC theorists assume the substitution effect of a real-wage increase (the increase in employment due to a higher real wage causing workers to substitute work for leisure) outweighs the income effect (the increase in leisure due to the increase in income of a higher real wage). RBC theorists apply this idea to changes in the real wage over time, arguing that workers work more in good times (when real wages are high) and less in bad times (when real wages are low).

e. Labor supply is directly related to the interest rate. When real interest rates are high, savings from work can be invested and earn a higher return than when real interest rates are low. This induces more labor to be supplied when real interest rates are high.

f. 1. Except for the oil shocks of the 1970s, no other technology shock has been identified that could be strong enough to explain business cycles.
    2. RBC models omit any explanation of price behavior.
    3. RBC implies procyclical fluctuations of real wages, but the data seem to indicate that there is no significant relationship between the real wage and real GDP.

g. market-clearing

the labor market and the product market

Workers have a choice about their hours of work; if real wages are falling, workers might choose leisure rather than working at lower wages.

Question 5

a. Production function (or total product curve).

b. *W/P*: 220, 215, 210; *Y*: 920, 970, 1,000

   The nominal wage rate; the productivity of labor (labor demand curve).

   $W/P = 210$; $Y = 1,000$; $P = 1.00$

c. *P*: 1.00, 1.024, 1.05; *Y*: 900, 940, 960

d. The demand-for-labor curve shifts leftward or downward. The production function (total product of labor curve) has pivoted down, becoming flatter, which means a lower marginal product of labor at every level of employment.

e. $W/P = 210$; The labor supply curve must be horizontal at the real wage of 210; $Y = 900$

f. $W/P = 205$; $Y = 940$

g. fall; $W/P = 200$; $Y = 960$

h. natural real GDP; smaller

i. the downward pivot of the production function; *B*; *Z*; 1,000; 960

j. decrease; decrease; *Y*; 960; 940; voluntary

k. flexible; *X*; 940; 900

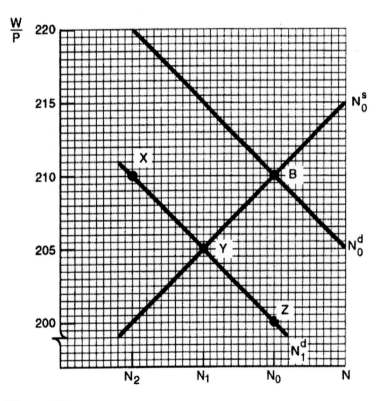

Figure 17B

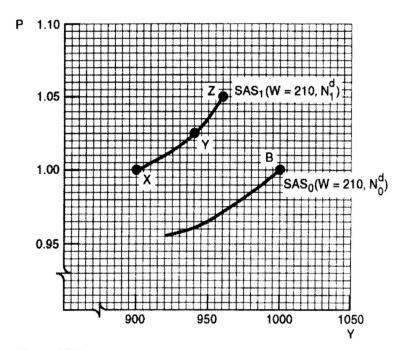

Figure 17C

Question 6

a. N_0; $W/P = 200$; $Y = 960$; natural level of real GDP

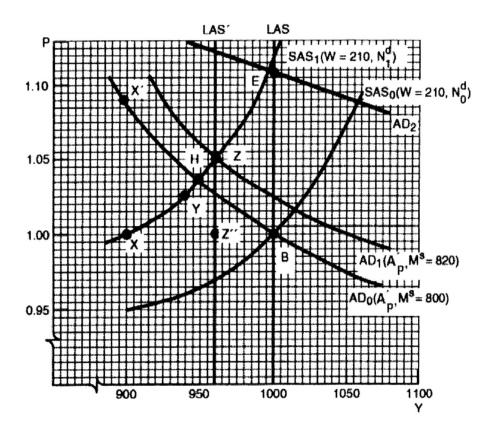

Figure 17D

b. *AD* doesn't change since neither A_0 nor M^s has changed.

$Y = 1,000; Y = 900$

excess demand; increase

c. $Y = 950; P = 1.035; M^s/P = 773; W/P = 202.9$

The actual real wage is greater than the equilibrium real wage

d. $N = N_0; Y = 960$

Yes. Point Z is on the long-run aggregate supply curve, *LAS'*.

e. $W/P = 210/1.12 = 187.5$.

$N > N_0$.

greater than; increase; shift upward

The price level would increase.

f. decrease; equal to; accommodated

g. $W = 220.5; N = N_2$; Yes

h. $Y^N = 900$

The Fed would have to decrease the money supply by an appropriate amount.

i. The short-run equilibrium level of output along AD_0 of 950 would be greater than the natural level of output of 900. Thus, there would be upward pressure on the nominal wage rate. The increase in *W* would shift SAS upward until long-run equilibrium occurs at $Y = 900$ on the *LAS* curve at 900 (not drawn).

lower; decrease; higher

j. $W/P = 200; W = 200$

The short-run aggregate supply curve would shift downward.

The Fed would have to decrease the money supply by an appropriate amount so that the aggregate demand curve passes through Z''.

Question 7

a. $P = 7.5 - 0.5Y$.

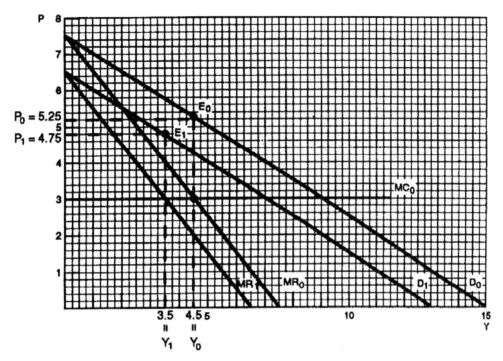

Figure 17E

$MC = 3$.
They are the same since there are no fixed costs.
$MR = 7.5 - Y$

b. $Y = 4.5$; $P = 5.25$; Profit = 10.125

c. $P = 6.5 - 0.5Y$; $MR = 6.5 - Y$

d. $Y = 3.5$; $P = 4.75$; Profit = 6.125.

Question 8

a. $MR_1(4.5) = 6.5 - 4.5 = 2$; fell; 2

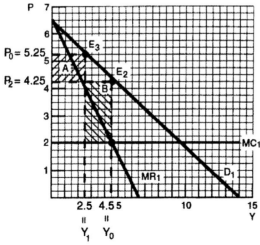

Figure 17F

$Y = 4.5$; $P = 4.25$; profit $= 10.125$

equal to; fall; remain the same

b. $Y = 2.5$; profit $= 8.125$

c. B is larger than A (4.5 > 2.5).

Profit rises by 2.

The amount by which B is greater than A ($B - A = 4.5 - 2.5 = 2$) is also the amount by which profit at P_2 is greater than profit at P_0 ($10.125 - 8.125 = 2$).

d.   menu costs; greater; 2

e.   leave price unchanged; decrease output

Question 9

a.   Nominal rigidities explain why wages, in general, do not adjust, while real rigidities concentrate on the movement of certain wages and prices relative to other wages and prices.

b.   Workers' productivity depends on the level of the real wage.

If firms decreased wages, productivity would fall, and the wage bill per unit of output would actually increase.

c.   The firm would be more willing to cut wages since it is the real wage relative to the real wage of other firms that is crucial.

d.   If nominal GDP fell by 5 percent, all firms would lower wages by the same amount, say 5 percent.

Firms buy inputs from many sources. Since any one firm doesn't know for sure how other firms will react to the fall in the nominal demand, the firm would be reluctant to cut prices and wages without more information.

■ Chapter 18

Question 1

a. Prior to the Great Depression, the dominant school of thought, "old classical economics," emphasized the self-correcting properties of the economy. Changes in aggregate demand were thought to affect primarily prices, rather than real output. During the Great Depression, output fell dramatically and unemployment rose to record levels, and both remained in those states for several years. Consequently, economists sought explanations for these phenomena that could not be explained with the existing theory.

b. John Maynard Keynes.

c. It supported Keynesian economics because the tremendous growth in governmental spending caused output to soar and the unemployment rate to fall almost to zero.

d. Prices did not decline at all in the recessions of 1953–54 and 1957–58.

e. Inflation steadily accelerated.

f. No, because the Phillips curve hypothesized a tradeoff between inflation and unemployment, and there appeared to be no such tradeoff.

g. The tax cut was intended to stimulate the economy, which was in a recession when Kennedy became president. The tax increase was intended to help pay for the Vietnam War.

h. Temporary tax cuts did not lead to the increase in spending that was expected, as was supported by the permanent-income hypothesis. The legislative lag was 18 months for the tax surcharge.

i. The most notable features were twin peaks of inflation in 1974–75 and 1980–81, the twin peaks of unemployment in 1975 and 1982–83, and the twin peaks in interest rates in 1974 and 1980.

j. It was generally accepted that monetary policy was more potent than fiscal policy.

k. The major economic ideas developed during this period were new classical macroeconomics and the supply-shock analysis of inflation.

l. The food and oil price shocks of the 1970s.

m. The expectations-augmented Phillips curve was developed, in which the original Phillips curve was considered only a short-run phenomenon, while the natural-rate hypothesis determined the long-run Phillips curve.

n. The huge structural deficit led to a political stalemate that rendered short-term fiscal policy changes impossible.

o. The Fed was targeting monetary growth, abandoning any attempt to stabilize interest rates.

p. The severity of the recession of 1981–82.

q. The first new idea was the belief that fiscal policy had more of an impact on economic growth than on the business cycle. The second idea was that monetary policy had lost is potency.

r. The natural rate of unemployment turned out to be lower than the Fed had expected. The unemployment rate fell below 5 percent in 1994 with no increase in the inflation rate.

s.   The Fed raised interest rates in 1994 and cut them in 2001 in the effort to head off swings in unemployment.

t.   below and above the natural rate of unemployment.

That the NAIRU could change regularly.

Question 2

a.   It almost tripled from 5 percent to 13 percent.

b.   Each country would have independent monetary policy and chose the particular inflation rate it desired.

c.   Exchange rates were highly volatile.

d.   Economic dislocation caused by volatile exchange rates has caused many observers to look for ways to return partially or completely to fixed exchange rates. The formation of the European Monetary Union is an important example of this.

Question 3

a.   Economic growth cannot be achieved simply by investing in physical and human capital. Factors like geographic location and legal and political system play important role in determining growth.

b.   Productivity growth is often attributed to the high-tech investment; however, the U.S. productivity revival after 1995 and particularly after 2001 and the European failure during the same period puts this hypothesis in question. As a result, productivity growth remains leading puzzle for future research and debate.

c.   The answer to this question depends on the costs of inflation versus the costs of reducing inflation to zero. There is no consensus on the magnitudes of these costs.

d.   Various suggestions have been made, but recent research indicates that falling prices of computers and lower medical care inflation due to managed health care may have contributed to a reduction in the natural rate of unemployment. Improved measurement techniques have also reduced measured inflation relative to true inflation.

e.   Policy rules require a tight relationship between policy instruments and policy targets. Various kinds of shocks, however, disrupt that relationship, making the specification of feasible rules difficult or impossible. Discretion, on the other hand, is subject to the creation of policy changes that may have unintended consequences.

f.   Economists are still struggling with these questions because the science of comparative macroeconomics is just beginning to address them.